FUNNY, STRANGE, PROVOCATIVE

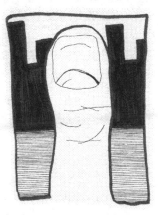

seven plays
from Clubbed Thumb

Edited by
Maria Striar and Erin Detrick

Playscripts, Inc.

New York, NY

Published by Playscripts, Inc.
325 West 38th Street, Suite 305
New York, New York, 10018
www.playscripts.com

Cover design by Michael Buchino
Front cover photo by Scott Adkins (picturing Meg MacCary)
Back cover illustration © 2005 Josh Dickens
Title page illustration © 2004 James Urbaniak

Text design and layout by Erin Detrick

First Edition: March 2007
10 9 8 7 6 5 4 3 2 1

Library of Congress Cataloging-in-Publication Data

Funny, strange, provocative : seven plays from Clubbed Thumb / edited by Maria Striar and Erin Detrick. -- 1st ed.
    p. cm.
Summary: "Anthology of seven scripts produced by Clubbed Thumb, an Obie-winning theatre company in New York City, including new plays by playwrights Adam Bock, Sheila Callaghan, Erin Courtney, Lisa D'Amour, Rinne Groff, Carson Kreitzer, and Ann Marie Healy"--Provided by publisher.
    ISBN-13: 978-0-9709046-2-1
    ISBN-10: 0-9709046-2-2
    1. American drama--21st century. I. Striar, Maria, 1969- II. Detrick, Erin, 1981- III. Clubbed Thumb (New York, N.Y.)
    PS634.2.F86 2007
    812'.608--dc22

                        2007005783

Contents

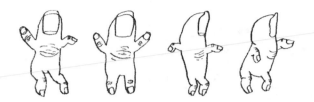

Illustration © 2001 Erin Courtney

3

Foreword

The ecology of a theater community is always fragile and unique. Theater artists are uniquely dependent on institutions to allow their work to flourish—painters may require dealers to sell their work, poets and novelists publishers to print and distribute theirs, but playwrights require theaters in order to make their work in the first place. Without a venue, a place to come together with actors and directors and designers and audiences, a playwright can't even fully practice their craft, much less grow to maturity as an artist. This places a special burden on producers and leaders of theaters: not only to make their company succeed, but to create a venue where artists can create and the new come into existence. Without such producers, no theatrical culture can hope to flourish.

Clubbed Thumb's indefatigable and brilliant leaders have shouldered this burden and joyfully, triumphantly, spent eleven years nourishing the American theater. If New York has been a fruitful and exciting place to be a playwright in the last decade, Clubbed Thumb can claim a real share of the credit. Their taste is broad-ranging and eclectic, yet somehow one can always recognize the writers they are attracted to: formally inventive, relentlessly curious, almost always funny, pop sensibilities linked with deeper, more serious concerns. From Erin Courtney to Carson Kreitzer, from Adam Bock to Ann Marie Healy, from Lisa D'Amour to Sheila Callaghan, Clubbed Thumb has consistently sought out the most exciting young writers in New York and, even more importantly, given them thoughtful, detailed, elegant productions. Their relationships with writers are not superficial, but rather long, involved and committed.

I first met Clubbed Thumb through a writer whose work I had grown to love, Rinne Groff. As I got to know Rinne's work and world, it became clear that Clubbed Thumb had recognized the beauty and power of Rinne's work years before I had, and had commissioned her, workshopped her, and produced her along the way. To me, this is a beautiful exemplar of what they do: recognize a brilliant young talent, give her resources and dedication and collaborative talent, and offer her up to the world. Clubbed Thumb is a major contributor to the American theater—long may they flourish.

—Oskar Eustis
Artistic Director
The Public Theater

Introduction

In 1996, some friends decided to put on a play. A funny picture in a book of palmistry made us laugh—so we named our company Clubbed Thumb. We rented a decaying firetrap for a month, invited pretty much everyone we met to put on their work too—before our show, after it, on dark nights—and became producers. Eleven years, 100 plays and 60 full productions later, we are still at it.

By now, we've defined our tastes. Clubbed Thumb plays are (as per the book's title) funny, strange and provocative. By provocative we mean you leave the theater with something to chew on, something unsettled; by strange we mean the work is formally inventive, that both the story and its telling are unusual; and by funny we mean funny. The plays always have three or more characters, run 90 *intermissionless* minutes or less, and have not yet been produced in New York. As actresses, Meg MacCary and I are confounded by the lack of roles for women. Clubbed Thumb plays attempt to redress this; they feature equally good and compelling roles for both sexes.

Over the years, Clubbed Thumb's commitment to new plays has intensified. We've gone from producing living American writers to producing *emerging* (i.e. not yet famous) living American writers, then on to producing *new plays* by emerging living American writers and then we started *developing* as well as producing new plays by emerging living American writers until ultimately we were commissioning, developing and producing new plays by living American writers. (The "emerging" is silent. That term gives us a headache.) Clubbed Thumb now offers its own commission, an annual development workshop, and we produce several plays a year. The writers we've premiered have been showered with virtually every accolade—MacArthur, Whiting, Tony, Susan Smith Blackburn, Obie, etc.— offered in the American theater.

A play is a thing on paper, a thing read; theater is an event. We choose plays that offer the most stimulating blueprint for making the latter, plays that insist on both interpretation and collaboration, and that demand imagination and virtuosity from the artists who will turn them into theater. We don't sand the rough edges off the plays we produce; that's where the charisma lies. A Clubbed Thumb play asks questions that we—producers, directors, designers, actors, and then audience members—are forced to answer.

We are parentally fond of every play we've produced. Clubbed Thumb has enjoyed long collaborative relationships with the writers of the plays in this book, so they are especially precious. They also highlight the qualities we most appreciate in new work. From the terse, staccato repetitions of *Inky*'s boxing rounds to the interplay of unfinished sentences and vocal tics in *The Typographer's Dream*, the plays are rooted in a rhythm as considered as the time signature in a piece of music. Their finely wrought language runs the gamut, from the tweaked vernacular of *Demon Baby* to the lyricism-on-steroids of *16 Spells to Charm the Beast*. (We use a monologue from this for auditions—if the actress can scale its Everest of commas, she's got the goods.) Like the 11-year-old who serves bleach in her doll tea set in *Crumble (Lay Me Down, Justin Timberlake)*, Clubbed Thumb plays toe the tightrope between ironic detachment and powerful emotion. They are populated by achingly compromised male and female characters, rendered with Chekhovian specificity and humor. Who is the most delightfully unlovable among the lonely, tormented trio of *Dearest Eugenia Haggis*? And we love a theatrical throwdown: *Freakshow* opens with a three-page audience address by a woman with no arms and no legs detailing her sexual prowess.

The only thing Clubbed Thumb asks of its audience (and now, its readers) is this: If we offer something worth engaging with, be willing to engage. These plays are worth it. Read them, grapple with them, and then…**put them on**.

—Maria Striar
Co-Artistic Director
Clubbed Thumb

Mission Statement

Clubbed Thumb commissions, develops, and produces funny, strange, and provocative new plays. Since its founding in 1996, the company has earned three Obies and presented plays in every form of development, including over 60 full productions. Clubbed Thumb is an incubator for artists and their work, staging plays to critical acclaim while supporting an ever-growing creative community. Our core producers are Arne Jokela, Michael Levinton, and Co-Directors Meg MacCary and Maria Striar.

To learn more about Clubbed Thumb and our current projects, please go to
www.clubbedthumb.org

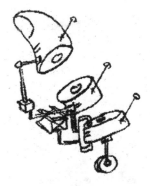

How to Get Performance Rights

If you wish to perform any of the plays in this book, you must do two things right off the bat: (1) Obtain a performance license. (2) Purchase enough acting editions for your cast and crew.

Conveniently enough, all of the plays in this book are licensed by the same company: Playscripts, Inc.

We look forward to hearing from you!

Erin Detrick
Publications Director

Playscripts, Inc.   Phone: 1-866-NEW-PLAY (639-7529)
325 W. 38th Street, Suite 305   Email: info@playscripts.com
New York, NY 10018   Web: www.playscripts.com

Copyright Basics

These Plays are protected by United States and international copyright law. These laws ensure that playwrights are rewarded for creating new and vital dramatic work, and protect them against theft and abuse of their work.

You'll find all of the official fine print on the next page, and these are the most important rules:

- Do *not* perform these Plays without obtaining prior permission from Playscripts, and without paying the required royalty.

- Do *not* photocopy, scan, or otherwise duplicate any part of this book.

A play is a piece of property, fully owned by the playwright, just like a house or car. You must obtain permission to use this property, and must pay a royalty fee for the privilege—*whether or not you charge an admission fee.* Playscripts collects these required payments on behalf of the author.

Anyone who violates an author's copyright is liable as a copyright infringer under United States and international law. Playscripts and the author are entitled to institute legal action for any such infringement, which can subject the infringer to actual damages, statutory damages, and attorneys' fees. A court may impose statutory damages of up to $150,000 for willful copyright infringements. U.S. copyright law also provides for possible criminal sanctions. Visit the website of the U.S. Copyright Office (www.copyright.gov) for more information.

The Bottom Line: If you break copyright law, you are robbing a playwright and opening yourself to expensive legal action. Follow the rules, and when in doubt, ask us.

The Fine Print

11

THE TYPOGRAPHER'S DREAM

by Adam Bock

BIOGRAPHY

Adam Bock's plays include *Five Flights* (Rattlestick Theater, 2004; San Francisco's Encore Theater, 2002; Glickman Award winner; published in *Breaking Ground*; American Theater Critics Award nominee; Elizabeth Osborn Award nominee; two BATCC Awards); *Swimming in the Shallows* (Shotgun Players; 2000 Bay Area Theater Critics Circle Awards for Best Original Script, Best Production; Clauder Competition Award-winner; L. Arnold Weissberger Award nominee; LA Weekly nominee; GLAAD Media Award nominee; TimeOut NYs Top Ten; Second Stage's Uptown Series in New York City, summer 2005). Mr. Bock helped Jack Cummings III develop *The Audience*, nominated for three 2005 Drama Desk Awards including Best Musical. Other plays include *The Shaker Chair*, (Actors Theater of Louisville, 2005 Humana Festival; Kesselring Prize nomination); *The Typographer's Dream* (produced in New York City, San Francisco, Edinburgh Fringe Festival, Berkeley in 2006); *Thursday* (produced in San Francisco with a 2003 NEA grant); *The Drunken City* (Kitchen Theater in Ithaca, New York, 2005); *The Thugs* (premiered at Soho Rep in NYC, 2006); *The Receptionist* (workshopped Perry-Manfield and the O'Neill, 2006). Mr. Bock is an artistic associate at Shotgun Players and Encore Theater, a member of MCC's Writers Coalition and a member of New Dramatists.

Other Clubbed Thumb credits: *Medea Eats* (Summerworks 2000); *Thursday* (Boot Camp 2002).

ACKNOWLEDGMENTS

The Typographer's Dream was originally produced by Clubbed Thumb as part of Summerworks 2002, and subsequently received a winter production by Clubbed Thumb at HERE Arts Center in New York City during February 2003. It was directed by Drew Barr, with the following cast and staff:

Summerworks Cast:

MARGARET	Meg MacCreary
ANNALISE	Kate Hampton
DAVE	Tim McGeever

Production Cast:

MARGARET	Meg MacCreary
ANNALISE	Kate Hampton
DAVE	Dan Snook

Sets	David Evans Morris
Lights	Juliet Chia
Costumes	Kim Gill
Sound	Kai Harada

CAST OF CHARACTERS

MARGARET, the Typographer
ANNALISE, the Geographer
DAVE, the Stenographer

SETTING

A long, shared desk at the front of the stage. Three chairs.
In front of MARGARET, paper. A pen. Pencils. A ruler.
In front of DAVE, a steno machine.
Each of the three has a glass of water.

PRODUCTION NOTES

Most of the play is direct audience address in real, present time. As if the characters have been asked to come to this room to talk to this audience about their jobs. Be better if this is the first time they've done something like this.

Be good if the characters notice the audience's reactions. Perhaps the audience is lit.

It is best if lighting and sound not be stagey. Be better if the lights didn't "create stage spaces" for example*. Sounds normally found in a space like this would be more interesting to me than a soundtrack. Pipes clanking maybe. A light that blinks oddly that they notice. Is this a space that has been borrowed? When ANNALISE exits to get her props, does she leave the theater and go to her car? When they are offstage can we still hear them? What I want to avoid is the idea that all of this has been directed/rehearsed for the audience.

* The exception being the flashbacks obviously, which would need to be in "last night." Lights and sound might help create a sense of that.

Tim McGeever, Meg MacCary, and Kate Hampton
in *The Typographer's Dream*.

Produced by Clubbed Thumb at The Ohio Theatre, 2002.
Photograph by David Evans Morris / Juliet Chia

THE TYPOGRAPHER'S DREAM

1.

> (DAVE, ANNALISE, *and* MARGARET *enter. They sit at the desk,* MARGARET, ANNALISE, DAVE *stage right to stage left. They get ready.*)

2.

MARGARET. I'm a typographer.

ANNALISE. I'm a geographer.

DAVE. I'm a stenographer.

(*Full stop.*)

Well. I'm a court reporter.

No. A stenographer. Stenographer. Typographer geographer stenographer. Say stenographer. It's.

3.

MARGARET. Typography um

ANNALISE. Geography is a science.

DAVE. No. Say court reporter. It's, it's more

Yeah. Say court reporter.

No. Say either one. Doesn't matter, court reporter stenographer court reporter.

4.

MARGARET. A typographer is someone who um I um who specializes in the design of, um in the choice of, the arrangement, the um of ah the um. Everything of type. Type. Letters and. And also.

ANNALISE. Geography is a science. It's the study of the earth itself. The whole thing. We study the earth's shapes. The earth's spaces. What's on the land? What's in the water? What's in the air? We study plant and animal life. Humans. And. Or. Their industries. Migrations. Weather. Tectonic plates. Ice floes. All of it.

It's a broad science.

DAVE. Stenographers type.

5.

MARGARET. I place type.

ANNALISE. As a geographer I guess I guess I
I explore the idea of place. Different types of places.

DAVE. Stenographers type. A lot. In lots of different places.

>   (*Pause.*)

You gotta like to type.

6.

MARGARET. Typography um

ANNALISE. Geography was my favorite subject in school. When I was a little girl in Saskatoon. Which is in Saskatchewan. Which is in Canada. I love maps. Love maps. Love. I think it was the colors on the maps that first caught me. That Russia could be pink. That that big pink shape could be Russia, and that Russia was a country, a country! a country next to a green Finland, another country, and a sort of yellowy strange yellowy Poland, again, another country. But then on another map pink could instead be England, not Russia at all, isn't that strange, England is pink! or even the whole British Empire could be pink and pink would be everywhere all over the whole map. And why was Poland still yellow then? I was instantly, constantly intrigued when I looked at maps. Where the hell was Finland or Poland and why is Poland always yellow? Yellow! Why?

DAVE. And you gotta like to type fast. Because stenographers type fast.

7.

MARGARET. Typography um

ANNALISE. You can imagine my excitement.

DAVE. You type fast.

8.

MARGARET. Um

ANNALISE. It's very easy oh it's easy to get excited about geography.

DAVE. If you blink, you'll miss it.

>   (*Types fast.*)

9.

MARGARET. Um
Don't interrupt me.

ANNALISE. What?

MARGARET. Don't interrupt me.

ANNALISE. *Pause.*

MARGARET. Don't.

ANNALISE. I didn't mean to—

MARGARET. *Pause.*

ANNALISE. Ok. Ok.

MARGARET. *Pause.*

ANNALISE. *Pause.*

DAVE. *Pause.*

10.

MARGARET. I love typography.

ANNALISE. (*Pause.*) Geography

    (*Pause. Mutters.*)

Ok then.

    (*Pause.*)

Geography is pretty important to Canadians. Because Canada is a really big country, second biggest in the world. That's right, second! That's something to be proud of there, eh.

Americans are more into history. A lot of things have happened down here in the States.

The difference? Geographers think: time passes, and places change. Historians think: time passes, and things change. For example: when the Union of Soviet Socialist Republics, all of a sudden, it was gone eh? In the States there was a lot of excitement, historians were saying: we called it! we called it! we knew it was going to happen! In Canada we were saying: uh huh ok so now a whole bunch of maps are now completely junk.

DAVE. Used to be you were called a court stenographer. Now: You like to be called, you should call yourself, you do, you call yourself a court reporter. It's a little more glamorous.

11.

MARGARET. Um. Ah.

ANNALISE. (*Pause.*)

Used to be, at first, geography was all about discovery. Imagine Columbus and his geographer talking.

Columbus goes: Hey! There's India!

But his geographer says: That isn't India.

And Columbus says: Yeah it is.

His geographer says: No it's not.

Yeah it is, no it's not.

Yes it is.

No it's not, it's nothing like India, India has Indians.

So Columbus says: Those guys could be Indians.

But his geographer says: Those guys aren't Indians. Those guys are nothing like Indians.

So Columbus says: You sure?

And he's disappointed.

> (*Pause.*)

But then Columbus says: Hey! Well I guess then we discovered something eh?

DAVE. Whatever you call yourself it's typing. But.

12.

MARGARET. I'm just going to um

Because now I'm all

You just

ANNALISE. (*Pause.*)

Then after it was all about discovery, geography was also and maybe more about exploration and cartography. Cartography equals maps maps maps I love maps.

DAVE. The typing a court reporter does is different from the typing you or any old anybody does say on a computer or on a typewriter. Unless of course you happen to be a, unless you're a court reporter too. But then you'd probably know me.

13.

MARGARET. Typography is an art.

> (*Taps her pen on the desk. Five times.*)

ANNALISE. Then it evolved into an organizing, descriptive discipline. Geographers had to know, oh hell you know, the Bay of this, the Strait of that, what the hell is the difference between a Bay and a Strait. Or a Gulf even, eh?

DAVE. We're a pretty tight crowd.

> (*Pause.*)

As a rule. Well. You work alone. When you're an independent like me. So.

But it's like a fraternity, really. Even if you don't know another court reporter, you still know them. So.

14.

MARGARET. (*Taps her pen on the desk. Five times.*) Or maybe, more accurately, typography is a craft.

(*Taps her pen on the desk. Five times.*)

ANNALISE. Now:

MARGARET. I guess really. Really it's a. Really it's a business.

ANNALISE. Now: I'd say the draw to geography is, well

MARGARET. I guess everything is a business. Everything is. Right? Some just make more money than others.

ANNALISE. I'd say the draw to geography

MARGARET. It's a goddamn business.

ANNALISE. Now: I'd say the draw to geography is, well it's useful for analysis and decision-making—what would happen if we put this here? what does that over there effect over here, or over there?

Or alternatively, it can be used as a tool that lets you critique—why the hell are you doing that over there, because look what's happening as a result over here!

How you want to use it, one: analysis and decision-making, or two: critique—well I guess that would depend on what space you're in, yourself, inside or outside.

If you're inside you'll maybe say: we're making a decision.

If you're outside looking in, you're gonna say: what the hell are you doing?

Makes for. It's it's it's thrilling. It's a dangerous science. It's it's. It's probably why they tried to make it part of, just tried to hide it in social studies. Right? Just hide it. Geography, who's going to miss it? Right?

Social studies. I mean. What the hell is that?

DAVE. As a court reporter, you're the official witness. To a legal proceeding, a deposition, a hearing, a trial, any proceeding. You're the official witness to what was said, everything that was said by all the people present. It's kind of a responsibility.

MARGARET. It's a goddamn business.

DAVE. It's a big it's a big They're counting, counting on you to get it all So there can be a record of the event What you capture becomes the official record before the law. It's it. So it has to be right.

Which is a lot of pressure on you.

15.

MARGARET. It's a goddamn. Crap. Crap.

ANNALISE. Social studies.

DAVE. The only way you can get all that talking down on paper is to use stenography, which is which well "definition": any system of writing that uses contractions and arbitrary marks in place of normal "normal" writing, making writing fast enough to keep up with talking.

That's why you need one of these. This is a CAT steno machine. This, this is the. Oh thank god for.

CAT stands for computer aided transcription and

There are four banks of keys. At the top you got the number bar, then here's the upper bank, the lower bank, then vowel keys, they're a little lower for your thumbs. These, the upper and the lower banks, are divided into initial, asterisk, final. Initial and final are for consonants. The vowel keys, they're for vowels. The asterisks are just that. Asterisks. They're for corrections, you know for when you make a mistake, they're like the delete key on your computer. Stroke, oops, asterisk, equals delete. That's what it's called as you're typing in steno, stroking, the mark that's made, is called a stroke.

It's it's really compact. This little machine it's.

Single keys are used sometimes, U the letter U is for you, E he, T on the initial side is for it, the word it, T on the final side is the, for the, the word the, but mostly the keys are pressed down, stroked in groups, like on a piano. Sort of like chords on a piano. A group of keys at once. And then the group of letters you've stroked means a word or a phrase.

It's kind of like music except you're hearing it then writing it, instead of writing it and then hearing it.

It's important you get it right.

16.

ANNALISE. I didn't move down here to the States to do social studies.

DAVE. (*Looks at audience:*)

Sometimes the pressure can get to you.

17.

ANNALISE. They folded geography into social studies in the schools and geography as a science for all intents and purposes disappeared.

DAVE. (*Looks at audience.*)

18.

ANNALISE. At least I think that might have been the hope. Because we geographers are unpolitic. We chronicle consequences. And to acknowledge consequences is unpolitic.

Not always. The earth moves and a volcano is formed. That's ok. Absolutely. Hey look the earth moved and there's a volcano! Consequence equals knowledge and no one's responsible for anyone getting hurt.

But. An oilwell is sunk and people make a lot of money and there's energy sure, but a geographer says "that oilwell was sunk and," and then says "an environmental infrastructure is now shredded and the wildlife is destroyed and." Then the oil people think: Maybe we should teach social studies.

Or. "Let's create a buffer state here, don't worry that this group is Muslim and that group is Hindu, they'll they'll they'll, this boundary, this border, this line of ink from a MonteBlanc pen at a high-level and very historic meeting, this line will hold, or, we'll make this boundary, this border, we'll make this line of ink hold. That's decided." And the geographer says "Ahh. Hey—"

And the thought is: Social studies.

DAVE. Of course the pressure can be exciting, too.

19.

ANNALISE. Gimme a second.

　　　(*Exits.*)

DAVE. You can be sitting there and people are They can be raising their voices they can be shouting they can be and you're flying and the noise and the and you can just

There can be a thrill.

20.

DAVE. When your friend says to you, "Dave, Dave I don't think, I don't I don't," that's just how she sounded I remember it exactly, "I don't think court reporting is as glamorous as you think it is, I don't I don't I just get," and so you say to her you say "Gail why don't you think about doing something else, you could be a, you could type for realtime TV, type captions for the deaf for example and still use your skills. Since you don't like it." Because it doesn't make any sense not to like your job. Right?

I don't know what she's doing. These days. Gail. I think she might still be court reporting though. Which.

21.

DAVE. Although you can totally understand why she's. Cause it's a hard job. You have to be really, you have to be really, you have to be organized. You have to be able to concentrate when you need to and then just go with it when you can.

And some people aren't. And can't.

MARGARET. Typography.

DAVE. Some people don't fit their jobs.

22.

MARGARET. Typography. Is an art. It's the art of um it's the art of designing letters and, of designing text, text and letters so they can be read easily so they can

Typography is also a tool. Of communication.

When we talk, the words float out, language is ephemeral and intangible, it's hard to capture, it can disappear as soon as it's out of

It's a breath which

Written language, on the other hand, is language captured. It's captured in a visual and a spatial

The letters are put down and they can be read back. But. But. How do you capture the emotion in the sounds? How do you capture the play of feelings in language or the impact of thought or. That's where the art of typography can be

Um.

So. In typography, the basic elements of typography, what we have to use, our tools are small and are simple. We have upper case letters, capitals, caps. We have lower case letters, small letters. We have numbers, one two three four five six seven eight nine zero. We have punctuation marks, comma, semi-colon, exclamation point, etc etc etc period. Period.

This is the beauty of, where the art in typography is hidden, is cradled in moss, like a white egg in moss. We have only these few small elements and our ability to place them, and with them we capture breath, we capture language on a page.

It's.

>   (*Long pause.*)

It's.

>   (ANNALISE *enters. Holds up a diagram of a choke point.*)

ANNALISE. Look at this.

DAVE. Look. Court reporting isn't for everyone. Some people

>   (*Pause.*)

You start with typing. In high school maybe, you're all sitting, row after row after row of typewriters was the way it was when I got started, me here, Monalisa Garalletti next to me, Toby Moore behind me whispering, and you're typing asdf asdf asdf fdsa fdsa fdsa asdf asdf asdf fdsa fdsa fdsa and some people, well, that's enough to make them crazy, Monalisa, and they end up doing something with their feet instead of their hands like soccer or postal worker or waitressing, Monalisa, or something with their ears instead of their hands like phone operator or sound engineer.

But,

if you like it, you keep going and then it's "type the copy exactly as it is given below. Spell, space, begin and end each line, each paragraph, punctuate and capitalize precisely as shown. Make no erasures" and if that makes you crazy, well maybe you like doing things with your hands but you want to be less precise, and so you go and you work on an assemble line, or you work as a surgeon or you work as someone who replaces window panes, Toby.

But,

if you like it, you practice, you might do drills, like alphabetic drills, rhythm drills, alternate hand drills, you might make "most frequently used word lists" and then practice them and you get good. You get really good at it. And fast. Hundred and twenty words a minute junior in high school and people are looking at you. And people are mentioning it to you. And to each other. And. And you hear about court reporting and you think Hm.

And then you find out.

Court reporting. It's an entirely different world.

23.

MARGARET. When people start noticing the amount of type around them, not only in publications, in newspapers, magazines, the instructions that come with everything, your microwave, your prescriptions, when they see it being used in advertising and

When they realize how much we depend on type to understand what to do, how to do it, when to start, where to go– they realize a world with different typography would be an entirely different world.

ANNALISE. If people paid attention to geography, if they really paid attention, if they paid

We'd probably have an entirely different world.

DAVE. Because court reporting is stenography.

24.

MARGARET. But.

ANNALISE. But.

DAVE. And.

25.

     (MARGARET *taps her pen on the desk. Five times.*)

ANNALISE. But they don't eh. People don't pay attention.

DAVE. And stenography is a different story.

26.

ANNALISE. This is a diagram of a choke point.

DAVE. Turns out becoming a court reporter requires a real commitment. A lot of people don't get past that.

27.

ANNALISE. At some point between its point of origin, where it left from, and its point of destination, where it's going to, a ship, merchant or military, will often have to get past, to pass through, will have to be funneled through, a narrow bit of water, a strait, a passage or a sound. Typically this narrow bit of water is a natural deep channel at the head of a gulf or and enclosed sea, or between two islands, or between an island and the mainland. It might be artificial, like the Panama Canal.

That's a choke point.

DAVE. It takes a real commitment of time and money and effort.

You have to go to school. You have to start small and build up your skills and build up your speed all over again. You can't just walk in and assume that just because hey you were all great at typing in high school, your teacher Mrs. Golub is going think you're anything special because you're not and she's going to tell you that, she's going to tell you that "being a court reporter is a privilege not a right and you have to earn privileges" and that can sting.

That can sting and make you think: hey who needs court reporting anyway, but then you can think: well, life's not without its challenges, and Mrs. Golub is going on maternity leave sometime soon I think or that dress isn't such a great fashion choice for her,

and you apply yourself.

And you graduate and you borrow a lot of money from your Aunt Elizabeth who always wanted to be in the legal field herself and probably should have been, because can she argue! and did she ever have to, to convince your uncle Ray who isn't totally crazy for you anyway to lend you the money, right, and Thank God for Aunt Elizabeth! and you buy your first steno machine and the adventure, oh boy, the adventure begins.

You should hear the stories a court reporter hears.

28.

ANNALISE. (*Shows map of the Strait of Gibraltar.*)

This is the Strait of Gibraltar. It's where the Mediterranean meets the Atlantic. Ships, ships that want out of the Mediterranean and into the Atlantic or vice versa, they have no choice, they have to pass between the pillars of Hercules, which are the twin rocks that support the tiny colonies of Ceuta and Gibraltar. Ceuta is surrounded by Morocco, but it's controlled by Spain. The colony of Gibraltar is surrounded by Spain, but it's occupied by the British.

DAVE. You're typing and you hear: This one's mad at her boss. That one's mad at his neighbor.

This one's husband only let her talk when the football game wasn't on. Which was fine, until he got the Super ESPN package and the football game was always on. And then she had to shoot him, in the foot or in the mouth and she chose the foot.

29.

MARGARET. Um.

ANNALISE. This is a perfect example of a choke point.

MARGARET. Um.

DAVE. Then he came back from the hospital and he whacked her in the mouth. And broke her tooth. And so she had to break the screen of the bigscreen TV. Cause it was like a mirror and she was missing a tooth.

MARGARET. Um.

ANNALISE. Britain's colony is surrounded by Spain, Spain's colony is surrounded by Morocco, the Strait of Gibraltar is choked by Ceuta and Gibraltar.

MARGARET. Um.

DAVE. The kid just wanted to watch his show on the bigscreen TV and he can't, so he goes and shoots the neighbor's cat.

MARGARET. Um.

ANNALISE. Everyone is always holding their breath, just waiting to see what's going to happen.

MARGARET. Um.

DAVE. They're all in court to see if they can keep the kid out of counseling.

ANNALISE. Is the ship going to get through? Will Britain and Spain let it pass? Will they? Or will there be a blockade? With rockets flying and blood and sorrow and death?

MARGARET. Um.

DAVE. That's what they were focusing on, on the kid.

    (MARGARET *breaks through the verbal choke point Annalise and Dave have her in.*)

MARGARET. Um when people notice that there is so much type everywhere around them, at first, um, at first they think, it's just letters. It's just numbers. And they move onto another thought or another realization, they move onto what they think is another bigger problem, a more complex and more. And what they might not realize is, what they do not realize is, is that power can be in the details, power and the ability to change might be hidden, can be hidden in the small small

ANNALISE. If we just paid attention, we'd see that there are choke points all around us.

DAVE. They're all talking. And it's hard to know who to listen to.

30.

MARGARET. Because if you look really closely at type, if you really look, if you really look closely at, you see that caps and small letters and numbers and punctuation, while they are the primary

they're joined by secondary characteristics, small caps, accent marks, foreign punctuation marks like umlauts and ring accents and cedilla, and special signs like dollar signs and copyright marks and brackets, and suddenly as you keep looking, a whole landscape reveals itself. A landscape of voices and demands and sounds and

Italics send the reader tilting into a dream world. A word in bold typeface shouts.

It's it's

And then you realize that this typeface is different from that one, it's more lyrical, it's rougher, it's more frank or the letters are spaced too far apart or the letters are too close together and and and

And then you realize that there are all different kinds of typefaces and there are so many different ways they can all be used, and there must be so many different choices being made everywhere and all the time everywhere, and

Someone has chosen this type over that one.

Someone. Has chosen this one. It didn't just happen.

And that's when people realize that how the text is shown is a choice, that someone has decided that this story should be told this way, should be shown to the world this way, not that. That this story would be better served by being told in a quiet tone of voice, or no rather instead it should be told loudly dramatically emphatically.

And then, if they continue to wander along this thought path, people realize that one: all stories are told and two: how they are told is on purpose for a reason and three: that the truth is colored by the way it is told and four: that someone, someone hidden, has made a choice to color the truth this way and therefore it is no longer the truth and it's now just an opinion. Pretending to be the truth.

If the typographer has done her job, this opinion will look like the truth.

(*Pause.*)

An unethical typographer can make lies look like the truth.

ANNALISE. Gimme a second.

(ANNALISE *exits.*)

DAVE. Thing that's interesting? You start connecting to the people whose stories you hear. Especially if they tell them well. It's impossible not to. You have to.

31.

MARGARET. And then people realize that if you want to change the world, change the way the story of the world is told. Is shown. Is set in type. Change the way a story is set in type and the story itself will change.

DAVE. First you think the kid's totally nuts, taking potshots at the neighbor's cat, and then you hear the husband and you're thinking "his wife's crazy! smashing the TV" and then you see her pull her mouth open and you think "she's got no tooth...he hit her? he shouldn't hit her!" and then the husband talks again and you think "she shot him in the foot! no wonder he hit her" and then you hear the wife and you're thinking "how does she live with him, if she's not allowed to say anything when the TV's on! No wonder she smashed the TV" and then you hear the son and you think "no wonder he's nuts" and you think "I better get all this down exactly because this, this is a mess."

32.

MARGARET. Typography matters. Sometimes the pressure can get to you.

DAVE. Stenography matters. Sometimes the pressure can get to you.

33.

MARGARET. Typography matters.

DAVE. The only way to beat the pressure is to know your job.

34.

MARGARET. Don't let anyone tell you different.

DAVE. You got to know that concentration is crucial. That an attention to detail is crucial. That proofreading is crucial.

You're there. You transcribe. And when a piece of evidence is entered, you take a sticker, usually it's neon and you number it and put it on the plastic baggie that the evidence is in, usually the evidence is in a plastic baggie, and you enter that number into your dogsheet and into your notes, you don't hold the evidence but you record it,

Oh. The dogsheet is where you write down everything that might give you trouble, the correct spellings of people's names, addresses, lawyers' names, anything, everything, anything that you might end up otherwise calling the lawyer in the middle of the night and waking him or her up, like you do when you're first starting out. And of course they yell at you. Who wouldn't, the middle of the night.

There's a lot to it.

So you transcribe and this,

>   (*Points to steno machine:*)

this is a great help, you take the diskette and put it in your computer and the CAT program translates the strokes into almost English and you read it and then there's the scoping phase when you add in anything you missed and make it readable, and you proofread it again and correct it and then print and bind it, and send copies to the lawyers. Not the originals. That, you wrap the steno tape around that, with your notes and your dogsheet and you store it all somewhere dry. Not your attic, not your attic, that's too humid, oh no yeah, that's way too humid, it's got to be there for seven years. You're the official witness to this for seven years.

And it's important to someone.

35.

MARGARET. It's hard to tell the truth.

DAVE. How somebody put something, how something was said, could change someone else's life.

36.

MARGARET. It's hard to tell the truth.

DAVE. It could change their life.

37.

MARGARET. I remember getting out of school. I loved typography, um everything about it. The rigor. The clarity. It was

I was in love.

And starting my first job. And being given the task of

Being asked to figure out which typeface should go on this packaging, in order to make this product appealing. And I remember hearing the client say "We want it to seem"

I remember hearing the client say "We want it to seem"

We want it to seem, to seem

Not "It is" or "Show our customers what it is" but "we want it to seem"
and I realized that I could choose a typeface that would make it "seem" a
certain way. I could make it look exciting, look serious, look fun, look
valuable, seem healthy.

So I did. Because that was my goddamn job.

DAVE. That piece of evidence that you didn't notice now, could be
important later.

38.
DAVE. So you work really hard.

39.
DAVE. You like your work.

40.
DAVE. You take pride in your work.

41.
DAVE. You do a good job.

42.

    (ANNALISE *enters. Carrying a book of maps.*)
ANNALISE. Look at this.

    (*Points to map of "The World that Nature Intended."*)
This is a map of

It's called "The World that Nature Intended." Oceans, seas, gulfs, bays,
lakes, rivers. Landmasses, mountains, deserts.

    (*Points to map of "The World of Nations and States."*)
And look at this one. "The World of Nations and States." Each of these
different colors is a different nation or. Each line represents a choice that
"this is where one ends and this other begins." Many of these lines are
disputed, here and here and here for example, choices that are still being
made

But. Each of these nations is a claim. That this is ours. From here to here.
This land is our land. This land is not your land.

Over time, we have gone from this place

    (*Points to map of "the World that Nature Intended."*)
to this place.

    (*Points to map of "the World of Nations and States."*)

Through millions of small choices. And claims.

DAVE. And you become your job.

> (*Pause.*)

and your job becomes you.

> (MARGARET *looks at audience.*)

43.

ANNALISE. (*Points to map of "the World of Nations and States."*)

This is the world we've chosen. Or the world we've let be chosen for us.

DAVE. For example: I'm a. Court reporter. You record what other people say. Then you play it back. Annalise here, she came over to our house last night for dinner, we had lamb couscous it was very good and Bob had gone to bed already, he was drunk again, had a little too much to drink again, and you know, you get talking about "he's had too much to drink again," not that you should get upset about that, and she last night she said "I never hear you use the word I."

> (*Pause.*)

And I said "What?" and she said "When you talk, I never hear you use the word I, or it's really rare. When you talk." and I said "Ok?" and

ANNALISE. (*In last night.*)

I never hear you use the word I.

DAVE. What?

ANNALISE. When you talk, I never hear you use the word I, or it's really rare. When you talk.

DAVE. Ok?

ANNALISE. When you talk, I never, I hear you saying things like "you know when you're going to the store and you see someone you're afraid you're going to have to talk to and you"

stuff like that.

DAVE. And ok. So?

ANNALISE. So I never hear you say "I went to the store and I saw someone I was afraid to talk to." I hear you say "You know when you're going to the store and you blah blah blah" and it seems like you avoid using the word I. That's all.

DAVE. Really?

ANNALISE. Why do you think you do that?

DAVE. And you really think that's what?

ANNALISE. Well listen to yourself sometime.

DAVE. Is this a joke?

ANNALISE. No Dave. I was listening to you all night, and I noticed that the whole time I don't think you ever used the word I and then I realized that you barely mentioned anything about yourself and Bob did most of the talking until he blacked out.

DAVE. He was tired. He fell asleep.

ANNALISE. Ok. Sure. But still.

Fine. Sure Ok.

Dave.

DAVE. He was tired.

ANNALISE. Dave.

DAVE. You know how it is, you've had a long day at work, he had a long day at work, and you come home and maybe you have too much to drink.

ANNALISE. You're doing it again.

DAVE. What.

ANNALISE. Bob's not my point. Bob can Bob can I don't care what Bob

DAVE. Well good because he's fine. He's

ANNALISE. You on the other hand you don't I never hear you use the word I and I wonder

And then I thought maybe it's because you're shy or

But I don't think it's, I wanted to mention it to you so you could notice it too because I think it's kind of important and

DAVE. (*Back in the now.*)

You know when you hear something and you know it's important? And you feel the world stop and get quiet. That's how I felt.

MARGARET. I'm not my job.

44.

MARGARET. I'm not my goddamn job.

45.

MARGARET. I'm not my job.

ANNALISE. Margaret.

MARGARET. I'm not my job. No I'm not.

DAVE. When you say something like "You're your job" you don't necessarily mean

MARGARET. I heard you. I heard you. I know what you meant.

I'm not my job. I'm not not this this I'm not

> (*She knocks over her glass of water. It falls off the desk and smashes. They all look at it. Shocked.*)

(*She stands up. Exits.*)
(ANNALISE *pauses, then exits.*)

46.
DAVE. (*Pause.*)

47.
DAVE. (*Starts to try to learn to use the word I.*)
So when ah
so when someone says something like that to you
so when Annalise said all that to me, you have to
I had to think about it.

48.
DAVE. You start listening to yourself.

49.
DAVE. I started listening to myself. And I heard what she was talking about.
        (*Pause.*)
And I thought about my work. How when you're a court reporter, you just capture and repeat what other people say and you're practically not even there. You're just neutral.
        (*Pause.*)
How since I'm a court reporter, I'm neutral. And maybe I don't tell my own side of
        (*Pause.*)
And it's hard it's a hard it's hard for me to
I have a hard time, my tongue gets tripped up.
And if you go just a, if I go just a little bit farther with it all, I can see that, when I've been talking like that, I've been putting myself over there, and it's as though I've been talking about someone else all the time, as if I've been talking about that person. Not about me, but about that "you" person. The whole time.
So then.
Where have I been? I guess that's.
        (*Pause.*)
Where have I been?
        (*Pause.*)

Where have I been? All this time?

>　(*Pause.*)
>
>　(*Exits.*)

50.

>　(*No one on stage.*)

51.

>　(MARGARET *enters.*)

MARGARET. Seven years ago, about six or no six or seven maybe seven years ago, seven years ago I think it was, it was in the spring, in the early spring six years no no no no no it was seven years ago because I was working at

yeah no it was seven, seven not six, no half dozen, no three and three, but seven

>　(*Smiles.*)

and

It was early spring seven years ago, in that early time when the air and the earth,

after a dry winter, after shoes tied tight or boots and wool

It was early spring and I hadn't escaped the winter yet, I was still in the darkness of the

It was early spring. I thought, maybe it's time to do something new.

I woke up early every day, and each day, every day, each day I designed a new version of the letter A.

An uppercase A. Each of the 26 letters is unique, is a unique combination of

A for example is a strong, has a triangular, is

>　(*Holds her hands in a peak, and then slashes the crossbar.*)

Three strokes.

But. And this is

A letter can be bold or light, can be wide or heavy or as narrow as a path through the woods, can be can be can be sans serif or serif, can be

Can slant. Can

Day after day, week after week, month after month, into the summer, into the fall, every morning I woke up and I drew a new a new A.

>　(*She stands up.*)

Each day, every day was new.

>　(*Exits.*)

52.

(ANNALISE *approaches the desk. Walks along behind it, trailing a finger along the desk and up and over and down each chair, as if they were mountains.*)

ANNALISE. If we just paid attention, we'd see there are landscapes all around us.

(*She takes her seat.*)

53.

ANNALISE. In my neighborhood there is a woman who walks around our streets picking up bits of garbage. Litter. Trash.

She wears rubber gloves and her house slippers. She stoops over. She looks angry. She picks everything up: paper, cigarette butts, bottles, crap, food wrappers, any any any any any bit any bit of this or that that she finds. She has a route. When she sees someone litter, she yells at them.

Obviously she sees the streets as an extension of her home, and that it's dirty?—disturbs her.

We see her and we see that, a disturbed person.

54.

ANNALISE. I love maps. Love maps. Love.

When I was six, was I six? Six. Six, was I six no I couldn't have been, no no no no no I was nine. I was nine. I was nine. I looked at a map and asked my teacher why there were lines between the different countries, and she said "that's how we know who owns that part of the world." And I asked her "how come some people own those parts of the world and some people don't?" and I asked her "who told them they could own it?"

But I was asking all this during math class. So.

(DAVE *enters. Sits down.*)

55.

ANNALISE. Each bit of land on this good green earth has been claimed. All of it, every. And while we'll use anything that will give our claims weight eh, National Security, National Interest, Science, God, the Queen, it is so entirely clear from geography that, the disturbing truth that geography reveals is, is we've only borrowed it. We're only borrowing the earth. These lines are going to move.

DAVE. While you were

While I was

While you were training to be a stenographer, you'd use the "postem scoring" method to check for mistakes in your exercises right after you'd finished them.

P, o, s, t, e, m

P is for the number of errors in punctuation, caps, I don't know why, because caps is "c" not P but still ok, and paragraphing—P is also for paragraphing, it's for punctuation, caps and paragraphing

O is for omitted words

S is for substituted words or added words, again "added," S, "added," S? I don't get it but.

    (*Shrugs.*)

Ok.

T is for the number of typographical errors

E is for erasures

M is for misspellings

P O S T E M!

It's diagnostic. It helps you go back and figure out how many of each kind of mistakes you're making. It also helps you know that common, the most common mistakes during transcription are typing, spelling, punctuation, grammar, word division, numbers, format, caps, abbreviations, erasures, omissions.

    (*Ticks them off in his head.*)

That's about it, pretty much covers it. And if you go back and check those, you're probably going to be ok.

Proofreading is crucial.

56.

ANNALISE. Why do we create choke points? How does a boundary get set? How do we decide who owns what? When I started studying geography, really seriously started studying it, those were the kinds of questions that really interested me. Still do they still do.

DAVE. You get really good, I got really good at proofreading.

57.

ANNALISE. My studying keeps me awake. In the world. I guess I guess I

DAVE. I'm good at being careful.

58.

ANNALISE. My studying keeps me asking questions. Makes me a pain in the ass. I don't mind that!

DAVE. I'm probably too good at being careful.

59.

ANNALISE. I love my job.

DAVE. What I like about my job, I like that you, I like that I have these skills I've honed. I've been doing it so long that I have these

I know how to examine a transcript and I can find the problems in it. And if I can find the problems, I can work on them.

60.

ANNALISE. I'm lucky. I used to hate my job. I used to hate all my jobs.

DAVE. I'm lucky. I like my job.

61.

ANNALISE. I worked at a mortuary. I worked scooping ice cream at a stand in front of the Tontine Mall. I worked in a greenhouse. I was the office manager for an eyeglass store.

DAVE. It's an interesting field. Well, it's the only field I've ever been in. But it's interesting.

62.

ANNALISE. The mortuary was interesting at first. Dead people. Black clothes, quiet voices. Sorrow.

I didn't like being inside all the time.

Scooping ice cream, well at least I was outside. But I could only eat so much ice cream, eh. And it depressed me, how many people always had the same flavor. Vanilla vanilla vanilla vanilla. Vanilla.

I killed a lot of plants in the greenhouse.

I am very grateful to the Perry Eyewear Store, "We've got our eye on you!" Allen Perry "Call me Uncle Al!" was a complete dope. "You gotta give'm what they want and then convince'm they want a little more!" And "Blink and these glasses'll be gone!" "Great glasses in eye'll two!" "Eye'll bet you need new glasses!"

That job was so awful, I had to really look at what I was doing.

DAVE. So, so when you say, when you say that you never hear me use the word I, what exactly do you mean by that? That's exactly what I asked Annalise last night. I said:

(*In last night.*)

So, so when you say, when you say that you never hear me use the word I, what exactly do you mean by that?

ANNALISE. What?

DAVE. What are you trying to tell me?

ANNALISE. That you never use the word I.

DAVE. But what do you mean by that?

ANNALISE. I mean you never use the word I.

DAVE. But what do you mean by that?

ANNALISE. What do you mean, what do I mean?

DAVE. What do you mean, What else are you trying to tell me? what do you mean.

ANNALISE. Dave.

DAVE. You must be trying to tell me something else or else you wouldn't have brought it up.

ANNALISE. I wasn't trying to tell you something else. I was trying to tell you that.

DAVE. That's what you were trying to tell me.

ANNALISE. Half the time you're talking I don't know who the hell you're talking about.

DAVE. Really? Really. No.

ANNALISE. Yes.

DAVE. No.

ANNALISE. Ok. No.

DAVE. Really?

ANNALISE. You say something like "you know when you're at the gym, do you think you should blah blah blah" and I'm thinking "I don't go to the gym" and then I think "oh no, he's talking about himself, when did he start going to the gym? he doesn't go to the gym" and then I think "oh no, he's talking about Bob. He's talking about Bob. Going to the gym."

DAVE. I go to the gym.

ANNALISE. Fine. Is there anymore wine?

DAVE. I haven't been going recently because I hurt my shoulder.

ANNALISE. Ok Dave.

DAVE. Annalise. It's sore.

ANNALISE. Hey I don't go either.

DAVE. It hurts when I go like this.

ANNALISE. Dave? Is there more wine?

DAVE. You guys finished off both bottles.

ANNALISE. Bob finished them off.

DAVE. Do you think I look fat? Is that what you were?

ANNALISE. This is what you always do.

DAVE. What?

ANNALISE. Look, Dave. If you don't want to think about it, fine. I just wanted to tell you, so I'd know, so I could be sure you'd heard it from someone. Since I'm your friend.

63.

ANNALISE. Working with Allen Perry "Call me Uncle Al" made me realize I couldn't just work just anywhere. I had my limits. His wife Monica, Monica Perry, "Call me Monica." She and I didn't really get along.

She wanted me to wear the eyeglass frames around the store, because "people are easily led." I'd tell her "I'm more of a contact lens person."

DAVE. (*In last night;*) Let's say I

Let's say I never used the word I, which isn't true, as you can tell, since I'm using it right now, well what would be the problem with that?

ANNALISE. What do you think the problem would be with it?

DAVE. It's irritating?

ANNALISE. I'm so tipsy.

DAVE. You are?

ANNALISE. I should never

Trying to keep up with Bob is always, boy oh boy oh what a mistake that is. I should of eaten more couscous. It was very good.

DAVE. Do you feel sick?

ANNALISE. No. Just. No I'm fine.

DAVE. You sure?

ANNALISE. I'm fine.

       (*Sighs from her stomach. Rubs her nose into her face. Pops her eyes open.*)

I'm fine.

DAVE. You ok?

ANNALISE. I'm kind of critical. I'm critical.

DAVE. You're not critical.

ANNALISE. I know I am.

DAVE. Annalise.

ANNALISE. Dave. It's ok. I'm critical. It's a blessing and it's a curse. A blessing for me. Curse for everyone else.

       (*Laughs.*)

DAVE. You're not so bad.

ANNALISE.

(*Purses lips. Blows air into her cheeks. Lets the air out. Elbow on desk, heel of hand in nose. Head lifts, everything else doesn't move. Eyes go from friendly to alien.*)

You're a liar You're sneaky You make people feel bad. And you don't even know it!

DAVE. What?

ANNALISE. Yeah.

DAVE. You're drunk.

ANNALISE. Yeah.

DAVE. You're drunk.

ANNALISE. So?

DAVE. You wouldn't be saying this if you weren't drunk.

ANNALISE. I would too It's the truth.

DAVE. You're just like Bob "When you're drunk you can tell the truth You can cry You're allowed to make friends with the fucking waiter!" You can do that when you're not drunk.

ANNALISE. It's still the truth!

64.

ANNALISE. Then they started playing that song Rose Colored Glasses over and over and over in the store and Monica started singing along Rose Colored Glasses and I knew I better

And I better do it quick cause I wanted to tell Uncle Al and Monica especially exactly how But Uncle Al was a friend of my Dad's so I just said "Thanks a lot, I'm going back to school." And I got the hell out of there.

DAVE. (*In last night.*)

(*Pause.*)

That was kind of harsh.

65.

(*In last night.*)

(*There is a dance music song on. Loud. ANNALISE is dancing. DAVE is sitting.*)

(*ANNALISE almost falls over.*)

ANNALISE. Whoa! Whoa. Whoa. Ha. I can't feel my teeth!

(*Laughs.*)

DAVE. That was harsh.

66.

ANNALISE. (*In last night.*)

  (*Sits down.*)

It was.

DAVE. It was.

ANNALISE. It was. I agree. It was.

DAVE. Is that what you really think?

ANNALISE. Yeah.

DAVE. Does everyone think that? Is everybody saying this?

ANNALISE. Everybody who?

DAVE. Like Margaret? Does she think this too?

ANNALISE. No I don't know maybe.

DAVE. Has she said that?

ANNALISE. Dave.

DAVE. Great. Great. Does Bob?

ANNALISE. That's not the point.

DAVE. Great. Great. Bob's got another thing coming if he thinks.

ANNALISE. Come on Dave.

DAVE. How would you feel if your best friend told you you were a liar.

ANNALISE. And sneaky.

DAVE. This isn't funny. You'd think Bob at least would
Bob thinks that?

ANNALISE. I don't know what Bob thinks. Bob's not Bob not even

DAVE. This doesn't have anything to do with Bob.

DAVE. Who is it you think I lie to then?

ANNALISE. You lie all the time.

DAVE. Oh. Oh. Oh. All the time now.

ANNALISE. Well.

DAVE. Fucking Bob!

ANNALISE. What I said, Dave, what I said, is what I think. Not what
Margaret thinks. Not what Bob thinks. What I think.
This is classic you.

  (*Pause.*)

Did Bob have a dentist appointment last Tuesday?

DAVE. What?

ANNALISE. You said you called his work and you told them he had a
dentist appointment.

DAVE. He wasn't feeling well.

ANNALISE. He wasn't feeling well?

DAVE. He wasn't!

ANNALISE. Right.

Did you like Margaret's last haircut? The one before this one?

DAVE. No.

ANNALISE. You didn't?

DAVE. The one with the flip flip thing? No. Did you? No. It was horrible.

ANNALISE. It was. Horrible.

     (DAVE *laughs*.)

ANNALISE. She thought you did. She said you said you liked it.

DAVE. You're not going to tell her you don't like her haircut.

ANNALISE. She was nervous to change it, she thought you thought it looked so good. She kept saying "Dave likes it. Dave told me it looks great." I had to make her go and get it recut.

DAVE. Oh big deal.

ANNALISE. Right.

DAVE. That's a big deal. I lied about her hair. Guilty.

ANNALISE. Is there more wine?

DAVE. You guys finished it.

ANNALISE. No we didn't.

DAVE. You drank both bottles.

ANNALISE. I saw three bottles in the fridge.

DAVE. Then why're you asking?

ANNALISE. You're a liar Dave.

DAVE. You've had enough to drink. You said so yourself.

ANNALISE. You're a liar Dave.

DAVE. You had plenty to drink.

ANNALISE. You sneak around. You watch everything. It's like you have a, that dogsheet thing in your head and you're keeping track. Bob did this. Bob didn't do this. Annalise did this or that. Keeping track of everything and then you bring it up and

I've seen him squirm and

DAVE. (*Quiet:*)

Annalise.

ANNALISE. That's not the friend I used to.

DAVE. I have to.

ANNALISE. No you don't.

DAVE. You don't

ANNALISE. No you don't. That time when you guys went off the road and with the fruit stand and the peaches and the nectarines and olive loaf

(DAVE *laughs.*)

ANNALISE. (*Laughing:*) I know and the garden trolls with the peaches "I'm going to eat your peach!" and the flamingos and you made it into such a great story.

DAVE. I'm going to eat your peach!

ANNALISE. I'm going to eat your peach!

(*Not laughing.*)

You did good you made it all ok. Bob sits there when you tell that story. That shouldn't have happened.

DAVE. He wouldn't let me drive.

ANNALISE. You shouldn't have been in the car with him.

DAVE. I didn't drink.

ANNALISE. Oh.

DAVE. What if he'd really crashed hard?

ANNALISE. What if he'd really crashed hard?

DAVE. He could have been really hurt.

ANNALISE. You could have been hurt. You would have been in the car.

DAVE. You're going to let someone kill himself?

ANNALISE. There's something wrong with you, Dave. Not Bob. Bob's got his.

But I don't care. Bob's Bob's Bob. You're my friend and there's something wrong with you that you'd let him, that you'd go down with him.

And that you'd keep hurting him by refusing to look at it. On top of it all.

DAVE. (*Laughing.*) Annalise.

(*Pause.*)

ANNALISE. (*Pause.*) Ok.

67.

(MARGARET *enters. Sits.*)

MARGARET. At my work Six months ago.

A consultant came in to work with my company, where I work. He was going to help us make the business grow. Bring in more business. Bring in new business. Get us to act more like a business that did business. Made sense. He was a business consultant. He was focused on the business of business. Of our work. He's been working with us, on us, to get us to focus on it too. We've focused on the business so much, we've forgotten to work.

ANNALISE. I remember when I left the Perry Eyewear Store, I quit, I walked out the door, Uncle Al and Monica were just looking at me, and I stood outside on the sidewalk and I

I had no job. If someone came up to me in that moment and said "What do you do?" I'd have had to say "nothing." That was a scary feeling.

(DAVE *looks at audience.*)

68.

MARGARET. I get so nervous about the numbers, the quarter, the projections, the numbers, the numbers, the numbers

I forget why I work.

ANNALISE. I was in a no man's land. I didn't have "I'm the office manager at the Perry Eyewear Store" any more.

(DAVE *looks at audience.*)

69.

MARGARET. When I'm working on a type problem, when I'm wandering around, between the letters, around in the spaces between the letters, letter space letter space letter word word word

When I'm in that space I can feel myself open I can

That's where I'm supposed to be.

This business consultant wants me, wants all of us to join him in his

It's hard, it's impossible to serve someone else's god.

I can feel myself

I disappear.

ANNALISE. The lines on our maps reveal a drive towards ownership. A drive to capture territory, to reassure ourselves that "Here we are, and we are staying here." "I own this, or this is where I belong, this is who I am." Reassurance that if there's not enough to go around, well, at least we'll have ours.

DAVE. My friend Monalisa is a waitress. She says when people come into her restaurant they can be really foul, in really foul moods. She says it took her years to realize why. She says it's because they're hungry. Well yeah, but they're panicky and they get nasty because they're afraid she won't bring them any food. At some deep level, they don't think they're going to get fed.

She says people are afraid like that all the time all over the place all the time. She learned that from waitressing.

70.

MARGARET. I was driving home across the bridge. I thought What would happen if I swerved into that concrete pylon? How much broken glass would

there be? Would my airbag open? Could I disable my airbag? How fast would I have to be going to really smash my car up?
ANNALISE. Margaret.
DAVE. Margaret.

71.

MARGARET. When I have thoughts like that, I used to get, I would, all nervous, all nervous.
Now I know, when I think things like that, I'm telling myself: I don't like who I am being. I don't want to be where I am. I don't want to be here. Simple as that.
> (*Pause.*)

I gotta get a new job.
DAVE. You think I'm a liar Margaret?
MARGARET. Oh yeah Dave.
DAVE. You do?
MARGARET. Sure. You're a huge liar.
> (*Pause.*)

Did Annalise tell you that?
DAVE. So
Great. Great. What am I supposed to do about this?
MARGARET. Oh don't worry Dave.
DAVE. Great.
MARGARET. You don't need to worry You're great at solving problems. You just never knew what the problem was.
ANNALISE. (*Laughs:*) Right!
DAVE. Great.
MARGARET. Dave.

72.

MARGARET. That business consultant is a bully.
ANNALISE. You should get a new job.
DAVE. Great.

73.

DAVE. I'm sorry I said you were your job.
MARGARET. No Dave.
DAVE. No I am.

MARGARET. No. Dave.

Dave. Dave. Dave. Look at me Dave. Dave.

DAVE. I am.

MARGARET. I am my job. I don't care. I know that. It's what I do all day. I am my job.

I got mad because

It's ok you said that. It was the truth.

ANNALISE. You should quit your job.

MARGARET. I should quit my job. Dave should question his relationship. You should stop thinking you know what everyone should do.

ANNALISE. I'm not saying I know

MARGARET. You are too you are. Of course you are.

Dave's an idiot because he lets Bob just.

ANNALISE. Dave's not an idiot.

MARGARET. He's "misguided."

ANNALISE. He hasn't noticed.

MARGARET. He's "not paying attention."

DAVE. Hello I'm right here. You're talking about me I'm right here.

ANNALISE. Well you're not.

MARGARET. He is. He's doing what he needs to

ANNALISE. He's not

MARGARET. He is he is

DAVE. I'm right here.

MARGARET. Dave. Stop.

Annalise he is. Or it doesn't matter if he isn't he's gotta

ANNALISE. It matters!

MARGARET. According to you.

ANNALISE. It does. All of it does!

MARGARET. It's his life!

ANNALISE. It's so easy down here. In the States we say anything that works for us. Each plastic bag each piece of trash each bit of crap matters. The crime we've created is—we believe it doesn't! We say— "oh it doesn't matter, my bit of trash won't be noticed, my bit can pass because it's mine and I needed it!"

MARGARET. We're not talking about trash, we're talking about Dave, Annalise.

ANNALISE. Same thing.

DAVE. I'm right here!

MARGARET. He's right here.

ANNALISE. You know what I mean.

MARGARET. It's none of your business.

ANNALISE. It is too!

MARGARET. It isn't!

ANNALISE. It's all the same thing. The States is on drugs!

MARGARET. Annalise.

ANNALISE. It is Margaret. It's on speed, it's on stuff, on sex on ok religion whatever, it's on it it's on it's on, and I've seen it, and I've been there and I don't want to be there, even though it's exciting and you might think "oh I can't live without it" "I can't live without Bob" it catches you up and it denies itself and you're in the middle of it

But

every now and then there are moments when it all falls away for a moment, the celebrity, the pop the jazz the moving fast the business it all falls away and what is left is grace! is silence! is clarity! is understanding! and you think "maybe I could live without it"

But then it's broken by a car alarm wrang! wrang! wrang! wrang! or a cell phone or a motorcycle or siren or a person talking too much too loud too long about something anything that really really really matters to them and then you are lost in it again

and you forget that

MARGARET. Annalise.

ANNALISE. You forget that

MARGARET. Annalise.

ANNALISE. You forget that you forget "maybe this isn't all good for me" Maybe this big dump of crap over in that county is going to be a problem when it slips into their groundwater and drifts under the county line into my county into my groundwater. Because groundwater doesn't notice the county line!

MARGARET. Annalise.

ANNALISE. I'm supposed to just let him get himself killed?!

MARGARET. Annalise!

DAVE. What?

ANNALISE. His drunk boyfriend! Just smash him in the car! Just Just Just! I should shut up?

MARGARET. Yes!

ANNALISE. Because I'm going to be the one crying!

DAVE. What?

MARGARET. "You should quit your job!"

ANNALISE. What?

MARGARET. "That's what you should do!"

ANNALISE. You should!

MARGARET. It's all so easy for you to say! You sit there and you just say it say it You just say whatever you You should quit your job! You should do this! You should do that! It's so easy to say!

ANNALISE. You said that guy's a bully! You've been complaining about

DAVE. Maybe.

MARGARET & ANNALISE. Dave!

MARGARET. It's all the same You with your

And Canada and the States

Oh Canada wouldn't do that, the States shouldn't be doing this or that

Oh Canada oh Canada

DAVE. Yeah. Ha. Canada!

ANNALISE. What?

MARGARET. Canada!

DAVE. Yeah. Canada!

MARGARET. HA!

ANNALISE. What?

MARGARET. The United States is a big bully!

ANNALISE. It is!

MARGARET. Bob's a big bully, my business consultant is a big bully, the United States is a big bully!

ANNALISE. Well yeah eh?

DAVE. Bob's not a bully.

ANNALISE. Dave.

MARGARET. Dave.

And poor old Canada just sitting up there looking down and saying "if only if only" "They should"

ANNALISE. What's Canada supposed to do?

MARGARET. Just remember it's partly because Canada just sits!

and

because all over the place people are letting the States be a big bully because even though the bully is scary, and we try to contain it, we actually hope we might get to be one of them ourselves—Maybe I'm going to get to yell at the cook "get in the kitchen!" or maybe

Just like Bob has a problem and Dave won't look at it

DAVE. Bob doesn't have a problem.

MARGARET. Just like Dave has a problem and he isn't going to look at it either

DAVE. I don't have a problem.

MARGARET. Because maybe he's too scared to look at it

DAVE. I don't!

MARGARET. Because maybe he's not ready yet

DAVE. I don't have a problem!

MARGARET. Ok Dave!

ANNALISE. Sure. Dave. Fine.

MARGARET. Ok!

ANNALISE. Margaret.

MARGARET. Because Canada's getting all the stuff too. Sitting next to the bully. Sharing all the toys!

> (*Pause.*)

And I agree with you I gotta get a new job. Cause I'm not going to be that one any more. I know that! I know that! I know that!

ANNALISE. Well then you should

MARGARET. Maybe it's scary to stand up to the bully

ANNALISE. You should

MARGARET. Maybe it'd be easier to just get mad at you for pointing the bully out!

ANNALISE. You should

MARGARET. Stop saying it as if you know what I should do You should do this You should do and I don't, I'm some sort of stupid Who doesn't have any idea what she should

ANNALISE. Margaret

MARGARET. Stay on your own side of the fence!

ANNALISE. Margaret

MARGARET. Because when you talk like that you make people feel bad. You make me feel And you don't even know it!

And it's hard enough Without getting mad at your friends

ANNALISE. Ok.

> (*Pause.*)

Ok.

> (*Pause.*)

You're right.

74.

MARGARET. I'm a typographer.

ANNALISE. I'm a geographer.

I'm gonna go home.

I'm gonna go home.

DAVE. (*Silence.*)

75.

MARGARET. The typographer's dream: Ink on paper.
To typeset a book. To have a civilized deadline. To work at a slower pace.
Oh. To see the metal type kiss the paper. To use quality ink on archival acid-
free paper. To have time stop.

    (*Pause.*)

I've got a book that was printed in the seventeen century. It's still good.

76.

    (*Final blackout.*)

End of Play

CRUMBLE
(LAY ME DOWN, JUSTIN TIMBERLAKE)
by Sheila Callaghan

For more information about rights and permissions, see p. 10.

BIOGRAPHY

Sheila Callaghan's plays have been produced and developed with Soho Rep, Playwright's Horizons, South Coast Repertory, Clubbed Thumb, The LARK, Actor's Theatre of Louisville, New Georges, and Moving Arts, among others. Sheila is the recipient of a 2000 Princess Grace Award for emerging artists, a 2001 LA Weekly Award for Best One-act, a 2001-02 Jerome Fellowship from the Playwright's Center in Minneapolis, a 2002 Chesley Prize for Lesbian Playwriting, a 2003 Mac Dowell Residency, a 2004 NYFA grant, a 2007 NYSCA grant with Clubbed Thumb, and is a 2007-2008 Finalist for the Susan Smith Blackburn Award. Her plays have been produced internationally in New Zealand, Norway, and the Czech Republic. She has been commissioned by Playwright's Horizons, South Coast Repertory, and EST/Sloan. Her full-length plays include *Scab*, *The Hunger Waltz*, *Crawl Fade to White*, *Crumble (Lay Me Down, Justin Timberlake)*, *We Are Not These Hands*, *Dead City*, *Lascivious Something*, and *Kate Crackernuts*. Several of her plays are published by Playscripts, Inc. She has taught playwriting at The University of Rochester, Spalding University, The College of New Jersey, and Florida State University. Sheila is a member of the Obie winning playwright's organization 13P and a resident of New Dramatists. Visit her at sheilacallaghan.com.

Other Clubbed Thumb credits: Boot Camp 2003; *Roadkill Confidential* (2007 Commission).

ACKNOWLEDGMENTS

Crumble (Lay Me Down, Justin Timberlake) was originally produced by Clubbed Thumb as part of Summerworks 2004 at the Ohio Theatre in New York City (with support from the Jerome Foundation). It was directed by Katie Pearl, with the following cast and staff:

JANICE	Flora Diaz
MOTHER	Effie Johnson
BARBARA	Annie McNamara
DAD/JUSTIN TIMBERLAKE/ HARRISON FORD	David Brooks
THE APARTMENT	Michael Stumm
Sets	Andrew Cavanaugh Holland
Lights	Garin Marschall
Costumes	Jessica Gaffney
Sound	Sxip Shirey

The play received its official world premiere at Moving Arts in Los Angeles, October 2005. It was directed by Larry Biederman, with the following cast:

BARBARA .... Evie Hammer
JANICE .... Lily Holleman
DAD/JUSTIN TIMBERLAKE/
       HARRISON FORD ....Jeffrey Johnson
THE APARTMENT... Stephen Kline
MOTHER ....Amy Thiel

The play was previously developed with Manhattan Theatre Source in New York City in 2000.

Special thanks to Chad Stutz and Manhattan Theatre Source for their initial support in the creation of this play.

CAST OF CHARACTERS
THE APARTMENT
FATHER / JUSTIN TIMBERLAKE / HARRISON FORD, male, 20s–40s
JANICE, girl, age 11
MOTHER, female, mid-late thirties
BARBARA, female, early 40s

PRODUCTION NOTES
It is advised not to be literal with the portrayal of The Apartment; the device
of the anthropomorphized dwelling is best handled creatively, simply, and
theatrically (as budget and imagination will allow).

Flora Diaz
in *Crumble (Lay Me Down, Justin Timberlake)*.

Produced by Clubbed Thumb at The Ohio Theatre, 2004.
Photograph by Carl Skutsch

CRUMBLE
(LAY ME DOWN, JUSTIN TIMBERLAKE)

OVERTURE.

Lights up on THE APARTMENT, BARBARA, MOTHER, FATHER *and* JANICE, *all in separate spaces.*

MOTHER *is in a chef's apron, cutting vegetables.*

BARBARA *is opening a can of tuna.*

JANICE *is listening to her walkman.*

FATHER *is falling through space and time.*

End OVERTURE.

THE APARTMENT *is the floor. He listens to his voice echoing.*

THE APARTMENT. OOOOOOOH.

Cavernous.

OOOOOOOOHHHHHH. Echooooo.

OW OW OW OOOOOOOH.

Musty. I stink. Creak all the time... My back. Strings of dust... fffft. Appalling.

Oh. Alright that was a RAT, I just felt a. Possibly a mouse. Unngghhuuuuhhhhaaaa. Cannot TOLERATE. Dirty dirty little paws... mouths, little rat-mouths, with the the.

(Creak.)

It's gone.

NEGLECT. Frigid. NO HEAT. Capacious fireplace in the den, no one uses. And DISREPAIR? I was a mansion once. A KEPT mansion. Young women with their young hands, oh small fingers splitting apart to feather my crevices. So gentle. They would kneel, their knees pressed into my wood—is there anything more delicious than a servant girl's knees? Damp stiff horse-hair brush along my spine back and forth, faint scent of orange rind... and the giggling, laughter like little bursting soap bubbles... Back then. People hired HELP. Defined themselves by their CLEAN LIVING SPACES. POISONED THEIR RODENTS.

(Creak.)

(MOTHER enters in her coat. She has some bags of groceries. She begins unloading the bag.)

THE APARTMENT. Well GOOD AFTERNOON, Baroness.... you look, hmmm. Holiday tired. Sit down, rest your little footsies...

(MOTHER *sits.*)

Look up. Look up. Look up. Look up. Look up.

(MOTHER *glances absently up.*)

What do you see?

(MOTHER *looks slightly concerned.*)

How do you suppose it got there?

(MOTHER *looks bewildered.*)

What does it resemble? A vein? A tributary? A tree branch? Or just a plain old CRACK? Have you any IDEA. How DISGUSTING. I am BECOMING.

(MOTHER *sighs and looks down again. A piece of plaster falls from the ceiling by her feet. She regards it without interest.*)

FFAAAHHHH! And this?

(*A piece of wallpaper begins to peel in the corner.* MOTHER *smooths it out with her hand slowly, lovingly. It curls back immediately.*)

PASTE, woman. Not a lot. No I would never DARE to imagine you'd commit the energy to a whole new PAPER JOB. Paper takes TIME. Paper takes EXERTION. Paper takes all the FUN out of living, yes? But who needs FUN here. No, we sink and sink. We crumble to bits. We shove our fists into our mouths at night to keep those around us from hearing our sobs. Don't we.

(MOTHER *shivers and puts her scarf back on.*)

(*Creak.*)

For what I am thinking, and for the actions I am prepared to take heretofore... let it be known. I had no other choice.

(MOTHER *sighs and begins to cut up vegetables.*)

MOTHER. Janice? JANICE?

JANICE. WWHHHHAAAAAAAAAAT?

MOTHER. OFF.

(JANICE *turns her walkman off.*)

MOTHER. Do you have the list / for me yet

JANICE. The list the list the list list / list list list list ...

(JANICE *dances mirthlessly around her mother.*)

MOTHER. (*Overlapping:*) I don't have time for this, Janice...

JANICE. LIST LIST LIST...

MOTHER. JANICE MIRANDA LOUISE PATRICIA ANN!

(JANICE *stops and stares at* MOTHER.)

THE APARTMENT. How does one cultivate such an odd human?

(JANICE *calmly retrieves a much crumpled piece of paper from her sock and hands it to her mother.*)

MOTHER. Thank you. Three more shopping days... ludicrous... you have any idea what the lines will...

(MOTHER *reads it. She falls silent a moment.*)

MOTHER. I don't understand.

(JANICE *stares at* MOTHER.)

MOTHER. Janice...

JANICE. I have homework okay.

(JANICE *turns to leave.*)

MOTHER. Since when do you do home—wait. Are you eating dinner tonight, I'm making something light. Ah, starting with bruchetta and an olive tappenade, and then pork tenderloin glazed with a brown sugar and bourbon sauce topped with a honey Dijon, and a roma tomato salad with fresh basil and garlic on the side. And peach bread pudding for dessert. And I made some mint lemonade spritzers. So. I'll expect you at the table at seven. Put on something warmer. They still haven't fixed the heat.

JANICE. You haven't. Called them.

MOTHER. What about that sweater Aunt Barbara bought you for your birthday. With the duckies in snowsuits. Yes it's hideous but it's wool. Go.

(JANICE *hesitates.*)

MOTHER. Go on, now...

JANICE. (*Carefully:*) I would rather bleed to death in an open field slathered in manure.

MOTHER. Don't be melodra— Janice, it's frigid in here, you'll catch pneumonia or strep, we really don't need that this year, and put some socks on, your toes will fall off, you know the radiator was banging all morning, the pipes are, I don't know, contracting maybe, I can't turn the darn thing on because it will leak like last time and ruin the floors so GO Janice and PLEASE close your bedroom door so the heat stays in. NOW. I'm so tired. And don't spend all night on your computer. You'll, your eyes will. You'll go blind, or. Stop looking at me like that.

JANICE. MY TOES ARE FALLING OFF. HOLY CRAP. SOMEONE CALL AN AMBULENCE.

(JANICE *exits into her room and sets up her dolls.* MOTHER *stares at the paper. She begins to hyperventilate.*)

MOTHER. ... oh dear Lord...

THE APARTMENT. And here she goes. Breathe...

MOTHER. Breathe

THE APARTMENT. Breathe

MOTHER. Breathe.

THE APARTMENT. Super.

(*A beat.*)

THE APARTMENT. Look up. Look up. Look up. Look up. Look up.

(MOTHER *does not. A large piece of plaster falls from the sky.*)

(*To calm herself* MOTHER *does Pilates.*)

(JANICE *appears to be having a tea party with some dolls. She pours bleach into their cups.*)

JANICE. (*Singing:*)
Mama I dropped the candy
Mama could I have another one please
That beast gots the sticky behind his knees
Say oooh ah oooh-oooh ah

Slather my body in manure
Cook me over an open flame
I'd rather die die die die die
Than wear that ugly sweater, babe

That butt butt butt ugly
butt butt butt ugly
butt butt butt fucking fucking nasty-ass butt fucking
snowsuit duckie-fuck butt butt butt butt
what what what what butt butt butt butt

(*She works herself into a frenzy. She then pours each cup of bleach into a pot, one by one.*)

(*A shadow or silhouette of* FATHER *appears somewhere, in his work clothes, moving slowly.*)

(BARBARA *is holding a can of tuna.*)

(THE APARTMENT *begins to drip.* MOTHER *tends to is as she speaks on the phone to* BARBARA.)

BARBARA. It must be hard

MOTHER. It is

BARBARA. For you both

MOTHER. Yes

BARBARA. The holidays

MOTHER. Very

BARBARA. She's had a rough time of it

MOTHER. Yes

BARBARA. Children often do
At times like these

At times
MOTHER. Like these
I need your help
BARBARA. I'm here, Clara
MOTHER. I know
BARBARA. Talking helps
MOTHER. To talk
BARBARA. It really does
MOTHER. Hurts/
BARBARA. It really does.
          (*A beat.*)
BARBARA. I bought tuna today…
MOTHER. What?
BARBABA. Tuna?
MOTHER. Oh.
BARBARA. And you wouldn't believe how much they're charging…
MOTHER. Oh.
BARBARA. I bought it as a treat…
MOTHER. Oh.
BARBARA. I don't think I'll be doing THAT again…
MOTHER. You aren't listening
BARBARA. Oh. I thought you were done.
          (*A beat.*)
BARBARA. Go on
MOTHER. She wrinkles differently in daylight these days
BARBARA. Oh
MOTHER. her voice tilts with a purple cast
and sometimes her hair is wire
BARBARA. I see
MOTHER. And sometimes her breath is yellow
BARBARA. Like
MOTHER. Napalm
like rotting fruit and stomach acid
as though she swallowed a pear months ago
but can't digest it
BARBARA. Since when
MOTHER. Since the/

BARBARA. Calamity?

MOTHER. Yes

BARBARA. I see

MOTHER. She made a list last night

BARBARA. Of what

MOTHER. Seven things

BARBARA. What things

MOTHER. Strange things

BARBARA. Gifts.

MOTHER. Yes.

BARBARA. I see.

MOTHER. Girls that age should care

BARBARA. About

MOTHER. Make-up. Clothes. Gossip.

BARBARA. Indeed

MOTHER. What does she need

BARBARA. To talk

MOTHER. I've tried

BARBARA. To me

MOTHER. She won't

BARBARA. I know things, Clara

I know what to make of small girls

I know what they think of at night as they watch the squares of moon prowl
across their ceilings

I know what they think of in the bathtub when they wash behind their knees
with a new soap

MOTHER. You always did know things

Just like Mother

BARBARA. I intuit like no other

MOTHER. It's worth a try.

BARBARA. I'm hungry

MOTHER. We have left-overs... Janice doesn't

BARBARA. Eat much

MOTHER. These days,

BARBARA. What'd you make?

MOTHER. Um, bistro onion tarts to start with vegetable saté and then
chicken breast breaded with pecan nuts in a pineapple green peppercorn
sauce with a European cucumber mint salad and a rice wine vinaigrette on

the side. And chocolate espresso cheesecake with dark rum for dessert. And I made a non-alcoholic, um. Toddy.

BARBARA. Perfect.

> (BARBARA *disappears.*)
> (FATHER *vanishes.*)
> (MOTHER *begins cutting vegetables.*)
> (JANICE *is arranging her playing dolls.*)
> (THE APARTMENT *is the window sill.*)

THE APARTMENT. Clean me. Clean me. Fix me.

> (*A large chunk of the windowpane falls off and hits the ground.* JANICE *whirls around.*)

THE APARTMENT. Touch me.

> (JANICE *returns to her dolls and talks in different voices.*)

JANICE. Hey Janice, you know those jelly bracelets you wear, they're a symbol of sex.

Shut up. I have them because they look cool and well I think they're awesome. And I don't give a shit what you think.

They're idiotic. We always talk about them. And other stuff. Like how your breath stinks and don't wash your hair. And you probably eat boogers.

I know, and hey guess what, I don't care.

And like you always bring weird food to lunch

My mom's a cook, okay it's her JOB.

> (THE APARTMENT *blows a cool wind toward* JANICE.)

THE APARTMENT. Touch me...

> (JANICE *shivers and runs to her closet. She retrieves the duckie/snowsuit number and puts it on.*)

JANICE. Uglyuglyuglyuglyulgy/uglyuglyuglyuglyug

THE APARTMENT. ...please...

> (JANICE *returns to her dolls.*)

JANICE. Nice sweater, asshole.

Eat me. You think you're so hot just because you have an eyebrow ring but know what it looks retarded and anyway it's FAKE.

Karen and me and my cousin think you're a Lesbian. And you're on crack. My mom said your mom stopped buying Mountain Dew because you're too hyper.

So?

So, you're hyper and weird and your apartment is shitty.

Whatever, Karen's apartment is smaller.

But YOUR apartment is a piece of crap, it's old and it smells like shit, and you smell like shit.

Yeah, but at least I know how to ice skate.

APARTMENT. Your apartment is going to kill you. Your apartment is a murderer.

JANICE. Our mom told us we can't stay there anymore. There's asbestos and ghosts.

Shut up, there's no asbestos.

There's asbestos and mold and stuff. And your mom is crazy.

She's not crazy. She's. She's, like. She hyperventilates sometimes. That doesn't mean she's crazy. And she won't let us leave. But she won't fix anything. She doesn't even try. But. I'm going to change everything, okay. So she'll be happy again, I mean we both will. Because like, I'm very powerful.

Crazy.

Fuck you.

Crazy crazy.

You're a bitch.

Fuck you crazy bitch.

Fuck you asshole.

Fuck you.

Fuck you dick licker.

Fuck you.

> (BARBARA *enters, eating a plate of food.*)

BARBARA. Hello there, Janice. You look lovely today. What a beautiful sweater. I got you that, didn't I? Well how adorable it looks on you!

> (JANICE *doesn't answer.*)

BARBARA. Your mommy is SUCH a wonderful cook. You are one lucky little girl.

> (JANICE *doesn't answer.*)

BARBARA. So, what have we here? A tea party? May I play?

> (JANICE *doesn't answer.* BARBARA *grabs a doll and speaks in a doll-voice.*)

BARBARA. Hey there, pal. Looks like you got something stuck in your craw. Why not tell me about it. We're girlfriends, aren't we?

> (JANICE *stands and walks over to a pair of shoes. She begins taking the laces out and tying them together.* BARBARA *makes the doll drink from a tea cup.*)

BARBARA. Mmm. Nummy.

> (BARBARA *notices the teacups. She picks one up and smells it. Her doll voice drops.*)

BARBARA. (*Alarmed:*) Bleach. Janice? Are you drinking bleach?

(JANICE *doesn't answer.*)

BARBARA. JANICE.

JANICE. I'm not drinking bleach.

BARBARA. Then what are you doing with it?

JANICE. Cleaning.

(*Pause.* BARBARA *places the teacup down.*)

BARBARA. Janice honey... Mommy says your hair is wire and your breath is napalm. Mommy says you asked for seven really strange gifts this year. Your poor Mommy is so worried. You know how she gets. You don't want to give Mommy a lobotomy, do you?

Are you thinking of Christmas last year? You can talk about it. Hm?

(FATHER *appears again, as a shadow, moving slowly. He hammers a phantom nail.*)

(BARBARA *suddenly gasps in recognition.*)

BARBARA. Oh, I think I know... I was eleven once too... I had a Secret Crush. Mickey Forinelli. Never told a soul, not even my best friend. I watched him eat lunch every day. That boy could eat... do you watch boys eat

(*JANICE says nothing.*)

BARBARA. It's all right, it's perfectly healthy. Boys. Feelings about boys? Watching the poster of the boy on your wall come alive at night? He floats over to you like a question mark, lays his boy hands on all your new parts...

(JANICE *looks blankly at* BARBARA.)

BARBARA. You don't have to answer, your face says it all. Well, now we're talking, this is Girl Talk. Good good. Feels good to talk. Clears the noggin like a blast of freon. Ahhh.

(*Silence. And more silence.* BARBARA *is at an utter loss. She grabs the doll from before and reverts back to doll voice.*)

BARBARA. How about it, buddy? Is there a boy out there in Boyland gotcha down? Tell me tell me tell me...

(JANICE *grabs her doll and makes her speak to* BARBARA's *doll.*)

JANICE. Lady Sue with your dirty yarn hair and your mouth stitched shut in a perma-grin

Do you know how your eyes were made?

A needle poking into your head again and again

A million tiny holes in your flesh

How do you feel about that

(*A pause.* FATHER *vanishes.*)

BARBARA. Well, I suppose I wasn't too keen about it at the time...

(*A pause.* BARBARA *drops the dolls voice.*)

You're shy about it. That's okay. You'll talk when you're ready.

(BARBARA *exits. She moves back to her space and begins opening many, many cans of tuna, placing them around her feet. She saves the last one for herself and eats from the can with a fork.*)

(MOTHER *is still cutting vegetables.*)

(JANICE *continues intently with her project.*)

(THE APARTMENT *steps out of himself a moment.*)

THE APARTMENT. I was a mansion once. This was an aristocratic neighborhood of course, back in the early eighteen—Well, first it was a cabbage field. Sold for six shirts, two pairs of shoes, six pairs of stockings, six axes, six knives, two scissors, and six combs. But AFTER... pillows, divans, rugs, merchants' wives lolling about in my parlor awaiting news from their husbands at the trading docks. My plush, decadent, lounging ladies. Never a ruffle out of place, never a stray hair or a—and me as well. Drapes beaten, mattresses aired...

Then, yellow fever. I survived of course. Barely. A time of tears and soot. Time One of Disrepair. Swore I would never allow myself to descend into squalor again...

But AFTER... ladies again, ladies ladies... stronger perfumes and bolder laughs oh and naughty? Supremely naughty. Mattresses EVERYWHERE... All night, every night, my rooms thumping and swelling. Those ladies, well. Not the classiest but they had. Mmmm. And they trimmed me in shiny black. And they papered me in velvet-red. And their knees on my boards and perfumed knickers and.

But then, of course. A fire. Electricity, my wires all... tried to warn them, flicker flicker, but who knew from wiring back then. Time Two of Disrepair. Tears and soot.

THEN, ladies again. Well, one lady. Millie Putnam. Stinking of wealth—the tastiest stink. An eighty-year old woman in high heels. Playing a clarinet. Badly, but it hardly mattered... Millie was. Shhweee. And they all knew it. The record would spin and spin, and she'd be tilted sideways in her chair spitting into her clarinet, bodies moving slower and slower until they simply slumped to the floor. But they always cleaned in the afternoon. Drained the gin from my tub and washed themselves in it, two and three at once, scrubbing each other first, then of course, me.

Poor Millie. Twenty years I had her. Then, tears. But no soot.

More ladies, for a little while. Six. All pursuing degrees in law. Trim, muscular, shoulder pads and pantyhose, everything ironed. They smoked but never indoors. They swept regularly. Drank white wine. Carried purses. Wore slippers. Called their parents on the telephone. My occasional creak, then two of them in silk pajamas and a flashlight clinging to one another. Several painful and borderline obscene adjustments… fixed.

Then, one by one, rooms were emptied. Milk crates and scarves and vanilla candles and file cabinets and hangers. Poof.

And now… One creepy, tedious pre-teen with terrible hygiene and a mouth like a trucker. And a mother so flooded with sorrow she can't see past her nose.

It wasn't always so … Little Princess never smelled so bad. She tap danced in patent leather shoes and pretended she was a child star. She laid on my carpet face down and whispered this:

> (THE APARTMENT *becomes the carpet.* JANICE *lays down on it. A whisper.*)

THE APARTMENT.	**JANICE.**
"I want my birthday.	"I want my birthday.
Could you bring it to me."	Could you bring it to me."

> (JUSTIN TIMBERLAKE *flies in.*)

JUSTIN TIMBERLAKE. Hello, Janice

JANICE. Justin Timberlake

JUSTIN TIMBERLAKE. It is I

> (JUSTIN TIMBERLAKE *grabs* JANICE *and sweeps her up into the most dramatically romantic kiss this side of paradise.*)

JUSTIN TIMBERLAKE. There. You like those. I'm very good at them.

JANICE. You are.

JUSTIN TIMBERLAKE. The best

JANICE. The only

JUSTIN TIMBERLAKE. Yet, you do not smile…

JANICE. I can't

JUSTIN TIMBERLAKE. Why not

JANICE. My face doesn't work right

JUSTIN TIMBERLAKE. May I?

> (*He holds her chin in his hand.*)

JUSTIN TIMBERLAKE. Smile.

> (*She does, shyly.*)

JUSTIN TIMBERLAKE. You are still the prettiest girl in the contiguous sixth grade

JANICE. Am I?

JUSTIN TIMBERLAKE. Indeed. I could gaze at your nose until time folds in on itself and never miss an hour

JANICE. Would you?

JUSTIN TIMBERLAKE. Alas, I have a show tonight

JANICE. Oh.

JUSTIN TIMBERLAKE. But I shall return, I promise

(*He takes her right hand and holds it up.*)

Ahhh. The right hand

The angel hand

First the damage-doer

And last,

The hand that shall mend it all

Are you going to tell her your plan?

JANICE. She's not handling things well right now. I don't think she'd get it.

JUSTIN TIMBERLAKE. You're probably right. Not many people would. But I do.

JANICE. You do?

JUSTIN TIMBERLAKE. Of course.

JANICE. Do you think I'm doing the right thing

JUSTIN TIMBERLAKE. Yes.

JANICE. Tell me why

JUSTIN TIMBERLAKE. Close your eyes.

(JANICE *closes her eyes.*)

JUSTIN TIMBERLAKE. Picture the smell of his neck the second he gets off the train. Picture his good black shoes tossed in the hallway by the mat. Picture the hamper filled with his dirty work clothes. Picture his crooked blue silhouette in the light of the den as he bends down with a small grunt to kiss you goodnight.

(*A pause.*)

JUSTIN TIMBERLAKE. You know what's right.

JANICE. I do.

JUSTIN TIMBERLAKE. I have to fly now

JANICE. You can fly?

JUSTIN TIMBERLAKE. Naturally

JANICE. How?

JUSTIN TIMBERLAKE. I hold my breath and my chest puffs up like a marshmallow and I rise into the air, and then the backs of my heels split and tiny propellers snap open like umbrellas and buzz me through the sky.

JANICE. Justin Timberlake, you're magic

JUSTIN TIMBERLAKE. I am

(*Singing:*)
I'm a story spun from silk
I stand up there with my moonglow hair
And I draw every song from powdered sugar and milk.

> (JANICE *swoons.* JUSTIN TIMBERLAKE *kisses her right hand, first the back and then the palm.*)

Until next time.

JANICE. Good bye Justin Timberlake

JUSTIN TIMBERLAKE. Goodbye Calamity Janice.

> (JUSTIN TIMBERLAKE *holds his breath and floats away.*)
>
> (JANICE *touches her right hand, staring at it.*)
>
> (*She then pours some granulated sugar into a bowl with water and drops the shoelaces in. She takes another bowl and puts globs of Vaseline into it.*)
>
> (THE APARTMENT *is still the carpet.*)

THE APARTMENT. For what I am thinking, and for the actions I am prepared to take heretofore... let it be known. I had no other choice.

> (JANICE *begins to hum the "Butt Ugly Sweater" song.*)

MOTHER. How did it go

BARBARA. Are you still looking for a place, Clara?

MOTHER. A place, an apartment? Well yes, but. I mean the holidays, and Janice's school...

BARBARA. Find another apartment, Clara.

MOTHER. It used to be a mansion/ you know

BARBARA. The draft is terrible. The faucets leak, the floor boards are warped/

MOTHER. Barbara. Janice?

BARBARA. Yes. She's a very precocious child

MOTHER. Yes

BARBARA. Highly intelligent

MOTHER. Yes

BARBARA. But troubled.

MOTHER. Yes?

BARBARA. Tormented, even

MOTHER. Oh no

BARBARA. But not about what you're thinking

MOTHER. No?

BARBARA. No

MOTHER. Then what?

BARBARA. Boys on the brain

MOTHER. Is that all?

BARBARA. It seems. But I set her straight

MOTHER. How

BARBARA. Girl talk

MOTHER. So she's okay

BARBARA. She'll be fine

MOTHER. Oh Barbara, you don't know how much this means

BARBARA. What are sisters for?

MOTHER. So now what

BARBARA. Meaning

MOTHER. What do I do

BARBARA. About

MOTHER. The gifts

BARBARA. The gifts.

MOTHER. Yes.

BARBARA. Indulge her

MOTHER. Indulge

BARBARA. She needs nurturing

She needs to know that some things

Are okay

Like Christmas

Christmas is okay.

Christmas provides.

MOTHER. Alright. But.

BARBARA. But what.

MOTHER. She doesn't drink coffee but she asked for filters.

She doesn't go to church but asked for a prayer candle.

Only one item on the list makes sense to me.

BARBARA. Which

MOTHER. Does it matter?

BARBARA. Why not talk to her?

MOTHER. I.

BARBARA. Are you afraid?

MOTHER. I.

BARBARA. Of your own daughter?

MOTHER. Yes.

BARBARA. Clara

MOTHER. She has eight different laughs

I haven't heard one of them in such a long/

BARBARA. Clara.

Do you hear yourself

You are unendurably fraught

Didn't Gary ever complain about your endless worrying?

> (*A pause.*)

MOTHER. (*Quietly:*) Yes.

BARBARA. What did he say?

> (*A pause.*)

MOTHER. You're always so damn tense, honey

Your back is so taut if I had fifty of you I could make a fence

BARBARA. Here is the Objective Eye, Clara.

Here is the Voice of Reason.

Are you listening?

MOTHER. Yes.

BARBARA. Janice is an average girl at an awkward age. She is of average intelligence and has average proclivities/

MOTHER. But you said/

BARBARA. Let me finish.

All unusual behavior heretofore may be considered average and, here's the cherry, TEMPORARY.

MOTHER. You're right. You're right. I know you're right. Thank you Barbara

BARBARA. What are sisters for

MOTHER. You would have been a wonderful mother. If things had... you know... worked out. If nature had been kinder to you.

> (*A pause.*)

BARBARA. What are sisters for.

MOTHER. Are you eating

BARBARA. Yes

MOTHER. On the phone?

BARBARA. Yes

MOTHER. You know I hate that

BARBARA. Sorry

MOTHER. Chewing noises...

BARBARA. I'm hungry

MOTHER. What is it

BARBARA. Tuna

MOTHER. From a can?

BARBARA. yes

MOTHER. Would you like to come over for /dinner

BARBARA. No

MOTHER. I made.

> (*A beat.*)

BARBARA. ...what...

> (MOTHER *is lost.*)
>
> (MOTHER *appears in different circle of light, wearing a scarf and a coat. She holds* JANICE's *list in her hand, squinting at it, and a shopping bag filled with wrapping paper and boxes in the other.*)
>
> (JANICE *lays the shoelaces out to dry and stirs the Vaseline.*)

MOTHER. ... so what's the difference between this and a regular thermometer?... density of a liquid? Why would one need to know that?... How odd... Oh no, for my daughter... Eleven... She's very precocious.

> (MOTHER *disappears.*)

JANICE. (*Singing:*)
something left to pulverize
a rotting fruit between my thighs
won't you try some of this soup
maggots soaked in formaldhyde

> (MOTHER *re-appears with the list, bags, scarf, and more boxes. She squints at the list.*)

MOTHER. ... a preservative?... no, I suppose botulism isn't a pleasant disease... actually, I know plenty about raw meat, this is for my daughter... eleven... She's very precocious...

> (MOTHER *disappears.*)

JANICE. (*Singing:*)
how's that for a marinade
everything is filth now
everything is filth now
but isn't it about time

> (MOTHER *reappears, consulting the list.*)

MOTHER. N-S-Y-N-C... it's a band... oh, *that's* how you pronounce it, hee, the capital letters threw me... my daughter... eleven...

Girls that age... what can I say

JANICE. Hey Janice...

> (JANICE *retrieves one of her dolls. She speaks to it and through it, as before.*)

(MOTHER *enters halfway through the song.*)

What?

Wanna hang out tonight?

But you hate me.

We're just jealous because you're cooler than us.

Oh. But. I have to finish. He's waiting for us.

But what if he isn't?

Oh.

JANICE. (*As the doll, singing:*)

Hey let's see a movie.

    (No.)

Hey let's go hold hands.

    (I can't.)

Go see an all-ages band

    (Which one?)

Get our hands stamped at the door

    (Well…)

Scream like crazy for more

    (Okay…)

Let's kiss on a stoop and giggle

    (Yeah!)

Eat granola bars in my bed

Drink Mountain dew and stay up all night

Paint our toenails blue

And then I'll write a poem about you

And then I'll write a poem about you

And then I'll

    (MOTHER *smiles at* JANICE. JANICE *looks down at her doll. She pops the head off the doll and peers inside the body cavity through the neck opening with an appraising eye.*)

JANICE. Butt butt butt butt butt butt…

    (JANICE *exits.*)

    (MOTHER's *bedroom.* THE APARTMENT *is the radiator.*)

    (MOTHER *enters with a bag full of wrapped gifts. She is exhausted. She takes off her coat and scarf and collapses onto the bed.*)

THE APARTMENT. Touch me…

    (MOTHER *shivers. She puts her scarf back on. She approaches the radiator and regards it.*)

THE APARTMENT. Touch me…

(MOTHER *strokes* THE APARTMENT.)

THE APARTMENT. … yes… it's been… so long…

MOTHER. A thousand years ago

Her sweet weight new to our arms

Two adults were struck witless

At the fruit we had rendered

And our throats gnarled in terrible love-agony,

The heaviest of all hanging things

Her eyes crunched like two anguished caterpillars

Her mouth a hot blossom, lips shivering

Impossibly tiny pieces of body tensing and releasing

To a tune played in infant-time

For a thousand years we stood

Choking on our warm blood orange without the peel, our daughter,

And somehow we could not swallow

Her shadow grew and tossed its round mountain on the wall

We shrank and shrank

Until we were lima beans slipping on the tile floor

And from within the center of our salty flood

The words we found, the only words,

Gaping-eyed and hollow

Were these:

"Please let no harm come to this child."

THE APARTMENT. My lady making another lady right there in my arms. Could anything, anything in the world be more perfect…

Turn me on.

(*The radiator begins to bang.*)

MOTHER. (*Quietly:*) Stop it.

(*It bangs louder.*)

MOTHER. Stop it… please… I don't know how to fix you…

(*Louder.*)

THE APARTMENT. Turn me on. Do it. Quickly!

(*The radiator bangs out of control.* MOTHER *loses it.*)

MOTHER. I can't take it I can't take it WHY are you banging! You never banged when he was here!!

THE APARTMENT. I cannot make it stop, it's my heart!

(MOTHER *begins to slap the radiator violently, hyperventilating.*)

THE APARTMENT. STOP IT STOP IT STOP IT STOP IT STOP IT!!!

MOTHER. STOP IT STOP IT STOP IT STOP IT STOP IT!!!

(MOTHER *darts from the room and returns with towels. She shoves them beneath the radiator and turns the knob violently. A loud hiss emits, along with steam.*)

(*A long beat.*)

THE APARTMENT. (*Quietly:*) I needed that...

(MOTHER *slumps to the floor and leans against* THE APARTMENT.)

(HARRISON FORD *appears.*)

HARRISON FORD. Hey kiddo, why so glum

MOTHER. Oh Harrison Ford, I don't know... I'm a mess. I'm an enormous unavailing glot of nerves.

HARRISON FORD. She's your daughter, of course you're worried

MOTHER. But I'm supposed to be a rock for her

HARRISON FORD. You're doing super

MOTHER. I haven't heard her laugh in so long

HARRISON FORD. It's only been a year

MOTHER. And I'm doing Pilates and they aren't working... And I don't know how to fix anything around here, HE always fixed everything... Oh, and they want to make me head chef, less work but I need to rebuild the entire menu and then supervise all the... And we used to LAUGH. She and I. Not like *they* did, of course... I was jealous, can you imagine? So playful and easy, while I clunked along behind.

HARRISON FORD. Perfectly understandable...

MOTHER. When she was seven she fell down the front steps and broke her collar bone. I sobbed the entire ride to the hospital. He showed up with a whoopie cushion. I want that, I want to be that but my tongue is a brick and my arms are wrecking balls and my heart is a monkey thrashing in its cage and I don't know how to make it stop

(HARRISON *approaches* MOTHER *and massages her shoulders.*)

MOTHER. Oh. That works.

HARRISON FORD. Give her time. She'll find her eight different laughs one by one.

MOTHER. I know... but... sometimes... this is terrifying... she looks at me... and her eyes are filled with bile... and the bile has a bubbling voice of its own...

HARRISON FORD. What does it say

MOTHER. Your fault. Your fault.

HARRISON FORD. Now Clara. You're just projecting your own fears onto her.

MOTHER. Am I

HARRISON FORD. You know it's a lie

MOTHER. Tell me

HARRISON FORD. There is no fault. The moment has a life of its own.

MOTHER. Oh Harrison

HARRISON FORD. You're a good mother

MOTHER. I want to be

HARRISON FORD. You're doing everything right

MOTHER. You really think so

HARRISON FORD. I really do.

Now relax.

MOTHER. Okay. And the apartment is falling apart/

HARRISON FORD. RELAX.

You're so tense

Your back is so taut if I had fifty of you I could make a fence.

Breathe.

> (*She breathes. He whacks her on the back.*)

HARRISON FORD. Deeper. Breathe all the worry out, let it drift from your tongue like a cloud of bad dialogue.

> (*She breathes.*)

HARRISON FORD. Good. Do you feel better?

MOTHER. Yes.

HARRISON FORD. Lie down.

> (MOTHER *lies down on the bed, her eyes closed.*)

HARRISON FORD. I'm going to stay here and stroke your hair and talk to you until you fall asleep. Okay kiddo?

MOTHER. Okay.

> (*He strokes her hair.*)

HARRISON FORD. Okay. Clara. You are doing everything right. You are a rock. Everyone who knows you is amazed at how strong you've been. The angel was crooked, you were right. You didn't know the floor had a broken board. Christmas decorations are dangerous. Too young for a make-up set. Your eyes will stay that way. You'll cut off your. You'll go deaf if you. Finish your.

Clara. You were right. About everything.

You asleep?

MOTHER. Yes.

HARRISON FORD. I'll go now

MOTHER. Will you fly?

HARRISON FORD. Yes.

MOTHER. I always knew you could fly...

(HARRISON FORD *kisses her on the forehead and flies off.*)

(JANICE *sneaks into the room, spies the bag of gifts, grabs it and sneaks off again.*)

(BARBARA *is at home sitting by the phone, not working on her watercolor.*)

BARBARA. Well. I'm certainly not going to phone *her*. Don't look at me that way, Darwin. Go eat your Fancy Feast. Persephone, don't hog the dish. I don't care if Melvin says you're too skinny. A lady never snarfs her Gourmet Beef-and-Liver.

What is it, Trudy? I'm too hard on my sister? When did you become so mortally amicable? No, Violet, she's a good mother. She's just a little twangy sometimes.

That's not true, Vladamir. Clara was a fearless little girl. She was the first kid in our neighborhood to swim in the lake after that boy drowned. Used to scare the fried oysters out of all of us. But she's so small now. A peanut. A frightened little mother-person.

What, Garrison? *I'm* a better mother? It's not a competition... Well, thank you. I know you don't need a Daddy. I never said you did. No, he left before you were born. No, he was bad news. A big black fog of bad news.

What's that? ... I have a sexy voice? Stop it Leon, you're flattering me. Well, meow to you too. You're the meowiest. You too, Angela. And you, Zachary. And Clementine and Buster and Augusta and Francis and Caroline and Euripedies and Rita and Ernest and Opus and Jerimiah and Jaquelin. And Douglas and Murphy and Charlene and Heinrick and Rory and Tad and Constance and David and Hope. And Edward and Fiona and Darryll and Andrew and Chadrick. And Bocephus. And the twins. All of you are the meowiest. You're the meowist children a mommy could have.

(BARBARA *pours herself a drink and tries to finish her watercolor. Then she begins opening cans of tuna once again.*)

(*In* JANICE's *room, an elaborate set-up is now strewn on the floor; the headless doll, shoelaces, two mixing bowls, hydrometer, pot with bleach, glass with a coffee filter on top, and a small jar of a white salt-looking product.*)

(THE APARTMENT *is the lighting fixture. He regards the mess quietly.*)

(JANICE *is quietly re-taping her gifts. She then consults a ratty, much-folded piece of paper, then the mess on the floor. The lights flicker.*)

THE APARTMENT. Alright I have NEEDS. And they are simply. Well they're not being met. So. And I suppose the blame falls mostly on. On myself. I suppose in all honesty the blame in this case, yes. But you see, I had not anticipated. Okay YES, he repaired things, he was very. Handy. The occasional hinge was oiled, the occasional. Trim painted and so forth. I assumed, wrongly perhaps, that. That it was by choice, not by. Necessity. But now it seems. And actually it's worse than I could have ever imagined, you see not ONLY am in a state of utter calamity but you. Neither of you. You don't ENJOY me. Nor do you enjoy each other. It is unbearable. I am sensitive you see, I need. Little bursting soap bubbles. Bodies being bodies with each other, warmth. That sort of. But. No. So.

(*The lights flicker.*)

THE APARTMENT. Look up.

(JANICE *looks up.*)

THE APARTMENT. Behind my fixture. Two loose wires. Touch them. It will only hurt a moment. Your body will be thrown to the ground or perhaps against the wall, but you will not feel it... your hands will be burned but you won't feel them. You will look down and notice you are transparent. You will be amazed. Then you will be gone.

I shall be as kind to her when the time comes...

(JANICE *looks down.*)

(*The lights flicker again.* JANICE *looks up, contemplating whether or not she should try to fix it.*)

THE APARTMENT. I survived yellow fever. I survived an electrical fire. And I shall survive you as well. Touch the wires... or I will find another way.

(JANICE *looks down again and begins counting and measuring and sizing up her creation.*)

(*The lighting fixture drops a bit, now hinging from two wires.* JANICE *looks up a third time. She grabs a chair and stands on it. She inspects the wires.*)

(JUSTIN TIMBERLAKE *appears.*)

JUSTIN TIMBERLAKE. How's it going

JANICE. Oh,... I feel like I forgot something

JUSTIN TIMBERLAKE. Did you filter the potassium chloride through the bleach?

JANICE. Yes

JUSTIN TIMBERLAKE. And you soaked the shoelaces in the chlorate and sugar solution?

JANICE. Yes

JUSTIN TIMBERLAKE. And you dissolved the Vaseline and wax in the campstove gas

JANICE. Yes

JUSTIN TIMBERLAKE. All you need is this...

(*He produces a lighter. He flickes it on.*)

APARTMENT. (*Terrified:*) AAAHH!

(JANICE *takes the lighter from him reverently. She sways it like she's at a concert.* JUSTIN TIMBERLAKE *jumps on a chair and responds in kind.*)

JUSTIN TIMBERLAKE. (*Singing:*) It's almost time

JANICE. It is

JUSTIN TIMBERLAKE. (*Singing:*) It's all going to happen

JANICE. It is

JUSTIN TIMBERLAKE. (*Singing:*) Remarkable

JANICE. Yes

(JUSTIN TIMBERLAKE *touches* JANICE's *face as though she were in the crowd.*)

JUSTIN TIMBERLAKE. (*Singing:*) You're remarkable

JANICE. I am

JUSTIN TIMBERLAKE. I think about you all the time

JANICE. I think about you all the time

JUSTIN TIMBERLAKE. I see you in the ocean of faces beneath the colored lights each night

JANICE. I see you in the squares of moon across my ceiling

JUSTIN TIMBERLAKE. I taste you in the salty drops that bleed down my fabulous sideburns

JANICE. I taste you in my blood when I bite my tongue

JUSTIN TIMBERLAKE. I smell you in my own boy-body smell/

JANICE. I smell you in your dirty work clothes thrown in the hamper/

JUSTIN TIMBERLAKE. Your hot head into my hands your hair tangled around my knuckles/ your

JANICE. Your neck when you get off the train your good black shoes/your neck

JUSTIN TIMBERLAKE. Your neck to my lips/ your lips

JANICE. your lips to my stomach/ you writhe

JUSTIN TIMBERLAKE. Writhe/

JANICE. Stain/

JUSTIN TIMBERLAKE. Spill/

JANICE. Spin/

JUSTIN TIMBERLAKE. Love, love/

JANICE. Lay me down, Justin Timberlake

JUSTIN TIMBERLAKE. I will

JANICE. Lay me down

JUSTIN TIMBERLAKE. I will.

(*He blows out the flame and lays her down.* JUSTIN *and* JANICE *scream.*)

(*The lights flicker, a picture falls from the wall, the glass in the window cracks, the floor creaks, plaster falls.*)

(BARBARA *has finished her watercolor. She hangs it on a wall next to twelve other very bad watercolors of cats. She begins opening cans to tuna.*)

(MOTHER *is still sleeping.*)

(THE APARTMENT *quickly becomes the closet in* MOTHER's *room.*)

THE APARTMENT. She's making something she's making something with fire, I KNOW fire, I KNOW what fire does okay, and I can't stop her, I can't stop anything ... you must WAKE UP, woman, you must TALK to her IMMEDIATELY... I DO NOT WANT TO DIE, DO YOU UNDERSTAND...

(JANICE *enters, a bit rumpled, wearing her sweater, hiding her right hand.* JANICE *quietly returns the bag of re-wrapped gifts.*)

THE APARTMENT. Thank goodness. WAKE UP!

(*A wind blows and the closet door slams shut with a bang.* MOTHER *leaps up in a panic.*)

MOTHER. What is what's are you sick what...

THE APARTMENT. Tell her. Princess. Talk.

MOTHER. You. You want to talk? To me? Oh. Oh.

(MOTHER *and* JANICE *are both quiet. A beat.*)

THE APARTMENT. Why don't you tell her

MOTHER. Why don't you tell me what you told Aunt Barbara. About the boys.

THE APARTMENT. No, not/

MOTHER. Is it any boy in particular? That boy Brian? The skinny one with the gelled hair. He's called here a few times about vocabulary assignments...

(JANICE *shakes her head no.*)

THE APARTMENT. This isn't about boys...

MOTHER. This isn't about boys.

(JANICE *shakes her head no.*)

MOTHER. Has someone offered you drugs? You're not on the, the horse tranquilizers or the oxycotton ...

(JANICE *shakes her head no.*)

THE APARTMENT. Tell her what you are doing. In your bedroom. With the fire.

(*A long beat.* JANICE *looks as though she might say something. She does not.*)

MOTHER. Alright Janice. You're standing there, and, and I KNOW there's a, and I can't, I don't remember how to do this, I used to, I think, didn't I? We didn't. We never did this. Did we…

JANICE. No.

MOTHER. No. So.

THE APARTMENT. Go on. Talk.

MOTHER. Go on. Talk. I'm trying. How. How are you doing. Because I'm not doing so well myself. Falling apart, so… The breathing just takes over and I can't. Seem to.

(*Silence.*)

MOTHER. But this isn't about me. Um. He. Loved your nose, how strange… What did he used to, this is such a strange. He could stare at it until time folded or something…

(JANICE *slowly nods.*)

MOTHER. That's something true. And. Oh! Remember last September we went school shopping, the, the mall was infested with those obese squawking women, right? In in sweats? Dragging their spawn around by the hair? Um our arms ached from carrying bags and we we hadn't eaten since breakfast and no one in Buster Brown would help us, this is, wait this is a funny… So we were in the seventh circle of hell waiting for a pair of shoes, and. And you pulled your top lip down over your bottom and said "this is what I'd look like with no mouth."

(*She demonstrates.*)

MOTHER. And. Well it wasn't particularly witty, or. But we were so tired, and. We lost it. Remember?

(JANICE *smiles a little.*)

MOTHER. You were DROOLING. I was FLAILING, I knocked someone's Pepsi out of their hand, and um the manager came out to see if we were okay? And when we finally settled down? You let out this genteel little fart and started it all over again…

(JANICE *giggles for the first time.*)

THE APARTMENT. Bubbles…

MOTHER. Look at YOU. Laughing. I would have thought you forgot how… I need this again…

THE APARTMENT. Touch each other…

(MOTHER *and* JANICE *hold hands. After a moment…*)

THE APARTMENT. Tell her now.

(MOTHER *looks down at* JANICE's *hand and realizes it is covered in blood.*)

MOTHER. Oh my God

THE APARTMENT. Oh my God

(JANICE *snatches her hand away from her mother.*)

JANICE. I'm.

MOTHER. What is that? A cut? How did you get that? Where did it come from? Janice, don't do this to me, where are you hurt?

(JANICE *slowly pulls up her sweater and pulls on the waist of her pants so her mother can see.* MOTHER *peers anxiously into* JANICE's *pants. She shouts a nervous relieved laugh.*)

(THE APARTMENT *is horrified.*)

MOTHER. Your period! You got your period! When did this happen?

JANICE. Just now/

MOTHER. Janice, you're a woman now! My Janice is a woman. So fast.

THE APARTMENT. Oh my god…

MOTHER. We have to get you something. Go change your pants, I think I have some pads somewhere/

JANICE. It's not my / blood

MOTHER. But with everything I completely… what did you say

JANICE. It's not my blood

MOTHER. Whose is it

JANICE. His

MOTHER. Whose

JANICE. *His*

MOTHER. (*Quietly:*) What are you saying

JANICE. He's bleeding through me now. Because the angel wasn't crooked. Because.

THE APARTMENT. No

JANICE. Because the bulb inside the angel wasn't hot enough to set the tree on fire. Because he didn't have to. He didn't have to put the stool on the broken floor board to fix the angel.

THE APARTMENT. No…

MOTHER. Jan/

JANICE. But it's okay. I'm gonna to fix things. D-don't worry. You worry too much.

(JANICE *exits.* MOTHER *begins to hyperventilate.*)

THE APARTMENT. Breathe

MOTHER. Breathe

THE APARTMENT. Breathe

MOTHER. Breathe

THE APARTMENT. Breathe

MOTHER. Can't can't can't awful

(BARBARA *still opening cans of tuna.*)

BARBARA. Clara

MOTHER. Something awful

BARBARA. Go on

MOTHER. She

BARBARA. Yes

MOTHER. She thinks

BARBARA. Yes

MOTHER. Oh God, I don't know what she thinks, I don't know her mind, but I do and it terrifies me

BARBARA. Clara.

MOTHER. It's my fault

BARBARA. Your fault

MOTHER. Fault.

Mine.

All of it.

If I hadn't made a fuss over the angel

BARBARA. Clara

MOTHER. If I hadn't been afraid the tree would catch fire

BARBARA. Stop it Clara

MOTHER. Stop it Clara

Clara can't stop anything

It's on an infinite loop in my brain

The floor board snaps

(*Sound of a floorboad snapping.* FATHER *appears.*)

MOTHER. His left hand pops up like a waving clown and smashes through the glass window

His right hand clutches the angel

The right hand, the angel hand

As if its wings meant something

As if the feathers could flap and quietly lower him to the snow

But they never do

He slips and is gone

The tree tips a bit and rights itself

And I'm standing at the window as the icy breeze breaks in

The jagged glass a perfect frame for my new future

BARBARA. Oh Clara

MOTHER. I know things happen and people revolve around such things
And that the moment is everything
The perfect frozen film loop is all that truly exists
But tell me this, Barbara:
How can this body
This perverse apparatus of bones and muscles and other wet things
How can this little body wrap itself around such a moment
Without falling apart

> (*A pause.*)

BARBARA. (*Quietly:*)
I don't know

> (FATHER *disappears.*)

MOTHER. You don't know. You seem to know everything else. Why my daughter is disappearing. Boys, right? Why my hands are always shaking. Caffeine. Why I can't sleep at night, television, why my vegetable garden is dying, aphids… is there a goddamn thing you don't know?

BARBARA. Why are you yelling at me? I'm trying to help you!

MOTHER. Help me? You're pushing her farther away. You barely know her. You bought her a tea set for her eleventh birthday. And a sweater that would suit a child half her age. She got her *period* today, Barbara.

BARBARA. Oh.

MOTHER. And another thing. She is NOT average, like you said. She is ODD. She has ZERO friends. She rarely showers. She is doing terribly in school. She locks herself in her bedroom all day and sometimes? I hear her talking to NO ONE. Entire conversations. She makes up terrifying songs that I don't understand. I am losing her drop by drop, Barbara. So how can YOU try to fix things when you don't know how they work in the first place?

BARBARA. Listen, Ms. Mother, I PLENTY understand how things work

MOTHER. How can you say that? What experience do you have with a child?

BARBARA. You are not the only woman on the planet responsible for the lives of others

MOTHER. Your children are not children, they are *animals*

> (*A beat.*)

BARBARA. That is probably the most insensitive thing you've ever said to me.

> (*A beat.*)

MOTHER. I… I'm… Barbara, I'm…

BARBARA. Don't. Just… okay.

MOTHER. I'm sorry.

BARBARA. People don't choose some things, you know. Things like a defective womb. A defective husband.

MOTHER. I know. I'm sorry.

(*A beat.*)

BARBARA. I have to go feed my... my cats.

MOTHER. How. How are they.

BARBARA. I'll call you

(THE APARTMENT *is the broken floorboard.*)

THE APARTMENT. Oh... I can't feel my bricks. Funny, I hadn't noticed before now...

It's inevitable, I suppose... every building has its time.

But this... THIS is a downright pitiable way to go.

(JANICE *is stuffing a waxy substance into the doll's body with her right hand, still bloody.*)

(BARBARA *is counting fifty tiny wrapped presents, presumably cat toys.*)

(MOTHER *approaches* THE APARTMENT. *She kneels at his side.*)

MOTHER. Here we go...

JANICE. Here you go...

BARBARA. Fifty-one, fifty-two, fifty-three... who am I missing... Darwin.

THE APARTMENT. I would cry... but I can't get my sprinklers to work...

(MOTHER *strokes the floorboard.* JANICE *continues to work on her project.* BARBARA *unwraps a few presents and examines them.*)

MOTHER. Should have asked for this months ago...

BARBARA. Now I'm all confusterated... Darwin is allergic to catnip, not Reika. Reika is allergic to fuzz. And Glenda hates the smell of rubber. Or is it Kent? Damn. I should have done this earlier.

(JANICE *presses the shoelaces into the waxy doll center and begins mounting the headless doll on a wooden plank with duct tape.*)

(MOTHER *continues stroking the board.*)

THE APARTMENT. I mean I WAS planning on murdering you both... self-preservation... making way for the ones who would mend me. Nothing personal... keep stroking...

MOTHER. I want something from you this year...

THE APARTMENT. That feels... so nice... he was never this gentle... twisting this, banging that...

MOTHER. I am making an Official Christmas Wish...

BARBARA. She thinks I don't understand. What a joke. Someone has to feed you and change your litter and buy you toys and take you to the doctor when you catch—put that down! Not until tomorrow. You'll ruin the surprise. Good lord. And she thinks I don't understand...

THE APARTMENT. And LOUD? GAW GAW GAW GAW, sent the both of you into hysterics And he made noises when he slept, like, like an ANIMAL... And. And he touched you. He touched my lady. I simply could not abide it. And that board was already cracked... Killing him was so easy. But you... not you...

MOTHER. Tomorrow morning

Make me you.

Infuse me with whatever the thing was that made you two giggle so much together.

I want to be playful and easy.

I really think the morning will be easier to get through that way.

You can take it back when it's over...

BARBARA. She can have her Christmas morning with her delicate progeny. I won't be bitter. I have my own beautiful ones, fifty-seven of them, all devoted, all content. You'd never drink bleach, would you? That's right. You'd never talk back to me or wear my curtains in a school play or wet your bed in your sleep or draw on my kitchen table with permanent marker. And you won't break my. Heart.

(MOTHER *presses her face to the board.*)

THE APARTMENT. Oh Baroness... I shall miss you so...

MOTHER. Thank you, darling. Merry Christmas.

(MOTHER *kisses* THE APARTMENT.)

(JANICE *finishes mounting the doll. She then smears her bloody hand across the doll's chest.*)

(*She appraises her work quietly a moment, then looks around the room a final time.*)

JANICE. Shit I'm scared.

Okay.

I don't need anything.

I don't want anything.

Shed the things that make heavy my load.

Shed the things that make heavy my load.

And.... SHED.

Toasted almond bars

Grape magic markers

The Batman ride at Six Flags

Direct TV
The smell of wood
Baked beans and ketchup
My DSL
All of my dolls EXCEPT star-skater Barbie and Bridesmaid Midge
Halloween
Swimming lessons
My bear claw slippers
The Sims House Party Expansion Pack
Final Fantasy Unlimited, episodes 1 through 4 on DVD
Um...
My Justin Timberlake poster
The Simpsons
My seashell collection
My clarinet
Strawberry Hubba Bubba
Chocolate chip granola bars
Chocolate covered raisins
Chocolate milk
Swiss Miss hot chocolate with mini marshmallows
My birthday
Um...
My earlobes
        (*A pause.*)
That's all. I think.
        (THE APARTMENT *is the corner. He watches* JANICE.)
        (*A pause.*)
THE APARTMENT. (*Quietly:*) Goodbye Princess...
JANICE. Oh...
        (*She kneels by her bed and presses her cheek to the floor.*)
JANICE. Place where he put the little stool to read me Green Eggs and Ham a hundred million times.
        (*She moves to the wall and lays her cheek against it.*)
JANICE. Place where he drew little pencil lines each year showing how fast I was growing
        (*She stands on her bed and jumps, touching the ceiling.*)
JANICE. Place I've been staring for a year, pretending I could see the sky.
        (*She curls up in the corner, on the APARTMENT's lap.*)

JANICE. Place I go when my heart stops.

(THE APARTMENT *holds her.*)

(*Lights up on* MOTHER. *It is Christmas morning.* MOTHER *is seated with a pile of gifts at her feet. There is no Christmas tree.* MOTHER *is wearing hideous holiday accoutrements.*)

(THE APARTMENT *is the glass in the window. His mouth is full of glass. He cannot speak.*)

(JANICE *enters with a big wrapped box. She sits on the floor. A long pause.*)

MOTHER. Well.

(*Another long pause.*)

Well.

(*A pause.*)

Good morning and Merry Christmas. I didn't make breakfast because I figured you wouldn't eat it, so... I just... threw together some fresh fruit in a puff pastry with berry sauce and fresh whipped cream. Oh and a Devonshire double custard butter cup with crushed almonds and a light framboise glaze... and Peruvian hot cocoa with chocolate shavings and ground cinnamon, I've been up since 5 am, ha! Did... did you look outside? It snowed last night. The ground is completely covered. Maybe we can get the sled out later. Ha, wouldn't that be nice! You like to sled, don't you?

(JANICE *reaches for a cylindrical package. She unwraps it.*)

Be careful with that, it's glass, I don't want to have to drive you to the emergency room in the snow...

(*It is a prayer candle.* JANICE *retrieves the lighter given to her by Justin Timberlake.*)

Easy with the flame, don't want to ah set the apartment on fire. That would suck. Ha.

(JANICE *lights the candle.*)

Are you... praying now? I don't mean this second, I mean in general.

(JANICE *shakes her head no.*)

Are you planning to start? Not not that I'm I'm concerned or anything, I'm just curious.

(JANICE *shakes her head no.*)

MOTHER. Is it for Daddy? Is it Daddy's candle?

(JANICE *nods.*)

I see. Well, he'd like that. He always did like setting fire to things. I don't know why I just said that, it isn't true at all.

(JANICE *removes a flat, square package from the pile.*)

You, you might need a knife or something to open th, or maybe you can use your teeth, although I wouldn't want you to chip them, but then I suppose it would give your mouth uh character, ha

(*It is an *NSYNC CD. JANICE bites into the plastic with her teeth.*)

I was joking, don't do that, you'll get, you should, be care, oh. Okay

(JANICE *pops it into a CD player. "Bye Bye Bye" begins to play.*)

MOTHER. They have nice voices. Which one do you like the best?

(JANICE *points to someone on the CD cover.*)

MOTHER. What's his name?

JANICE. Justin Timberlake

(MOTHER *squints at the CD.*)

MOTHER. Very handsome... sort of looks like your father at that age. Only shorter. And less goofy.

(JANICE *retrieves the box she brought out and hands it to* MOTHER.)

MOTHER. You didn't have to get me anything sweetheart...

JANICE. I made it.

MOTHER. Really? In school?

(JANICE *nods.* MOTHER *unwraps the gift, a bloody headless doll strapped to a plank with duct tape.*)

Oh my. What... what is it? Artwork?

JANICE. It's a wish-doll.

MOTHER. Really? What does it do?

JANICE. It makes Christmas wishes come true

MOTHER. How wonderful. I could sure use this. How does it work?

JANICE. I'll show you.

(JANICE *places the gift on the floor. She dips the shoelaces into the flame of the prayer candle. The fuse slowly crawls up to the body of the doll.*)

MOTHER. It sparkles! How lovely!

JANICE. Now close your eyes and make a wish.

MOTHER. Okay...

(MOTHER *closes her eyes.* JANICE *takes* MOTHER's *hand.*)

(THE APARTMENT *is cringing.*)

JANICE. Are you wishing?

MOTHER. Yes...

JANICE. Keep your eyes closed...

(*The fuse gets closer to the doll. It is almost there.*)

When I count to three, your wish will be granted. Okay?

MOTHER. Okay...

(JANICE *closes her eyes, also cringing.*)

JANICE. I love you mom…

MOTHER. I love you too…

JANICE. Ready… one… two… three.

(*The fuse reaches the doll body. A beat. Nothing happens.* JANICE *opens her eyes.* MOTHER *does not.*)

MOTHER. Can I open my eyes now?

JANICE. I don't understand…

MOTHER. Janice?

JANICE. Shit!

MOTHER. Language!

(JANICE *grabs the doll body with her right hand. She and* MOTHER *freeze. They remain frozen like that,* MOTHER's *eyes closed,* JANICE *gripping the doll,* THE APARTMENT *shrieking silently in the window.*)

(*An explosion, or more like a firecracker popping.*)

(JANICE *remains frozen clutching the doll.*)

MOTHER. Barbara

BARBARA. Where have you been all day and night, I called seven times, your machine isn't on, it's Christmas for crying / out loud

MOTHER. I'm at the hospital

BARBARA. What? What's wrong

MOTHER. There's been an accident

BARBARA. Oh God, what/

MOTHER. It's fine, she's fine, we're all okay

BARBARA. What happened?

MOTHER. An explosion.

BARBARA. Explosion?

MOTHER. An art project. It burst

BARBARA. What?

MOTHER. Something Janice made. She mixed some things together and they were flammable.

BARBARA. But she's okay

MOTHER. They're keeping her here. She lost her hand. The right one.

BARBARA. Oh Clara, no

MOTHER. She doesn't know yet. They said she'll wake up in about an hour. I have to tell her.

BARBARA. Are you okay

MOTHER. I'm fine, but I need you to get some things from our apartment. You have the spare key

BARBARA. What do you need

MOTHER. Her pajamas. Her furry bear claw slippers. The hedgehog on her bed. Her toothbrush, her snoopy mug, her comic books… and on the way over could you stop at that Party store on 9 and pick up a whoopie cushion and some fake eyeballs

BARBARA. Are you serious

MOTHER. Completely.

BARBARA. Clara. You do not sound fine.

MOTHER. What do you /mean?

BARBARA. Your breathing is normal, your voice isn't shaking, you / have no

MOTHER. Janice doesn't need a wheezing ninny at her bedside when she wakes up. See if you can sneak some chocolate too.

BARBARA. All right

(BARBARA *disappears.* MOTHER *grabs her heart and begins to panic. She takes some deep breaths.*)

(THE APARTMENT *appears. He is the whole apartment.*)

MOTHER. Breathe out, breathe all the worry out, cloud of bad dialogue…

THE APARTMENT. Alive!

MOTHER. Breathe out

THE APARTMENT. Slightly scorched…

MOTHER. Breathe out

THE APARTMENT. Only in the living room…

MOTHER. Breathe out. Out.

THE APARTMENT. Very small area, really…

MOTHER. Out.

THE APARTMENT. And nobody's cleaned it, of course…

(*Slowly,* MOTHER *drops her hand from her chest. She is perfectly calm.*)

MOTHER. There.

THE APARTMENT. Someone please come home.

(*Lights up on* MOTHER. *She is in the apartment. The decorations she had put out for Christmas are scorched.*)

(MOTHER *approaches the apartment, who is the floor board, She opens a box and pulls out a drill.*)

THE APARTMENT. (*Incredulous:*) Is. Is that… A DRILL?

(MOTHER *kneels and examines the broken floorboard.*)

(JANICE *appears behind her. A bandaged stub replaces* JANICE's *former right hand.* JANICE *watches* MOTHER *quietly.*)

(MOTHER *turns. They share a look.*)

THE APARTMENT. ... you're fixing me...

(MOTHER *starts the drill.*)

THE APARTMENT. THANK YOU.

(THE APARTMENT *cringes blissfully.*)

(*Lights up on* JANICE, BARBARA, *and* MOTHER *seated around the dinner table. It is three weeks later.*)

(*She is struggling to cut her food with just her stump.* MOTHER *watches uncomfortably.*)

(THE APARTMENT *is the kitchen cabinet.*)

BARBARA. ... so it's kind of like a miracle, being that I had him neutered when he was a few months old. I guess nature finds a way. Darwin.

MOTHER. More cats...

BARBARA. I'm giving them away.

MOTHER. Wow. That's a first.

BARBARA. Yes... this is delicious, Clara.

MOTHER. Thanks...

BARBARA. Oh, and I love the new bathroom tiles...

MOTHER. Janice picked them out...

    (MOTHER *retrieves a glass from the cabinet. The hinge on the cabinet squeaks.*)

THE APARTMENT. Just a little WD40, or a little... although I'd be delighted with new hinges

BARBARA. ... but it's still a bit chilly in here...

MOTHER. They're coming tomorrow to fix the thermostat

BARBARA. Fabulous.

MOTHER. And I'm getting an appraisal for new insulation.

BARBARA. That'll cost you a fortune.

MOTHER. I know. But the realtor said it would never sell in this condition. We're just scraping by as is... but I'm trying not to stress too much. I'm doing hatha yoga.

THE APARTMENT. A marble countertop to match the mantle in my drawing room

BARBARA. Could you maybe pass his number on to me? The realtor I mean.

MOTHER. Why?

BARBARA. I'm thinking of moving too. Have been for about a month now

MOTHER. Oh. You haven't said anything...

BARBARA. I know...

MOTHER. But you're perfectly happy there...

BARBARA. Well. You could probably use some help now that you're at the restaurant full-time, and I'd like to be closer, so.

MOTHER. That's very sweet of you, Barbara...

BARBARA. And. I thought. You and I could. Maybe look at places. I mean, places for us. All of us.

(*A beat.*)

MOTHER. Goodness, Barbara...

BARBARA. Just for a while, on a trial basis... it would be cheaper, and I could help with the housework...

MOTHER. Your cats...

BARBARA. What about them

MOTHER. Fifty-seven, Barbara

BARBARA. We could... I don't know... work something out

MOTHER. You mean get rid of them?

BARBARA. No, I'd never get "rid" of them. I'd just keep them out of your way. Give them their own room. The attic maybe. They could have the entire space to themselves. God, they'd love that.

MOTHER. All fifty-seven.

BARBARA. A BIG attic. We'll it the Cattic.

MOTHER. The Cattic.

BARBARA. The Cattic, Clara! And Janice could play with them, she put them in strollers like she...

(*A beat.*)

BARBARA. No, I don't suppose you're into that nowadays. Well. What say?

MOTHER. I...

(JANICE *drops her knife to the floor and shouts.* MOTHER *is momentarily terrified. She systematically regains composure. A beat.*)

MOTHER. Watch it there... Stumpy.

(*It's the first time she's tried this nickname. All are quiet for a moment.*)

MOTHER. Oh... I mean...

(*A beat.* JANICE *slowly smiles.* MOTHER *and* JANICE *start cracking up.* BARBARA *does not.*)

BARBARA. That wasn't funny...

MOTHER. I know...

(*They stop laughing. A beat.* JANICE *and* MOTHER *erupt again.*)

THE APARTMENT. Bubbles ,,

(*After a few moments their laughter winds down.*)

BARBARA. Clara. Tell me you'll think about it.

(*A beat.* MOTHER *and* JANICE *exchange looks.*)

MOTHER. We'll think about it ...

(*A beat.*)

BARBARA. Good.

(*They eat in silence.* MOTHER *and* JANICE *exchange another glance.* JANICE *mouths the words "NO WAY."*)

(MOTHER *smiles.*)

THE APARTMENT. And... new doorknobs. Tremendous.

(*The women freeze. Then they vanish, taking all the furniture with them.*)

(*The apartment is left alone, and empty. He looks around, bewildered, then solemn.*)

APARTMENT. Oh.

(*He sighs heavily. And waits.*)

End of Play

DEMON BABY

by Erin Courtney

Required royalties must be paid every time this play is performed before any audience, whether or not it is presented for profit and whether or not admission is charged. To purchase acting editions of this play, or to obtain stock and amateur performance rights, you must contact:

Playscripts, Inc.
website: www.playscripts.com
email: info@playscripts.com
phone: 1-866-NEW-PLAY (639-7529)

Inquiries concerning all other rights should be addressed to the author's agent: Mark Christian Subias Agency, 331 West 57th Street, No. 462, New York, NY 10019.

For more information about rights and permissions, see p. 10.

BIOGRAPHY

Erin Courtney's plays have been produced or developed by Clubbed Thumb, The Public Theater (*Demon Baby*), The Vineyard and BRIC (*Alice The Magnet*), The Flea (*Mother's Couch*), The Actors Theater of Louisville (*Owls*), and Soho Rep (*Quiver And Twitch*). She has been a fellow at the MacDowell colony, a recipient of a NYSCA grant and a MAP Fund grant from the Rockefeller Foundation, and a member of the Soho Rep. Writer/Director lab. She is published by Playscripts, Inc and her play *Owls* is published by Smith and Kraus in *Humana Festival 2001: The Complete Plays*. As an undergraduate, Ms. Courtney studied with Paula Vogel at Brown University and as a graduate student she studied with Mac Wellman at Brooklyn College. She currently teaches playwriting at Brooklyn College. She is also a member of 13P, as well as the co-founder of the Brooklyn Writer's Space.

Other Clubbed Thumb credits: *Pricked* (Summerworks '97); *Summerplay* (Summerworks '98); *Downwinders* (Summerworks '99, Autumn '00); *Owls* (Winter '01); *Alice the Magnet* (Summerworks '06); Clubbed Thumb Affiliated Artist.

ACKNOWLEDGMENTS

Demon Baby was commissioned and originally produced by Clubbed Thumb as part of Summerworks 2002. It was directed by Ken Rus Schmoll, with the following cast and staff:

DEMON BABY	Abigail Savage
WREN	Effie Johnson
ART	James Urbaniak
SALLY	Anna Hayman
ALAN	John Wellman
CHARLES	Brian Quirk
CAT	Nina Hellman

Sets/Lights	Garin Marschall, Paul Olmer
Costumes	Kelly Hanson
Sound	Todd Griffin
Assistant Director	Annie McNamara
Stage Manager	Morgan Robinson

Demon Baby received a winter production by Clubbed Thumb at The Ohio Theatre in New York City during January 2004. It was directed by Ken Rus Schmoll, with the following cast and staff:

DEMON BABY .... Glenn Fleshler
ALAN ....Gibson Frazier
CAT.. Nina Hellman
WORKMAN* ....Leo Kittay
SALLY .... Polly Lee
ART.. Patrick McNulty
WREN ....Heidi Schreck
CHARLES... Mark Shanahan

Sets... David Evans Morris
Lights.. Garin Marschall
Costumes .... Kirche Leigh Zeile
Sound .... Michael Newman
Assistant Director ....David Myers
Stage Manager.. Leigh Goldenberg

*Please note: The scene which featured the workman has been cut from this version of the play.

The playwright wishes to thank all who have contributed to the development of *Demon Baby*: Effie Johnson, James Urbaniak, John Wellmann, Brian Quirk, Anna Hayman, Abigail Savage; Annie McNamara, Katherine Profeta, Morgan Robinson, Paul Olmer, Kelly Hanson, Todd Griffin, Mark Subias, Rinne Groff, Ami Armstrong, Bonnie Metzgar and Michael Kenyon from the Public Theater, Mac Wellman and the Brooklyn College MFA students, the actors who participated in the Clubbed Thumb boot camp, Ken Rus Schmoll, Scott Adkins and most especially, Arne Jokela, Meg MacCary, and Maria Striar from Clubbed Thumb.

The commission for *Demon Baby* was made possible by a grant from the Multi-Arts Production Fund at Creative Capital.

CAST OF CHARACTERS

WREN, An American woman

ART, Her husband, an American, an executive

ALAN, An editor, British

CAT, Skinny, smart, executive, not British, not American

CHARLES, British executive

SALLY, Skinny, smart, British

DEMON BABY, Looks like a Garden Gnome but with something a little bit different about it

Heidi Schreck and Glenn Fleshler
in *Demon Baby.*

Produced by Clubbed Thumb at The Ohio Theatre, 2004.
Photograph by Carl Skutsch

DEMON BABY

Scene 1

There is an empty apartment with spare, modern furnishing, a picture window and a balcony that overlooks a shared courtyard. Sounds of construction can be heard from the courtyard. CAT, ALAN, ART and WREN enter with suitcases.

ALAN. Here we go. Here we go, then. Watch your step there.

ART. Oh. Let me get that, Alan.

CAT. This is a lovely flat. Just lovely.

WREN. It's great.

ART. You like?

WREN. I like.

ALAN. It's very New York if you ask me. You've found yourself a very New York flat. Impressive. Impressive.

WREN. It's big. Bigger than New York apartments.

ART. Look Wren, I thought you could put a desk right here by the window

WREN. There's nice light. It's great.

CAT. I wish James could have come. He couldn't get out of that weekend training.

WREN. Big window.

ALAN. (*Looking out into the courtyard.*) Looks like they haven't finished up out there yet.

ART. It's a new development. It was supposed to be finished by now.

WREN. It's a little loud.

> (*Long Pause.*)

Thanks for picking us up Alan. I'm sorry about the mix up. I didn't realize that Art had organized for Cat to be there.

ART. I didn't realize that you had organized for Alan to be there.

WREN. An embarrassment of riches.

CAT. I told James that you absolutely could not be greeted by one of those corpses from Expatriate Management Limited.

> (*ALAN cringes. WREN and ART awkwardly smile.*)

When I was relocated here, that relocation advisor person just grated on my last nerve. Especially when you have jet lag. Beery robots, all of them. A paid companion but seemingly without a brain. Much better to be greeted by a normal person.

ALAN. If you'll excuse me, I have to get back to work.

CAT. Oh, how rude of me. What is it you do, Alan?

ALAN. I'm an editor. I'm an editor on a project that Wren is working on.

CAT. Oh Wren. How exciting. I didn't realize that you had work to do over here as well. What kind of project? A novel?

WREN. It's a children's book.

CAT. Fascinating. How admirable. A children's book.

ALAN. If you'll excuse me. Lovely to meet you Cat.

WREN. Thank you Alan. I'll see you in a month or so?

ALAN. We'll be in touch.

(ALAN *exits.*)

CAT. Should I show around your neighborhood? We could go out to eat? Or would you like some time to settle in on your own? Now, the horrible relocation drone was supposed to help you buy essentials. Bedding, television, an American coffee maker…show you around the shops.

WREN. Personally, I'm starving.

ART. Me too.

CAT. Excuse me for a moment , I'll just use your loo, and then I will show you around the shops.

(CAT *goes into the loo.* WREN *and* ART *let out the giggles they have been suppressing.*)

WREN. Oh, did you see Alan's face?

ART. He remained very calm.

WREN. Oh and Cat had no idea what she was getting herself into with that.

ART. I didn't have the heart to tell her.

WREN. Oh God. You can't tell her. She'll be mortified. Horrified!

ART. "Beery corpses!"

WREN. I saw all the blood drain from Alan's face.

ART. But he wouldn't admit it.

WREN. Oh never! Never.

(CAT *reemerges.* CAT *talks as they leave the flat.*)

CAT. Well, let's get you all settled in. There is a great cheese shop up the road. The best cheese shop in all of…And there's one or two restaurants on the high street…and the Waitrose, you'll do all of your shopping at the Waitrose…I know you've already seen the park…It's lovely… Art, you are just going to love it here. You won't regret it. Everyone is so pleased that you decided to come over…and Wren you can get so much work done on your book…It's a wonderful opportunity for both of you. A really wonderful opportunity…

Scene 2

WREN *is home alone. She stares out into the courtyard. She paces. She slumps onto the couch and stares out into space. She stares at the biscuits. She eats a biscuit.* ART *enters in business attire. He looks tired and frazzled.*

WREN. Hey sweetness.

ART. Hey.

WREN. How'd it go?

ART. Well Cat is driving me crazy. We're working on this little tiny project and it should only take about three hours to do the whole thing. I mean I could get this whole thing done in three hours, but she wants me to write a proposal before we even start. Well, the proposal is gonna take five or six hours to write and then she's gonna wanna debate the whole thing. It's ridiculous. At home, I'd already have this thing done and finished. It's such a waste of time.

(*Pause.*)

She wouldn't stop talking. She just kept asking more and more questions.

(*Pause.*)

What?

WREN. I didn't say anything.

ART. I heard you say something.

WREN. I didn't say anything.

ART. Oh.

(*Pause.*)

What did you do today?

WREN. Nothing.

ART. Now, now.

WREN. No. Literally. Nothing.

ART. You got out of bed. You got dressed.

(WREN *glares.*)

WREN. I watched some television. They showed color home movies of Hitler on vacation. He looked so ordinary in his suit and hat staring over the railing at the hills of Bavaria. He seemed almost like he could be anyone.

ART. I thought you said that you don't watch television during the day.

WREN. I was feeling sick today. I wasn't feeling well.

ART. How's the book coming?

WREN. It's hard to work at home.

ART. Should we rent you an office?

WREN. God, no! That's a waste of money. All I need is discipline. I'm meeting with Alan in a month, so I'll have to have something done by then. A deadline is good.

> (*Long pause.*)

ART. Well, what else did you do today? Did you explore the city?

> (WREN *shakes her head no.*)

ART. Why not?

WREN. I was going to take the tube…

ART. But?

WREN. I couldn't walk down the tunnel.

ART. What?

WREN. I was frightened.

ART. By the tunnel?

WREN. It was too long………there wasn't anyone around.

ART. They have closed circuit TV's. They have people whose job it is to watch out for you.

WREN. It doesn't matter.

ART. It's just going to take some time. Hey, hang on…

> (ART *begins looking around the living room.*)

WREN. What are you doing?

ART. I'm looking for that book.

WREN. What book?

ART. The one from the beery corpses.

WREN. It's in the loo…

> (ART *exits and returns with the relocation manual.*)

ART. Hang on. Hang on. Right. Right here. (*Waving the relocation manual.*) The relocation manual!… (*Reads:*) You are in the anxiety stage.

WREN. How come you aren't in the anxiety stage?

ART. I get anxious sometimes.

> (*Long Pause.* ART *reads the relocation manual.*)

WREN. I did go to the corner store to buy toilet paper.

ART. Well, see, that's good.

WREN. But when I tried to give him change, I just stared at the coins in my hand and I couldn't count the change right and he was laughing right at me.

ART. No one is laughing at you. It's just going to take some time. You are just experiencing the anxiety stage.

WREN. Art, I'm not used to feeling this way.

ART. It's a stage. It will pass.

WREN. It doesn't feel like that.

ART. Come on, we'll go eat out tonight.

WREN. Oh, the foreman was down in the courtyard and he told me that they are going to get the roof garden finished in time for the bank holiday.

ART. So that's great news.

WREN. He said they just have to get the guardrails in place and put out the tables and chairs.

> (*Pause.*)

But then he said…"so, no diving off."

ART. He was making a joke.

WREN. So I said, "Well, I'm certain I won't be doing that." And he said "Good, Good, no diving off."

> (*Pause.*)

Why do you think he said that? Why did he say that? "No diving off?"

ART. It's a joke.

WREN. It's a fishbowl. They love to watch us.

ART. Nobody is watching us.

WREN. The workers watch.

ART. The same way that you or I do when we walk down the street peering into people's living room windows. Our eyes go towards things that are alive.

> (*Pause.*)

Oh, I almost forgot.

WREN. What?

ART. I got you something.

WREN. What ?

ART. Wait.

> (*He goes off. He comes back with a piñata.*)

ART. A piñata.

WREN. Where did you find a piñata here?

ART. Well, I was surprised to see one too. I know how much you like them so I bought it for you.

WREN. Thank you.

> (*He places the piñata in the middle of the room and they stare at it.*)

ART. Oh, also, James and Cat have invited us over for dinner. Charles too. Since they invited us, then they have to invite Charles. And Sally.

WREN. Well, you have to tell them I'm sick.

ART. If I call and say you are sick, they'll know we're lying. I told them you were having a hard time adjusting. Cat hated it here too in the beginning. When she first got here. They want to help. Let them help.

WREN. They just want to make sure that you're not going to jump ship and go back home.

ART. They wanna make sure you are okay.

WREN. I don't want to go. I don't want to leave the house.

Scene 3

SALLY, CAT *and* WREN *are sitting in the living room at Cat and James's house.* SALLY *and* CAT *are skinny and chain smoking. It is 2 A.M.*

CAT. It gets so cold in winter here and I swore that I wouldn't buy a hat. I won't buy a hat, I said. I'll buy a big scarf and gloves but I won't buy a hat. But finally it got so cold, that one Friday night I told James, I said "James, I'm going." "Where?" he said. "Out to buy a hat."

WREN. You lose a lot of heat through your head.

CAT. So what have you been up to?

WREN. Well, I work at home. I am working on a children's book but I've been having a difficult time getting work done. I think, oh, I'll just eat a cookie or have a gin or watch television for a few minutes.

SALLY. I think there are definitely two types of people, the people who can work at home and the people who can't.

CAT. Well, I have no problem working at home. Some days I prefer to work at home. James used to make fun of me because he would wake up at 5:30 in the morning and shower and go to work and I would get on the phone in my nightdress and start working and when he got home at 7:30 at night I would still be right there on the phone in my dressing gown. Working.

WREN. I also find it difficult to exercise.

CAT. Oh, I never exercise.

SALLY. Me neither. There is so much here to take advantage of. You really must take advantage of everything here. The museums. The theatre. You could take classes.

WREN. What kind?

CAT. Art history. I'm taking art history. Or French? You could learn French or gardening. Whatever you want. You've got to take advantage of this situation.

WREN. I am. I am.

CAT. Well, it's a great city and there is so much to do here.

(CAT *takes a drag off her cigarette and the women stare off into space.* ART *and* CHARLES *enter holding the butts of cigars.*)

ART. Wasn't that a great dinner?

CHARLES. Cat is great. She knows how to make loads of money. Did you know that? James is a lucky man.

CAT. Don't embarrass me.

CHARLES. She has great powers of concentration.

ART. That dinner was just great.

CHARLES. Yeah, Cat can pull money out of thin air and put it in her pockets.

WREN. Like magic.

CAT. You're embarrassing me.

ART. It's a compliment.

CHARLES. You're a great cook too, Cat.

ART. It was a wonderful meal.

WREN. Wonderful.

CAT. Where's James?

CHARLES. He's out there having a contemplative moment.

CAT. Surveying his kingdom.

ART. Something like that.

(*They all sit quietly.*)

WREN. How did you meet James?

CAT. Believe it or not, we meet at an Expatriate Management Limited cocktail party. You know James is from Scotland...so there we were and it was so ghastly there that James and I ended up sharing a bottle of gin...It turns out James hates gin...He was just drinking it to stay near me.

CHARLES. James is a whiskey man...(*In a Sean Connery voice:*) She's got a great ass.

ART. (*In a Sean Connery voice:*) She's got a great ass.

CHARLES. Sean Connery is absolutely the best James Bond.

SALLY. Absolutely.

WREN. And how old are your girls?

CAT. Sophie is four and Louise is two.

CHARLES. They are adorable. Luckily, they take after Cat and not James.

WREN. Kids are great.

CAT. You should do lots of traveling before you have them. You should go skiing. We do still go skiing but it's not as easy as it was.

ART. Well, the girls do look adorable in that picture.

(WREN *stifles a yawn. It is late and time for the guests to leave but everyone is too polite to make the first move.*)

Scene 4

WREN *is lying on her back on the floor of her living room. A garden gnome, the* DEMON BABY, *is sitting on her chest.* WREN'*s eyes open, frightened. The* DEMON BABY *stares into her face.* WREN *is paralyzed. She cannot move at all. She cannot speak. The* DEMON BABY *makes the sounds that* WREN *would make if she could.*

DEMON BABY. Oh Huh. Huh! Uh!

(*Some time passes like this.*)

Scene 5

WREN *and* ART *are standing alone in the living room.*

WREN. Thank God, you're here.

ART. What is it?

WREN. I lost time. I lost three hours, Art. From two to five. I can't remember anything.

ART. I am sure we can account for them.

WREN. No. No. I've tried. I can't.

ART. Tell me exactly what you remember.

WREN. I was napping on the floor and when I woke up, I couldn't move. I was paralyzed. I was frozen. I could see and think but I couldn't get my muscles to move. I felt a pressure on my chest and it was a demon baby, a demon baby sitting on my chest and it wouldn't let me up for hours. I thought I was dying.

ART. You were dreaming.

WREN. I wasn't.

ART. Wait. Wait. I remember reading something about this, it's…Oh! Wait! It's called… Sleep…Sleep…Paralization…no…Paralysis

WREN. What?

ART. Sleep Paralysis. That's what it's called. We read about it on the airplane over here. In the airplane magazine. It's a biochemical reaction.

WREN. I think this was real.

ART. People wake up frozen for a few minutes and they feel some kind of being pressing down on them. Right. And it's very interesting because in different places people see different things sitting on them. In Europe, people see witches. In Japan, it's a monster's foot. Now most American's think they see aliens, so you don't quite fit in with that. What did you say you saw?

WREN. A demon baby.

ART. What did it look like?

WREN. Don't laugh.

ART. I'm not going to laugh.

WREN. It's not going to sound scary when I tell you what it looked like.

ART. I promise to leave open the option of feeling scared.

WREN. It looked like a garden gnome.

ART. What does a garden gnome look like?

WREN. You know, those ceramic statues people put out on their lawns.

ART. So why are you calling it a demon baby, if it's a garden gnome?

WREN. Well, it had something a little bit different about it. Something stranger than a gnome.

ART. Was it bloody and mucusy?

WREN. No.

ART. Anyway, it's perfectly normal. I read about it in the airplane magazine. And the scientists think its chemical and the spiritualists think its spiritual and the UFO abductees— well, they really believe that they have been abducted by aliens. It's a very common phenomenon.

WREN. Well, it was terrible. And it wasn't a few minutes. It was hours.

ART. You believe everything you read. Everything you read turns into fact inside your head.

WREN. That's not true.

ART. You're highly suggestible. You read it in the airplane magazine and now you're living it.

WREN. You think I am that malleable.

ART. Sometimes.

WREN. Well, why don't you just reprogram me?

ART. Wren.

WREN. Do you want to reprogram me?

ART. Wren.

WREN. Stop saying my name!

ART. Do you think you might be pregnant?

WREN. What's that got to do with it?

ART. I thought maybe that's why you dreamed up this demon baby.

WREN. I'm not pregnant.

ART. I'd be happy if you were. If we were.

> (WREN *walks away from* ART *and sits at her desk. She stares out the window.* ART *stands for a while, sits, looks around the apartment.*)

ART. I think that if you left the apartment then you would feel better. Look, I'll pack a picnic.

> (*Long pause.*)

WREN. The ground is wet! It hasn't stopped raining for days.

ART. We have a plastic mat.

WREN. It's too heavy.

ART. I'll carry all of it.

WREN. People will recognize me.

ART. As what?

WREN. As someone who doesn't live here.

ART. Oh. I almost forgot!

(ART *disappears and returns holding a large object covered in white fabric.*)

Voila! Ta da!

(*He pulls off the fabric.*)

WREN. A cage!

ART. With a bird in it.

WREN. With a bird in it.

ART. To keep you company.

WREN. To keep me company.

ART. A pet.

(*Pause.*)

What do you think?

(ART *puts the cage down and they peer inside. Eventually, chirping sounds come from inside the cage.*)

WREN. What happens if we cover it back up?

(ART *covers cage.*)

ART. It stops.

WREN. Good.

ART. Oh, you know that night at Cat and James' house and James was outside and we said he was surveying his kingdom?

WREN. Yeah.

ART. He was actually pissing on his own yard. He was staring up at the stars watering the lawn.

(*They sit and stare at the covered birdcage.*)

Scene 6

The DEMON BABY *is sitting on* WREN. *They stare at each other for a long time.*

WREN. Ow.

DEMON BABY. Oh. Sorry.

WREN. Ow.

DEMON BABY. You felt that?

WREN. Yes. I feel that.

DEMON BABY. You aren't supposed to feel that.

WREN. I feel. A claw. Digging into my breast.

> (*Long pause.*)

Could you? Could you?

DEMON BABY. Move it.

WREN. Move it.

> (*There is no apparent movement.*).

Better.

DEMON BABY. You talk. You aren't supposed to talk.

Scene 7

> WREN *and* ALAN *stand in the living room. There is a manuscript on the coffee table.*

WREN. Alan, thank you for coming over.

ALAN. It's my pleasure.

WREN. Come in.

ALAN. Thank you.

WREN. Tea?

ALAN. No, thank you.

WREN. Gin and tonic?

ALAN. Thank you.

WREN. The manuscript is on the coffee table. Would you take a look?

> (ALAN *sits on the couch and picks up the manuscript. He studies the images closely.*)

ALAN. Wren, the illustrations are beautiful and the text starts off wonderfully well. The child is boarding the space ship and heading towards her new home, the moon. The father gives the sweet child a coloring book about the moon in order to prepare her for her new home environment. Preparation is very important and we want to stress that. The child stares at the window at the passing stars. However, it is this next image which seems to come entirely out of context here and...

> (*He looks ups.* WREN *is holding the gin and tonic and she is totally nude.*)

ALAN. Wren?

WREN. Yes?

ALAN. What's going on?

WREN. Well, I had an impulse to seduce you and I wasn't quite sure how to do it.

ALAN. The windows are open.

WREN. Yes.

ALAN. I would rather sleep with your husband.

(*She sits naked on the couch with him.*)

WREN. Really?

ALAN. Yes.

WREN. Are you attracted to him?

ALAN. Yes. Slightly, in a normal sort of a way.

WREN. Yes.

ALAN. Nothing to write home about.

WREN. And so you are not attracted to me?

ALAN. You may deduce that.

WREN. Are you in love with my husband?

ALAN. No. No. Just mildly attracted.

WREN. Oh, I see. Well. Let me put on a robe and we'll continue with the book.

ALAN. I should go.

WREN. I want to hear what you were saying about the book.

ALAN. Perhaps, we could reschedule a meeting.

WREN. No. No tell me now. You are here now, so you should tell me now.

ALAN. I don't think I should stay.

WREN. Nonsense! I'm putting on the robe. Continue.

ALAN. Right! Well, once this demon baby enters the book. Well, you seem to be going on a tangent. It's turned into a horror book. We've commissioned you for a book for children. "How to adapt to your new country" and we feel it should not have scary monsters in it.

WREN. Yes. But I made the new country the moon.

ALAN. Yes. Yes. We agreed to that idea, but this demon baby here. Well, I think this demon baby might give children...might put ideas in their head that people might rather keep out of their heads. This book is supposed to help them in their transition. The folks at Expatriate Management Ltd are a very literal bunch. I had to fight to even get the moon idea approved.

(*Reading from his notes:*) They wanted the child at their new home, the child at the new school, the child experiencing loneliness, the child eventually making friends— celebrating their differences, a party scene, inclusion. This demon baby is just too frightening. It's not going to ease the child's apprehensions.

WREN. Children love fantasy and metaphor. They aren't interested in the ordinary. You have to give them information in a fantastic way.

ALAN. Well, in this case perhaps it just isn't appropriate.

WREN. (*Offended:*) Interesting opinion. I will think about that certainly. I will certainly consider that opinion.

ALAN. May I venture another opinion?

WREN. Yes.

ALAN. On your seduction technique.

WREN. Yes.

ALAN. I think you should try to put a layer of suggestion between you and the nudity.

WREN. Oh, but I hate projection.

ALAN. Projection?

WREN. Oh, rejection.

ALAN. Yes, but perhaps it would be milder form of rejection if you had flirted first.

WREN. You may have flirted back.

ALAN. (*Blushing.*) Well, yes I may have.

WREN. And then I might have gotten the wrong idea about you.

ALAN. Yes. Yes.

WREN. This way there was no mistaking anyone's intentions.

ALAN. Yes.

WREN. And if you had been interested it would have been a very efficient form of communication.

ALAN. Yes, you do have a point there.

WREN. Will you try to sleep with my husband?

ALAN. There are plenty of fish in the sea.

WREN. That's a no?

ALAN. No.

WREN. Is that a yes?

ALAN. Let me be clear. I am not going to attempt to seduce your husband.

WREN. But you could do?

ALAN. Won't.

WREN. Won't. All right, then.

ALAN. Other than the Demon Baby, the manuscript looks very good.

WREN. Thank you for coming over.

ALAN. You should leave the flat sometime. There's so much to see.

WREN. That's a wonderful idea.

Scene 8

The DEMON BABY *perches on Wren's chest.* WREN *is lying on the floor.*

DEMON BABY. It's a beautiful day out today.

WREN. I wouldn't know.

DEMON BABY. It stopped raining.

WREN. It seems to have.

DEMON BABY. I can actually see the sun.

WREN. It seems odd that somebody died last night

DEMON BABY. Yes.

WREN. And the night before that.

DEMON BABY. And the night before that. People just keep dying and dropping like flies. They cannot stop themselves it seems.

WREN. From dying or killing.

DEMON BABY. Or being born.

WREN. Yes they do keep doing that too. Keep being born. Boring bunch. Boring cycle.

DEMON BABY. Are you bored?

WREN. I've always thought of myself as a take charge person. Like, I take charge of any situation and make it work out— make it fantastic— that's the image that I have of myself...I've never had a problem with subways before. I've always felt at home in cities— on subways— and...It is sunny today...very sunny. Almost enough to make you wanna go outside.

DEMON BABY. Bad things happen on nice days.

> (*Pause.*)
> (ART *enters.*)

ART. Hello honey.

WREN. Hello.

ART. Watcha doing?

WREN. Lying on the floor.

ART. Why?

WREN. No reason.

ART. How did it go with Alan?

WREN. He wants the demon baby out of it.

ART. Well, the demon baby is a bit creepy, honey.

WREN. We'll see. I think its gonna work. I think it needs the demon baby.

ART. You gonna sit up?

WREN. I can't.

> (ART *sits next to her on the floor.*)

ART. Maybe this move has been too much for you.

WREN. I'm going to be fine. I am starting to feel better.

ART. That's my girl.

DEMON BABY. Your husband is drunk.

WREN. Are you a little bit drunk?

ART. I had a few pints with Charles. We started at lunch and then we had two pints and then three so we didn't go back to work actually. We just stayed at the pub and had a few more. A long Friday lunch. When in Rome…

WREN. Right.

ART. But on the way home. On the tube. Oh Wren, you would have been truly disgusted.

WREN. What?

ART. Alright. Well. This man in a business suit.

WREN. Yeah.

ART. Was rolling around on the tube platform. Flopping like a dead fish.

WREN. A soon to be dead fish.

ART. You know what I mean. Just flopping there. Commuters passing by. Vomit on his face and business suit.

DEMON BABY. Guess he took a long Friday lunch too.

ART. Guess so.

Scene 9

> WREN *is alone on stage.*
> *She has a pile of sheets and towels that are neatly folded.*
> *The television is on.*
> *She eats a biscuit.*

WREN. Too much temptation.

> (*She covers the television with a towel.*
> *She covers the biscuits with a towel.*
> *She covers the couch with a sheet.*
> *She covers the birdcage and the chirping stops.*
> *She covers the piñata.*
> *She examines the room.*
> *She sits on the couch.*
> *She covers herself with a sheet.*
> ART *enters.*)

ART. I had no idea that we had brought this many sheets with us. I didn't even know that we owned so many sheets.

(ART *uncovers the birdcage.*)

ART. Hey Chirpic!

(ART *sits next to* WREN *on the couch.*)

ART. Wren! Sweetness! Let's go out tonight! Let's eat sushi! I'll get the scissors. I'll poke two eyes holes for you. No one knows us here. Who will care? Hang on a moment dear. Just a moment. Okay? Now let me feel for your eyes. Don't be scared. Got 'em. Okay. Okay. I'm going to cut so don't move and don't be scared.

(*He carefully cuts one eyehole out of the white sheet.*)

How do they get it so smooth? Probably cut it when it is flat. Off the body, not on the body. Okay! Cutting! Okay! There's my love! Right! So, what kind of shoes do you want to wear? Oh, hold on!

(*He looks under the sheet.*)

Okay! Yes! Well, that will do. That will do.

(*He goes and gets her shoes.*

He slips them on.)

Prince Charming, hey? Fit perfectly. Alright, off we go then.

(*He holds her hand and she rises from the couch.*

She walks to the living room center.

She drops hands and stops walking.

He circles her.)

Wren, Sweetness. Sweet Wren! They've promoted me. I'm in charge of fourteen departments now. Fourteen, Wren. I thought, Sushi to celebrate. I'll bring it home. Sake home too! Don't go anywhere.

(*He leaves.*

He returns.

He lifts the sheet off of WREN.)

Wren, why are you under the sheet?

WREN. It makes me feel more comfortable.

ART. I thought you would be happy here. You love cities and museums and bookstores and theatre and there is so much history here and beautiful hills up in the north— for walking—

I thought you would get so much work on your book done.

WREN. It's not even a real book. It's a pamphlet! It's not going to be published— it's just going to be printed and handed out with all the other useless information they give the expats. It's nothing.

(WREN *relaxes.*)

That's great that you are promoted. I'm really happy for you.

(*She leans over and kisses him.*)

Scene 10

The DEMON BABY *lounges on the couch smoking a cigarette.*

DEMON BABY. First of all, it's all in the timing. It must be just the right time and this is a skill that I have developed over the years. It becomes like second nature but it takes years to master. There is only the slightest moment between waking and sleeping. If you miss the window, you miss the moment, and you don't get another chance at one until they fall off to sleep again. Second of all, in order to do one's job well, one must take proper breaks and rests. A siesta. An August holiday.

(WREN *enters from the bedroom. She looks at* DEMON BABY *and then crosses towards the kitchen.* WREN *exits.*)

This is something that you Americans do not understand. You like to think about work endlessly. Even when you are not working, you like to have panics about it. You like to second guess yourself, as if this will make you more effective.

(WREN *re-enters.*)

WREN. But you have an American accent.

DEMON BABY. Oh, we all do. We all have American accents.

WREN. Huh.

Scene 11

The sheets still cover everything except for WREN. ART *has a slight British accent and he is very anxious now.* WREN *seems more relaxed.*

ART. They're coming Wren! Wren! They're coming!

WREN. Yes!

ART. Our guests! You still have all these sheets out. There's no food out! Is it in the fridge?

WREN. We're having drinks and biscuits.

ART. What?

WREN. Just drinks and biscuits.

ART. Great.

WREN. It's going to be fun, Art. It really is going to be fun. I am definitely feeling better. Let's have some fun tonight.

ART. We can't just serve gin and biscuits. When we went to their house, they served us a three course meal. There were courses and different drinks for each course. And an aperitif. You can't have people over and offer them nothing.

(*The doorbell rings.*)

WREN. We'll just say— it's an American custom.

ART. Wren!

WREN. An American Custom!

ART. Oh God. (*At door.*) Hello! Hello! Hello!

(SALLY *and* CAT *enter. They are already mildly drunk.*)

SALLY. The men are parking the car.

ART. Come in! Come in! What would you like to drink?

WREN. Ladies!

CAT. Gin and tonic.

SALLY. Oh, a white wine would be lovely.

WREN. All we have is gin and tonic.

SALLY. Well, a gin and tonic would be lovely then.

WREN. It's an American custom.

ART. An American custom.

WREN. To cover over household objects.

CAT. Really?

SALLY. I'm not familiar with that custom.

ART. In some regions.

WREN. Really all the regions. In every region there is some variation of this custom.

SALLY. I see.

CAT. Yes.

ART. Biscuit?

WREN. So the spirit of the object does not get out. It fetters the spirit of the object.

(*Doorbell rings.*)

ART. Hello. Hello. Hello. It's Alan here. It's Alan. Wren's editor.

WREN. Alan. Gin and tonic?

ART. Sally. Cat. This is Alan.

CAT. Why yes, we've met.

SALLY. Nice to meet you, Alan. Is it a novel?

ALAN. Children's book.

WREN. It's really just a pamphlet.

CAT. Delighted to see you again.

WREN. For Expatriate Management Ltd.

ALAN. Delighted.

CAT. That's a great service. Really. So helpful.

ART. (*Nervous:*) Let's sit. Shall we? Shall we all sit?

WREN. Yes. Yes. It's all right to sit on the shrouds.

> (*They sit for a long a time.*
> *Nobody talks to each other.*
> WREN *gets up to prepare another plate of biscuits.*
> ALAN *follows her.*)

ALAN. I've changed my mind.

WREN. You like the addition of the demon baby.

ALAN. About you. About that image of you. Your suggestion…

WREN. Really? How can that be Alan?

ALAN. Well, I'm both you see. It comes and goes at intervals. I feel very strongly one way and I think I won't be going back to the other way and then I find myself returning despite what I had thought previously.

WREN. I find that very hard to believe.

ALAN. I can't get that image out of my mind.

WREN. You see very efficient. Now, what about the demon baby?

ALAN. What about it?

WREN. I want to keep it in my book.

ALAN. That is not my decision. That came from marketing.

> (WREN *walks away from him.*)

WREN. Biscuits! Biscuits! Biscuits! Let's all go to the roof, shall we?

SALLY. The men are still parking the car.

CAT. Parking is terrible.

WREN. We'll leave a note on the door. Come on!

> (*They all go to the roof.*)

SALLY. Nice landscaping.

CAT. Good view.

ART. Is everybody warm enough? I brought the gin up.

ALAN. I'll have a little, thank you.

WREN. It's a full moon. It's perfect, Art. Isn't it perfect?

ART. Yes, I guess it is.

WREN. Oh, I just feel so much better! Let's all lie down and look at the moon.

ART. I don't think people will want to lie down.

SALLY. I will.

ALAN. Me too.

CAT. I'll keep an eye on things from up here.

WREN. I think we should play party games. Spin the Bottle. Two Minutes in the Closet. Who Can Get Closest to the Edge.

CAT. (*Sarcastic:*) Great choices.

(DEMON BABY *appears smoking a cigarette.* WREN *is the only one able to see him.*)

DEMON BABY. What a bunch of cold fish.

WREN. I know.

DEMON BABY. The world could lose a few of these.

WREN. We could play a game called…

DEMON BABY. Good People Versus Bad People.

WREN. …"Good People Versus Bad People."

SALLY. That sounds good. What are the rules?

DEMON BABY. Yes! What are the rules?

ART. Let's go back downstairs? What do you say?

CAT. Yes, let's.

WREN. The challenge of the game is answering the question; How can we tell the good people from the bad people?

ALAN. I think we can tell by people's actions.

WREN. Yes, but we can't always see what people are doing.

ALAN. Well, then we can tell by what we see people doing.

WREN. Yes, but that doesn't take away from what they are doing when nobody's looking.

DEMON BABY. So, how do we play the game?

CAT. So, how do we play the game?

SALLY. I'm not sure there is a game. I think it's a philosophical discussion.

CAT. I think you can often tell the good from the bad by what they wear.

ALAN. Oh, I don't think that's true.

CAT. In my experience, it's been empirically proven.

ALAN. If it were empirically proven, it would have to be through your own experience. You repeat yourself.

CAT. I was just trying to be clear.

DEMON BABY. What is wrong with these people? Can't they do something interesting?

ALAN. Interesting.

ART. She has a point. Like in the states, some people wear gang clothes and these clothes identify them as members of a gang.

SALLY. And some people just have a strange look about them. They look odd and then you cross the street.

ART. Yes, even in the U.S. almost everyone is wearing clothes that look like gang clothes.

SALLY. Like what kind of clothes?

ART. Oh, I don't know — Khakis.

DEMON BABY. Khakis!

CAT. Oh, that's no help. Everybody wears khakis.

ART. Exactly.

DEMON BABY. Khakis.

ART. Now, we have a criminal justice system that has a series of procedures to define the good actions from the bad.

SALLY. There's the United Nations.

(*Pause.*)

ALAN. If someone has bad thoughts does that qualify them as a bad person?

CAT. I say, bad actions, witnessed or not, makes a bad person.

WREN. And who decides what makes a bad action?

ART. Something that is harmful to others?

WREN. Also seemingly harmless actions can have exceedingly harmful effects.

SALLY. Sometimes I want to steal things.

(*Long pause.*)

Someone's coat off the back of a chair in a restaurant. A greeting card. Candy. Useless things. Walk out without paying for dinner. I did that once. It feels perfectly natural, like yawning, but I have to remind myself that I might get caught.

ALAN. You don't think about the fact that it might be wrong?

SALLY. No. I just think–I don't want to get caught doing this so I don't do it.

(*Pause.*)

I'm a little chilly. I think I'll go down and look for the men.

ART. This bottle's done, but there's another in the flat. Shall we?

CAT. Well, I could use a refresher.

WREN. I'll come in a minute

(*They all go downstairs except for* WREN *and* ALAN.)

ALAN. You look beautiful in this moonlight.

WREN. Do you consider yourself good or bad?

ALAN. Mostly good. What do you consider yourself?

WREN. Depending on the day, most days I would have to answer…

DEMON BABY. Bad.

WREN. Bad.

ALAN. You have a warped self perception.

DEMON BABY. Good.

WREN. That does add another layer to the discussion.

(ALAN *leans over and kisses* WREN.)

WREN. You change your mind often.

ALAN. All the time.

WREN. I wouldn't have thought that of you.

(WREN *kisses* ALAN. *An experiment—and then on to the next thing.*)

I dreamt last night that the end of the world was coming and everyone was very frightened because they were all looking to see what form the end of the world would take. We formed block patrols and watch parties, but nobody saw anything for a long time. Well, there was one firing squad that executed people at point blank range, but that was an isolated incident.

DEMON BABY. Anyway...

WREN. Anyway! It turns out the end of the world was coming in the form of a hard to see cult.

ALAN. (*Trying to caress her.*) A cult?

WREN. (*Ignoring the caress.*) This small group of people is brainwashing people and they brainwash you by putting eye drops in your eyes. The complete brainwashing process takes six days and on the sixth night if you find yourself in the company of six brainwashed people,... well it gets kind of confusing here, so stick with me...when a seventh brainwashed enters the room, this seventh person is programmed to kill all of the other six. The seventh brainwashed gets to live another six days until it's time to kill more of the converted.

ALAN. Hmmm.

WREN. The only way to stay alive is to keep killing the converted. In this way, the cult figured they could kill as much of the population as possible. Very efficient. Very organic.

ALAN. I think we are all brainwashed to a certain degree. We're brainwashed to go to our jobs. To be kind to our neighbors. To buy cars. To wear clothes

WREN. But in the end, it was a happy dream because I realized that I was part of the resistance movement. I had the power to not be brainwashed. There were others too, who had the power to not be brainwashed.

These are the options:

1. Allow yourself to be brainwashed, join the cult, and die.

2. Allow yourself to be brainwashed, and stay alive by killing other people.

3. Fight the brainwashing, fight the cult, and die trying.

Which would you choose?

ALAN. Which?

WREN. Would you choose?

ALAN. Number three.

WREN. No. You'd choose number one. It's not a coward's way. It's very practical actually.

ALAN. I disagree.

WREN. You dream about it tonight and see which one you pick.

ALAN. You think very little of me.

DEMON BABY. Yes. I rarely do think of you.

WREN. Yes. I rarely do think of you.

ALAN. We are going to discontinue the children's pamphlet.

WREN. What?

ALAN. Budget cuts and we can't spend anymore money— so we won't be using your piece— so I hope this won't affect our friendship— our relationship— or any future collaborations.

> (SALLY, CAT, and ART *return with fresh drinks.*
> *Everyone stands awkwardly around— not talking.*
> *Suddenly,* CHARLES *appears.*
> *He is drunk.*)

CHARLES. Sorry I'm late.

SALLY. Charles!

CAT. Where's James?

CHARLES. He's had an accident.

CAT. What?

CHARLES. Parking.

SALLY. Is he alright?

CHARLES. Wounded pride.

CAT. Well, where is he?

CHARLES. He drove himself to hospital.

CAT. Which hospital?

SALLY. Why didn't he come get us?

CHARLES. Oh, it's nothing. He didn't want you to worry. He told me to go back inside and enjoy myself.

CAT. I'll go meet him at the hospital. May I use your phone, Wren?

CHARLES. He didn't want you to miss the party. It's just a few cuts on his hand and a few stitches and he'll be good as new.

SALLY. How do you cut your hand parking?

CHARLES. He said we should we take cabs home. And he'd see you at home and not to worry.

CAT. Which hospital?

CHARLES. It's just a small thing.

ART. It's all sorted then.

SALLY. Perhaps we ought to call it a night.

WREN. Don't be silly. James drove himself out into the night to the hospital because he wants you to stay and have a good time. So, let's all have a good time.

CHARLES. Yes, James wants you all to stay.

WREN. You see. It's sorted.

SALLY. It seems so strange.

WREN. But it's what he wants.

SALLY. Yes.

WREN. Yes.

ALAN. Yes, well.

ART. Aaah.

CAT. Yes, I guess.

CHARLES. Yes!

    (CHARLES *pulls out a piñata.*)

I found this downstairs. Should we play?

WREN. Wonderful. Art, go get us a stick and a hankie for a blindfold.

ART. Do we really want to play hit the piñata?

SALLY. Why the hell not?

ALAN. Yes. A party game. Better than spot the evil one.

DEMON BABY. I heard that.

WREN. What are you waiting for, Art?

ART. I'm going. Going. Gone

    (ART *leaves.*)

WREN. Good.

CHARLES. Now, where to string it up? You do string it up, don't you?

SALLY. Don't play dumb. Of course you string it up.

ALAN. Not too close to the edge.

CHARLES. This is a perfect tree for it.

SALLY. I hope it'll hold it.

WREN. Let's try it.

CHARLES. Perfect. Let's string it up!

    (CHARLES *and* SALLY *string up the piñata.*)

CAT. May I use your phone, Wren? I'm going to try and reach him on his cell.

WREN. Of course, dear. Of course.

(CAT *leaves.* WREN *grabs* ALAN.)

WREN. Here's what I think. I believe that Charles has murdered James.

ALAN. Don't be silly.

WREN. Who cuts their hand parking?

ALAN. There will be a reasonable explanation.

WREN. No, there will not be a reasonable explanation.

ALAN. I think you are reading into this situation.

WREN. His eyes look hard. They look like a light went out.

ALAN. Great powers of exaggeration.

WREN. We'll see.

ALAN. If you think Charles murdered James, then why are you so cheery?

WREN. I just want to see what happens next.

ALAN. Great.

(ART *returns with a broom and the white sheet.*)

ART. I thought we could use the broom for a stick and I couldn't find a blindfold, so I thought people could just cover themselves with the sheet.

(WREN *gives* ART *a big kiss.*)

WREN. Thank you, Art! That's fantastic. Alright now, here are the rules when playing piñata. You put on the sheet and you swing until you smash the piñata. When you smash the piñata, candy comes flyin' out everywhere and everybody gets to scramble around picking up the candy.

SALLY. Oh good. I love candy.

WREN. People take turns.

ART. The problem is the winner never gets that much candy because they are blindfolded.

ALAN. Doesn't seem fair, then.

CHARLES. Who goes first?

WREN. I'll go first. So people can get an idea of how it is done.

(WREN *covers herself with the sheet.*

CAT *returns to the rooftop.*)

CAT. I was just in your bathroom. You have all those little candles lit, so I was just enjoying the soft glow of the room. I was orienting myself to the tenderness when I looked over the toilet, preparing myself to use it. Feeling very warm and nice, I looked down and on the back of the toilet I saw this beautiful pink surface. A gorgeous, inviting pink surface, and I thought, "Oh! What's that?" So, I looked closer as I was unbuttoning my pants and I, upon closer inspection, …I realized it was …tender…pink…vomit…It still looked nice somehow. Someone neatly placed the toilet seat on top of their pink vomit.

(WREN *takes the sheet off herself.*)

ART. Oh. Cat.

CAT. I'm leaving anyway.

WREN. Don't go, Cat.

CAT. I'm leaving the country.

CHARLES. What?

SALLY. Cat?

CAT. My marriage is over. I don't love James anymore. I'm bored and I can't stand this place. It's horrible. I miss my family. I miss my home. I'm going back.

SALLY. What happened, Cat? I didn't know.

CAT. I reached James on the cell phone. He's not at the hospital. He didn't have a parking accident. He's home. He couldn't stand to be near me anymore.

SALLY. What? He adores you.

CAT. I told him just today I was leaving the country. I told him I was leaving him. I'm taking the children. I don't want them growing up here.

(*Pause.*)

Charles, James didn't like your alibi. I told him no one believed you.

WREN. But, weren't you the one convincing me to stay here? That it wasn't so bad?

CAT. Things aren't always what they seem.

WREN. Apparently not.

CAT. And things change.

WREN. Things do change.

ALAN. Yes, they do.

WREN. Stay for the piñata, Cat. I am sorry about James, but why not stay and hit something with a stick?

CAT. I shouldn't.

WREN. You should.

CHARLES. It might make you feel better.

SALLY. Yes. Hit something with a stick

ART. Wren's right. It might make you feel better.

(CAT *takes the sheet and covers herself. She grips the bat firmly.*)

WREN. Wait.

(WREN *spins* CAT *to disorient her.*)

Okay.

(CAT *chokes up on the bat again and then begins swinging wildly*
She is nowhere near the piñata.
Her swings are forceful and uncontrolled.
As she swings, she moves toward the edge of the roof.
She falls off the roof.)

CHARLES. Oh!

ART. Oh!

ALAN. Oh!

SALLY. Oh!

WREN. I think I see her moving.

Scene 12

The DEMON BABY *is sitting on Art's chest.* ART *is asleep on the floor.*
He opens his eyes wide and then he cannot move. DEMON BABY *makes the*
noises that ART *would make if he could speak.*

DEMON BABY. Huh. Huh. UH UH. Huh Huh.

Scene 13

The DEMON BABY *is still on Art's chest. This* DEMON BABY *is very*
similar to Wren's *DEMON BABY, except this one looks like melted plastic*
in places and has a slight British accent.

ART. I hate my job. I hate the people that I work with. I have fantasies about hurting them. Scraping their soft fleshy cheeks across gravel. Dropping them down the elevator. They pay me too much money to leave. They give me everything I ask for. I have no idea what I am doing. I used to do things that I enjoyed. Things that made sense to me.

DEMON BABY. When was that?

ART. I don't know. I don't remember. I have pictures. I have a picture of us on a ferris wheel. We are so much younger and happy. We are smiling.

DEMON BABY. You're drunk in that picture.

ART. We aren't drunk. Tipsy. You look a little melted.

DEMON BABY. You could be happy again. It's a stage. It's hard to adjust, to accept, but once you do it's a wonderful place to be.

ART. Yes. Yes. I know.

DEMON BABY. It's perfectly natural to go through a difficult time at first. To rebel. But eventually, you begin to fit in.

ART. I don't like to get out of bed.

DEMON BABY. Yes.

ART. People are bumping into me, talking too loudly…

DEMON BABY. Yes! Yes! It's all perfectly normal! Biscuit?

ART. No. Well. Yes. Yes. Thank you.

DEMON BABY. You'll be alright.

ART. I…

DEMON BABY. Yes.

ART. I don't like to go outside.

DEMON BABY. As I said, it's all part of the process. It's horrible, but it ends.

ART. I want to go home.

> (WREN *enters from outside. She takes her coat off and puts her bag down. She does not see the* DEMON BABY.)

WREN. Whatcha doin' down there?

ART. Just resting.

WREN. You wanna sit up?

ART. How's Cat doing?

WREN. I didn't go. I just rode the tube to the end and then I rode it back. I saw the cutest baby on the tube. Big round face. Big cheeks. Big eyes. An absolutely gorgeous baby. And he just watched everything. And he watched everything with so much interest, I just thought, this baby must be a hundred years old. I mean this baby really seemed to know some things. And he looked at me, he looked right at me, and I thought —that baby knows exactly what I am thinking and exactly how I am feeling. And I felt all warm and absolutely perfect. It's so great when that happens. When you just feel exactly right some times. Oh! Everything about this little baby was fascinating and perfect. And then moments like that, you just feel great being alive. It's just great to be alive.

> (ART *continues to lie very still.*)

> (*The* DEMON BABY *continues to perch on his chest.*)

The baby's head wobbled just ever so slightly with the movement of the train and such delicate hand movements.

> (WREN *imitates the hand movements of the baby.*)

Something like that.

ART. Wren.

WREN. Hmmm?

ART. Let's go home. Wren?

WREN. Yes?

ART. What are you thinking about?

WREN. Nothing.

ART. Do you want to have a baby?

WREN. Oh no. That wasn't what I was thinking about.

ART. Oh. Did you hear what I said before?

WREN. Which thing?

ART. Did I say it out loud or just think it?

DEMON BABY. You said it out loud.

WREN. What was it?

ART. No. No. It's nothing.

(WREN *imitates the delicate hand movements of the baby.*)

WREN. It went something just like that.

End of Play

16 SPELLS TO CHARM THE BEAST

by Lisa D'Amour

Required royalties must be paid every time this play is performed before any audience, whether or not it is presented for profit and whether or not admission is charged. To purchase acting editions of this play, or to obtain stock and amateur performance rights, you must contact:

Playscripts, Inc.
website: www.playscripts.com
email: info@playscripts.com
phone: 1-866-NEW-PLAY (639-7529)

Inquiries concerning all other rights should be addressed to the author's agent: Val Day, William Morris Agency, 1325 Avenue of the Americas, New York, NY 10019.

For more information about rights and permissions, see p. 10.

BIOGRAPHY

Lisa D'Amour writes plays and creates collaborative, often site-specific theater. Recent projects include *Nita and Zita,* created with Katie Pearl and Kathy Randels (for which they received a 2003 OBIE Award); *16 Spells to Charm the Beast,* produced by Salvage Vanguard Theater (Austin); and *LIMO,* a performance installation commissioned by the Whitney Museum of Art. Ms. D'Amour has received funding from the Jerome and McKnight foundations, the Minnesota and Louisiana State Arts Boards, and the MacDowell Colony, and has received commissions from Children's Theater Company, The Guthrie Theater, and Playwrights' Horizons. She is a core member of the Playwrights' Center and a member of New Dramatists. Ms. D'Amour received her M.F.A. in playwriting from the University of Texas at Austin, where she was a James A. Michener Playwriting Fellow.

Other Clubbed Thumb credits: *Red Death* (Summerworks '02).

ACKNOWLEDGMENTS

16 Spells to Charm the Beast was originally produced by Clubbed Thumb as part of Summerworks 2001 at the HERE Arts Center in New York City. It was directed by Anne Kauffman, with the following cast and staff:

LILLIAN	Randy Danson
NORMA	Caitlin Miller
NED	Jon Krupp
MILLICENT	Cam Kornman
THE BEAST	Robert Alexander Owens

Sets	Louisa Thompson and Charles Goldman
Lights	Gwen Grossman
Costumes	Jenny Chappelle Fulton
Sound	Deniz Akyurek

16 Spells to Charm the Beast recieved its official world premiere from Salvage Vanguard Theater on February 21, 2003, at the Off Center in Austin, Texas. It was directed by Deanna Shoemaker, with the following cast and staff:

LILLIAN ....Lana Dieterich
NORMA...Monica Bustamante
NED..Harvey Guion
MILLICENT .... Cyndi Williams
THE BEAST .... David Jones

Production Stage Manager...Etta Sanders
Assistant Stage Manager..Wendy Meldrum
Scenic Designer .... Ann Marie Gordon
Costume Designer.. Marcia L. Rector
Lighting Designer.. Diana Duecker
Prop Master..Erim Randall
Sound Designer .... Buzz Moran
Composer...Graham Reynolds
Cellist..Ben Westney

This play was written with the generous support of a McKnight Advancement Grant from the Playwrights' Center in Minneapolis, Minnesota. It was subsequently developed through New Dramatists, and the Clubbed Thumb Summerworks Festival.

CAST OF CHARACTERS

LILLIAN DAVIS, a metropolitan housewife of a mature age.

NED DAVIS, her husband.

NORMA DAVIS, her daughter, aka NORMA RUST and NORMA PLYWOOD.

MILLICENT HICCUP, Lillian's neighbor from the floor below.

THE BEAST, a bona fide fairy tale beast, as in "Beauty and the Beast."

PLACE

Lillian Davis' apartment and the Beast's apartment, as described in the text of the play.

TIME

Is not an issue, except as it takes shape inside Lillian's head on the occasion of writing her Last Will and Testament.

NO SANDART ANYMORE, no sandbook, no masters.
Nothing in the dice. How many mutes?
Seventen.
Your question—your answer Your chant, what does it know?
Deepinsnow,
        Eepinno,
                I—I—O.

Paul Celan, from the collection Breathtum.

Randy Danson
in *16 Spells to Charm the Beast.*

Produced by Clubbed Thumb at the HERE Arts Center, 2001.
Photograph by Charles Goldman

16 SPELLS TO CHARM THE BEAST

One.

LILLIAN DAVIS' living room in a 3 bedroom, garishly decorated apartment on the 26h floor of a building in an enormous city which could be Manhattan. In the middle of the bright red carpet is a pile of snow. LILLIAN stands knee deep in snow: It is snowing only on her. THE BEAST comes in with his bloodshot eyes and his modest bouquet of flowers. He stands before her. She shivers. He stands before her. She shivers. Slowly, painfully, accompanied painful vocal gymnastics and snapping of bones, he gets down on one knee. She shivers. She shivers. She looks at him.

LILLIAN. I, Lillian Davis, being of sound mind and memory leave the following instructions regarding the distribution of my tangible personal property.

The set of hand painted china tea-bowls goes to Millicent T. Hiccup, who fondled them so discreetly during our many languid afternoons at tea.

My collection of handmade obelisks in the hall closet goes to my only daughter, Norma. (and that is all she gets. She is otherwise excluded from this will, an act that I perform in full knowledge of the consequences of doing so.)

The mysterious wooden crate in the back of the walk-in freezer goes to my dear dear husband Ned.

The tabby cat goes to the dear neighbor lady oh dear what's her name…

The ten Randy Warpohl prints are to be divided, equally among my 21 grandchildren in any manner they see so fit.

To Jonathon Keene Archipelago Redbreast: My cello.

(She turns to the beast.)

And you. Nothing for you. You can't have a piece of me even after I'm dead.

(Immediate, heartbreakingly sad reaction from THE BEAST. He is still in love with her. He gazes on her adoringly, lays his bouquet at her feet, stands himself up and leaves. She waits. She shivers. She looks off to where the monster went. She looks back. She shivers. It snows.)

(Blackout.)

Two.

LILLIAN and MILLICENT HICCUP at afternoon tea. LILLIAN is the perfect host, wardrobe and all. MILLICENT is an above-average guest and wears clunky, orthopedic looking shoes. MILLICENT fondles tea bowls discreetly throughout the tea. LILLIAN does not acknowledge this fondling until the proper moment arrives for her to do so. This scene is accompanied by the drone of the city that seeps in through the crack the sliding glass balcony doors: cars, busses, people, muggings, etc. However, we can't really see much city out the sliding glass balcony door: we can only the side of another high-rise apartment building.

LILLIAN. Yes well the problem with you see the problem with most cities is that most of their wealthy residents move out of the city and take the money with them. Take the money with them and move out of the city creating what I call an "empty city."

MILLICENT. When June (not the month, my daughter ha ha) went to her senior gala she wore this dress this dress which I swear was dyed with bona fide rosewater from bona fide roses from the Rookline Botanical Gardens.

LILLIAN. It's not just the white people I'm talking about its the money, the color Green I suppose being carted out of the city only not in a romantic or epic fashion such as when the Saralee Indians trudged across their country with their belongings tied to their backs creating a "trail of tears" no it's more pedestrian than that, pedestrian, I mean, in the "mundane" sense of the word, because they cart their money out in minivans and coupes and sedans, any kind of car they can get their hands on. There's no risk, really, no thought of *stakes*. They squeeze their feet into whatever shoes might be handy, chuck everything in the van and vamoose!

MILLICENT. The thing about the color of the dress was that the color of the dress was so faint that its effect was subliminal. More of a scent than a color. The scent of bona fide rosewater. She had men literally falling at her feet all about the auditorium.

LILLIAN. More tea?

MILLICENT. Just a spot. I mean she caused such a stir in that rosewater dress it hangs in the downstairs closet to this day inside the plastic casing that my drycleaner recommended a plastic casing he said he had specially designed for the last person who brought in a rosewater dress to be cleaned and I said *"the last person to bring in a rosewater dress to be cleaned?"* and pretended to be completely shattered that someone else might have thought of the idea of a dress dyed with bona fide rose water and my drycleaner said "yes, in 1938, when drycleaning was first invented, when my great Grandfather opened this shop an eerie woman in a black veil came in with a rose water dress, and gave a lot of questionable details about why she had such a dress— too many details, in fact. Even back then people never gave their drycleaners the whole story."

LILLIAN. The problem of this city is not EMPTINESS, of course. This city survives because we live so close together that we overlap, and so the money overlaps as well. You know there are some days when I think there is nothing more in the world that I want more than a bona fide rosewater dress.

The problem of this city is *not* that it is an "empty city" and this is what I am getting at you understand this is where I'm going.

MILLICENT. So I gave that drycleaner a knowing wink you know and said "yes but was that lady's dress dyed with BONA FIDE rosewater from the ROOKLINE BOTANICAL GARDENS" and my drycleaner chuckled and said "she said that it was but I didn't believe her, not for one second." And I said "but you believe me don't you?" And he said, "Ma'am, you have the face of an Australian Lemur, of course I believe you." And I gave him a knowing smile you know and walked out.

LILLIAN. No, the problem with this city is that this city overlaps so much so much that they are slowly but surely *taking away my view* . It used to be that with binoculars I had a clear view of the Statue of Offended Dignity but not any more, no, that building over there see right there, I watched it go up, floor by floor, for two years until one day my binoculars were a relic of a time gone by.

MILLICENT. June (not the month my daughter ha ha) comes home from time to time now that she has turned 40 and ditched her third husband and she just gets so upset when she opens that closet and sees the bon fide rosewater dress hanging there I means she is just a terror about it, screaming and tearing at her hair as though the dress is some awful skeleton in our closet, some outrageous symbol of some absurdity inherent in the fabric of our family you should see the way she carries on standing in front of the open closet door like that spouting off like a hot teapot. And I just stand there smiling that same smile, you know, that I gave to my drycleaner, and winking from time to time, you know, until eventually she crumbles to the floor, sobbing like a child and helpless and fragile as a pheasant for me to gather up into my arms and sing to her, the two of us on the hallway floor...

> (LILLIAN *opens the sliding glass door a wee crack. City sounds stop. A spell seeps in:*)

Twicesnow twolips

in the teartea

late babies thaw

fat suns

in the sea

> (*During the second time through,* MILLICENT *fondles her tea cup, and* LILLIAN *watches* [*i.e.* MILLICENT *fondles the tea cup for* LILLIAN]).

Twicesnow twolips

in the teartea

late babies thaw

fat suns

in the sea

(On the third time through, the ladies whisper along with the spell, looking at each other.)

Twicesnow twolips

in the teartea

late babies thaw

fat suns

in the sea.

(On the last line, LILLIAN quickly closes the doors. City sounds resume. The two ladies look at each other. MILLICENT smiles that smile, you know. LILLIAN smiles back. MILLICENT carefully puts down her tea cup. LILLIAN smiles. MILLICENT and LILLIAN stand. MILLICENT goes to the door. MILLICENT opens the door. She smiles one last time at LILLIAN, who smiles back. MILLICENT exits. LILLIAN suddenly feels like someone is watching her. She raises her binoculars towards her sliding glass window.)

(Blackout.)

Three.

THE BEAST *is in his apartment. His apartment is his cave, and should contain elements of both types of dwellings. Out of a tiny window in his apartment, you an see the outline of a city, and in the outline of the city, there is a clear view of Lillian's apartment. A telescope sits in front of the window. It is a fancy and expensive telescope. Everything else in the apartment is crappy and Cro-Magnon. THE BEAST sits at a crude table. He has scraps of paper and tiny children's scissors. He carefully folds the paper. He carefully places the tiny scissors in his large hands. He cuts five careful cuts, counting them all. He places the scissors down. He places the paper down. He picks up the paper in the proper fashion, so that it unfolds beautifully, into an extraordinarily intricate paper snowflake. He carefully walks over to another section of the apartment, and pulls aside a stained, raggedy curtain. Behind the curtain is a enormous sheet of these same snowflakes, linked together. He kneels (again, with great difficulty and bone-snapping). He picks up a needle and thread (again with great difficulty: the needle is far too small for his hands) and begins to carefully sew this new snowflake onto the bottom. As he sews he chants:*

Fingerhole

Skull

Ladysnow

Spine

Softleather

Skull

Yourmine

Spine
Mineyour
Skull
Leathersoft
Spine
Snowlady
Skull
Holefinger
Spine
Fingerhole
Skull
Ladysnow
Spine
Softleather
Skull
Yourmine
Spine

> (*He continues this mirror chant over and over as he sews, for as long as necessary, then the lights blackout.*)

Four.

Back in the Apartment. LILLIAN *and her daughter* NORMA. NORMA *is a grown woman. Through the sliding glass doors we can see the grand cityscape, unobscured. The* PAUSES *in this scene are not necessarily always long, but they are always heavy, like paperweights keeping all the papers underneath from flying away.*

LILLIAN. Devilish

NORMA. Cocksucker

LILLIAN. In

NORMA. Blue

LILLIAN. Smock.

> (*They suppress giggles, snorts.*)

NORMA. Unspeakable

LILLIAN. Tort. No, Tart. Tart.

NORMA. With

LILLIAN. Rank

NORMA. Meat.

(This time they can't hold it in, they laugh and laugh. LILLIAN *kisses* NORMA *gently on the forehead.)*

LILLIAN. Oh, I just love making up those nicknames for your father. How on earth did you think of that game.

NORMA. You thought of it, remember mother? We were standing in front of that Zipptchenstein called OOPS! when you said: my my my wouldn't that would be an appropriate nickname for the old man. And it started from there.

LILLIAN. I said that? God sometimes I glimpse my mean spirit so clearly I begin to despise myself.

(LILLIAN begins to weep.)

NORMA. Now now mother you know as well as I do that every human being is born with a mean streak embedded long and deep in one's soul. Personally I think its best to acknowledge and cultivate it in order to keep it in check. Pretending it just isn't there just makes it more wild and unruly. You are more civilized than half those miserable ants crawling around down there so its simply silly to despise yourself.

(LILLIAN stops weeping. They clink their vodka glasses.)

LILLIAN. Cheers.

NORMA. Cheers.

LILLIAN. It really is good to have you home.

NORMA. So I hear you've taken to sculpting obelisks out of clay.

LILLIAN. Oh, yes. It was your father Ned's idea, actually. I thought he had gone completely bonkers but then to my surprise I actually started to like it. Sculpting that same cryptic shape over and over gives one a feeling of vocation, of devotion to some mystic calling higher... higher than...

NORMA. Higher than this building?

(Dry, silent laughs.)

LILLIAN. Of course as soon as I started to like it then your father stopped liking it, though he does try his best to pretend he likes it, but you should see him, really, he looks at my obelisks the way one might look at a pile of dogshit. And as you can see:

(She opens up the closet door for a brief moment. We see it is filled with obelisks of various shapes, sizes and colors. She shuts it quickly.)

They are fine obelisks, more than fine, worthy of praise and even adoration.

NORMA. Why do you keep them hidden away in the closet?

LILLIAN. Hidden away? Hidden away she says. They are not hidden away, Norma They are on display in the most cutting edge way of being on display they are on display by NOT BEING on display.

(*They look at each other,* LILLIAN *looking to make sure her daughter gets it.* NORMA *pretends to get it.*)

NORMA. Of course. Oh mother aren't you the mint on the pillow. Now tell me about your days.

(*PAUSE.*)

LILLIAN. Those are nice shoes your wearing.

(*Norma looks down at her shoes.*)

NORMA. Thank you.

LILLIAN. Did you choose them yourself?

NORMA. (*Still looking down.*) Why yes, I did.

LILLIAN. They're nice.

NORMA. (*Still looking down.*) Thanks.

(NORMA *looks up.*)

NORMA. And your days?

LILLIAN. What about my days?

NORMA. You know, what have you been doing. with yourself and all that.

(*PAUSE.*)

LILLIAN. Well. There's the obelisks.

NORMA. Yep. On display.

LILLIAN. "On display."

(*PAUSE.*)

NORMA. And the skyline?

(*PAUSE.*)

LILLIAN. And the skyline?

NORMA. Has it changed much?

LILLIAN. Oh the skyline yes the skyline well of course the latest addition to the skyline is the PLAINTAIN BUILDING in mid-town, that's that building over there that looks like a giant, malformed penis, which penis is, of course, supposed to be a plantain. I can only assume that the scale model looked less like a penis or I can't believe they would have gone through with it. The entire city, I kid you not, has their lips zipped about it. Each of us thinks that we are the only person in the entire city who thinks the building looks like a penis, and so we're all afraid to say anything, because we don't want to get laughed at. So we all walk around on the street giving each other these sideways smirks, hoping against hope our smirk will be returned. Do you think it looks like a penis?

NORMA. I do.

LILLIAN. Thank God.

(*The two burst into laughter for a moment.*)

LILLIAN. It is so good to have you home.

(*Another burst of laughter, which ends.*)

LILLIAN. So. That's the skyline. Of course the Statue of Offended Dignity still stands, clear as day, on the horizon.

NORMA. You can see the Statue from here?

LILLIAN. Oh yes. Here. Take the binoculars.

(LILLIAN *takes a really nice pair of binoculars out of a case.*)

NORMA. These are really nice binoculars, mom.

LILLIAN. Thank you.

(NORMA *raises the binoculars to her eyes.*)

NORMA. Yep, there she is. Offended as always.

LILLIAN. But so dignified.

NORMA. Dignified, yet offended. Hence the name.

LILLIAN. Exactly.

(NORMA *hands the binoculars back to* LILLIAN. LILLIAN *makes a big deal of putting them back in, as though there is some joke to it, some old family joke that* NORMA *doesn't quite get.* NORMA *chuckles and agrees to it, anyway.*)

NORMA. So how is Dad?

LILLIAN. Dad is Dad.

NORMA. Good.

LILLIAN. He's either on my lap or absent as a peony.

NORMA. As a peony?

LILLIAN. You know—

(LILLIAN *performs some "absent as a peony" gesture.*)

NORMA. Of course.

LILLIAN. One day I will cause a great cello stir cello.

(LILLIAN *lightly touches or secretly strokes the place where her collarbone meets in the center of her chest and looks at* NORMA *as though she hopes* NORMA *will understand some sort of secret, subliminal reference but alas* NORMA *doesn't get it.*)

(*PAUSE.*)

NORMA. And Millicent Hiccup?

LILLIAN. Yes?

NORMA. Millicent Hiccup. Millicient Hiccup. That silly and altogether frazzled woman, Millicent Hiccup from the floor below does still come around?

(*PAUSE.*)

LILLIAN. Yes.

NORMA. And her downright petulant daughter, what was her name? February?

LILLIAN. June.

NORMA. Yes, of course, June. Ugh. I remember just before I moved out to go to college, Millicent Hiccup was always stomping up here in those pediatric-style shoes dragging June, freshly made up with some kind of off-brand of makeup, trying to get the two of us to "go out on the town," like I could ever truly enjoy an evening out on the town with a girl named June, a girl named June who was into Geodes, which fact was the only fact I knew about June, because the one time I deigned to visit her she said "What are you into, I'm into Geodes" at which point I stood up from her bed (I was in her bedroom at the time, which was filled with you-know-what) I stood up and walked out of the room without so much as a peep.

LILLIAN. I believe you meant orthopedic.

NORMA. What?

LILLIAN. Orthopedic. Millicent has an unfortunate problem with her feet, which she is working to correct with medical assistance. You said that Millicent wore "Pediatric style" shoes, when I think you meant "orthopedic."

NORMA. Whatever.

(NORMA *looks puzzled.*)

(*PAUSE.*)

LILLIAN. Yes, Millicent comes up from time to time. We recently initiated a quite regular tea, in fact.

(*All at once* NORMA *realizes that she's made a terrible mistake, insulting Millicent Hiccup, the woman who is now, apparently, her mother's only friend.* NORMA *pours herself another drink, wanders about, and looks out the window.*)

NORMA. Oh, it looks like there's some construction going on down there, just one block over.

LILLIAN. Oh, yes, I noticed that but I think they're going to leave it blank.

NORMA. Leave it blank?

LILLIAN. Yes, leave it blank.

NORMA. What do you mean, blank?

LILLIAN. Blank. Just Blank.

(NORMA *wanders around the room a bit more. She picks up an ashtray.*)

NORMA. Did you buy this ashtray on your trip to Kentucky?

LILLIAN. Yes.

NORMA. MOTHER, I CANNOT THINK OF A SINGLE THING LEFT TO TALK ABOUT THERE IS ABSOLUTELY NOTHING LEFF TO SAY EVEN THOUGH WE HAVE NEITHER SEEN NOR HEARD

FROM EACH OTHER IN OVER TWO YEARS AND SO HERE IT GOES I HAVE COME HERE TO TELL YOU THAT LAST YEAR I MARRIED AN ARCHITECT NAMED NAPOLEON RUST AND I AM NOW AT THIS VERY INSTANT PREGNANT WITH MY FIRST CHILD WE HAVE MOVED OUT OF THE CITY AND BOUGHT A HOUSE IN A TOWN CALLED "SOFTASAFEATHERBED" AND WE ARE QUITE NO WE ARE VERY HAPPY.

(*PAUSE.*)

LILLIAN. Well, aren't you the zit beneath the Bull's testicle.

NORMA. This is absurd…

(*She starts to leave.* LILLIAN *lashes out with a curse.*)

LILLIAN. YOU will find yourself prematurely withered.

YOU will not know your left foot from your right.

YOU will grow dull.

YOU will lose first an expensive ring and then an appendage in the garbage disposal.

YOU will lose your sense of smell as the result of some other horrible accident.

YOU will suffer the pains of labor 20 fold and suffer from complications in ever-increasing, excruciating increments, after which torment your husband will leave you.

YOU will eventually find the sight of their precious faces disgusting.

YOU will write your Will at age 55 and feel melancholy, then outrage, and then sickened at the wretch you have unwittingly become.

YOUR feet will never fill the shoes you choose.

YOU will die a quiet, uneventful death and go forever unremembered.

(LILLIAN *is breathless at the end of her curse. Gasping for air, she pours herself a glass of water, and drinks it.* NORMA *stands, shaken, feeling sick to her stomach.*)

LILLIAN. You KNOW how I feel about MARRIAGE. All the NOTES I slipped under your PILLOW. All my ADVICE.

NORMA. You don't want me to be happy?

LILLIAN. I want you to keep me company.

(NORMA *walks out the door.* LILLIAN *walks to the sliding glass door, gazing out.*)

(*PAUSE.*)

LILLIAN. Oh now really will you look at that enormous cock!

(*She bursts into laughter, which we hear even after the lights blackout.*)

Five.

THE BEAST's *apartment. We can see through his window that construction is encroaching upon his view of Lillian's apartment. He has propped his telescope up with phone books, and attached mirrors to it to try and get a better view. The sheet of snowflakes is now draped around the headless mannequin, pinned awkwardly. He is sitting at his crappy table, which is littered with rose petals and rose debris. He is making rose water by squeezing rose petals between his fingers and then dropping them in a bowl of water that boils on a hot plate. He squeezes petals (really hard!) and drops them in the bowl. He squeezes petals (really hard!) and drops them in the bowl. He squeezes petals (really hard!) and goddam it pricks his finger really deep on a thorn. He screeches, leaps up to suck his finger, and hits the table in such a way that he dumps the boiling water onto him. He screeches and hits the table in such away that the entire table breaks down. The hot plate falls on his foot, burning it. He screeches, leaping on one foot to pull the plug out of the wall, the act of which gives him a minor shock which runs through his body for a moment. When he recovers, he looks at the mess. A look of heartbreaking disappointment crosses his face for 2 seconds, then goes away. He looks at the mannequin. He can't bear to work on it. He sighs and looks to the window. He walks to the telescope. Perhaps he polishes the lens. He looks through the telescope for about 30 seconds. He comes away from the telescope a changed beast, almost giddy, with a spring to his step. He turns the rosewater bowl over on the floor, not even worrying about the hot plate. He squats on the floor, and begins squeezing the rose petals again, ignoring the fact that his workplace is in shambles. As he works he sings a ditty that has the quality of one of the seven dwarves singing "WHISTLE WHILE YOU WORK" to Snow White.*

THE BEAST. Ah Ba Doo Waaah

Ah Ba Doo Bee Doo

Lee Lee Lee Lee Lee Lay

Lab Lee Lie Low Luu

Lowry Lowry Lowry

Fish Rum Toe

Woebegone Humunculus

Otta-me Ottoman Ottomo

Tee Tee Tee Tee Tee Tee

Tiny

Ma Ma Ma Ma Ma Ma Ma

Hee Hee Hee Hee Hee Hee

He-li-um helium

HELIUM.

Ah Ba Doo Waaah
Ah Ba Doo Bee Doo
Moonman Lee Lee Lee Lay
Lah Lee Lie Low Luu.
(*Blackout.*)

Six.

The 10th anniversary of the completion of the building outside Lillian's window. The building completely blocks the view through her sliding glass doors. LILLIAN enters with a tray holding a bottle of champagne and two glasses. She pops the champagne cork. She pours the two glasses. She toasts:

LILLIAN. To a life unobscured.

(She takes a sip from the champagne. She looks sincerely wistful and nostalgic. Not sad, just sappy in that way when one allows oneself one dav to be silly and suppy about something one once loved and then lost. LILLIAN gets up, and makes her way over to the sliding door, half walking, half waltzing, creating detours as though she would like to prolong the anticipation of reaching her destination. From somewhere, she takes out a really nice binocular case. She playfully opens it, and makes a big show of taking a out pair of really nice binoculars, almost as though she was making a show of it for the benefit of someone else. A deep breath. She lifts the binoculars to her eyes.)

LILLIAN. My what a clear day look at all the people in Hummus Park roller skating and playing shuffleboard and picnicking and oh my I think I just saw a pocket picked poor sap oh well and look at the way the Fairweather Building stands so close to Fork Tower when you look at them from this angle they look like a pair of old drunkards "BRING BACK W BONNIE TO ME TO ME" Now if you direct your eye on a 40 degree diagonal down down from the tip of Fork Tower your eyes land on the marble statue of St. Pheobe of Guinea, which sits atop the historic St. Phoebe of Guinea Chapel, now this diagonal relationship between the tip of Fork Tower and the statue of St. Phoebe is said to be a secret, structural symbol of the long-term forbidden love between Horace Fork (the architect who designed Fork Tower) and Jane Plum, the headmistress of St. Phoebe's school for girls. Now many of Horace Fork's comrades and colleagues knew of his affair with the schoolteacher, and went to great lengths to hide it from the wife of Horace Fork but one day a tried and true friend of the wife of Horace Fork brought the wife of Horace Fork up to the tippy top of the Statue of Offended Dignity—which you can see standing in the distance on the Eastern horizon—anyway one day this friend brought the wife of Horace Fork up to the tippy top of the Statue, where the diagonal between the buildings can be viewed clear as day and said "LOOK MILDRED LOOK DON'T YOU SEE WHAT'S BEEN GOING ON RIGHT BEFORE

YOUR EYES DON'T YOU FEEL LIKE A CAST OFF DON'T YOU JUST WANT TO END IT ALL!" In an odd reaction, the wife of Horace Fork simply smirked a mysterious smirk and directed her friend's attention to a second diagonal, that's right a second diagonal formed the statue of St. Phoebe and the copper weathervane that sits atop the Fairweather Building well the revelation of the second diagonal allowed the friend to see that there was a TRIANGLE that's right a TRIANGLE formed by the three buildings and so the wife of Horace Fork descended the statue alone, wearing her mysterious smirk, leaving her tried and true friend atop the statue to contemplate the triangle and her role as a small, shortsighted speck in the vast matrix of the world before leaping to a quick and exhilarating death. Whether this is a true story or simply lore is unimportant, what is important is the TRIANGULAR RELATIONSHIP, which you can see, clear as day from my—

(*A knock on the door.* LILLIAN *is startled, perturbed, even. She lowers her binoculars, then raises them again. Another knock.* LILLIAN *resigns herself to opening the door. As she crosses to the door, there is another knock.*)

LILLIAN. OK, ok I'm COMING!

(LILLIAN *opens the door. A Man in a cheap plastic mask stands there. This is* LILLIAN's *husband* NED, *in disguise.* LILLIAN *doesn't recognize him at first, and she is surprised to find a man at her door.*)

LILLIAN. Oh. Hello. May I help you?

NED. Yes, I was wondering if you could show me your view?

LILLIAN. My view?

NED. Yes, I have heard that you have one of the best views in the city from you sliding glass door.

(LILLIAN *looks to the sliding glass door. She sees the only the building through the doors. She looks at the man. She looks back at the sliding glass doors. Oh, what the hell.*)

LILLIAN. Why yes, I do have a quite a lovely view, would you like to come see it?

NED. Why thank you.

(NED *enters. He can't see very well through the mask. He trips over things.*)

LILLIAN. Right over here. Over *here.*

NED. I'm sorry my Pink Eye is acting up. Could you escort me?

LILLIAN. Why of course.

(LILLIAN *escorts him to the window.*)

LILLIAN. Would you like a glass of champagne?

NED. Why thank you, a glass of champagne would be lovely.

(LILLIAN *hands him a glass of champagne.*)

LILLIAN. After your champagne, you can view the city through my binoculars, if you like.

NED. Why don't you look first. Ladies first!

> (LILLIAN *is delighted. She looks through the binoculars. As she speaks,* NED *lifts up his mask and chugs his champagne, which makes him choke.*)

LILLIAN. You'll notice that Rooster Avenue cuts a zig zag right through the heart of the city — is everything OK?

NED. Fine, fine, everything is fine.

LILLIAN. Are you ready for your turn?

NED. Sure.

> (LILLIAN *hands him the binoculars. He looks for a moment, repeating "Ah, Ah" over and over.*)

LILLIAN. What do you see?

NED. I see lots of things.

LILLIAN. Describe them to me.

NED. Well ah first of all I really like that dog over there with the pinstriped suit and then the way the Feathermore Complex has exactly 42 windows facing east which implies the 42 wives of Henry VIII and oh my the Anderson Building and all its strange Masonic reliefs and the wind through my hair in the evening brings with it thoughts of you and the boat and the tiny shoes—

> (LILLIAN *is utterly defeated with disappointment.*)

LILLIAN. Ned is that you?

> (*Silence from* NED.)

LILLIAN. Come on Ned. I know you're there. You got it all wrong.

NED. But baby—

LILLIAN. I'm not your baby.

> (NED *takes off the mask. His face is sweaty from being closed up behind the mask.*)

LILLIAN. I ask for one day a year.

NED. I missed you.

LILLIAN. One day. "My Pink Eye is acting up." I should have known from the beginning.

NED. I missed you.

LILLIAN. You just left an hour ago.

NED. I was just across the street. You looked so pretty from over there. I touched the glass like it was your face.

(Can NED *reach out and touch her face?* NED *can reach out and touch her face. He tries hard, but it is a forced and awkward gesture. Hold. Hold. He pulls his hand away.)*

LILLIAN. You didn't miss me. You're just jealous of Jonathon.

*(*NED *erupts.)*

NED. WHO'S JONATHAN!

LILLIAN. See?

(Ned composes himself.)

NED. Listen, Lillian. I just don't understand why our lives haven't been jiving lately. I mean when we first met there was such synchronicity. We didn't even need to wear watches we were so in sync. Now when I look at you, I am at a complete loss as to the thoughts circulating in your head. You were not always a cipher, Lillian, you were not always a distant planet, you were not always the cracked and mysterious teacup hiding in the back of the cabinet. And when I look around us and inventory all the things we have I can't help but think that with a little effort, Lillian, with a little gumption—

(Somehow, LILLIAN *silences him. I mean, turns down the volume. So* NED *is still talking, animated, but* LILLIAN *can move about freely.* LILLIAN *exits for a moment. She comes back in dragging an oblong wooden crate used to ship art in. She opens the crate. She pulls out an impressive hacksaw.* NED *continues to talk silently. As* LILLIAN *recites the following spell in a calm and straight forward fashion, she saws off her two hands and her two feet and leaves them in the crate.)*

LILLIAN. Present snow in bowls

Waiting for her small hands

to warm it into being.

A mouse on the ground

Ladybug on the mouse-back

See her gather wood.

See her pile the wood

Outside beside the snow bowls

For tomorrow's fire.

Her breath shapes the air

The bowls come to shape her hands

Silence shapes the night.

Snow before water

Air before the shape of air

Soundlessness before—

> (*She is finished sawing off her hands and feet. She closes up the crate. She exits again.* NED *continues his rant. She re-enters. Somehow, she turns* NED's *volume back on.*)

NED. And if you can reach down, down, down and stir up the gumption that snoozes in your core, I really think that you could pull yourself out of this this this this deeply personal sewer. OK I know, Lillian, that I do not have a way with words, and cannot charm you in the way you want to be charmed. But I can help but think that somewhere, somehow, sometime, someway, somewhich, somewho—

LILLIAN. Hold me Ned.

> (NED *looks surprised. then, he holds her.*)

NED. You're freezing.

LILLIAN. I've been in the freezer.

NED. We have so many things, Lillian.

LILLIAN. I know, Ned. I know. I shouldn't be so obsessed with my view.

NED. Oh sweet Lillian, you're crying.

LILLIAN. I'm not crying.

NED. There, there. it's all going to be OK shhhhhh.

LILLIAN. But, Ned, I'm not—

NED. Shhhhh, You don't have to talk. I'm right here.

LILLIAN. But—

NED. That a girl. Just let it all come out. When we cry we are Gods weeping floods upon the world. Let the rain come, that's it, shhhhh.

> (NED *comforts* LILLIAN. LILLIAN *still does not cry.*)
>
> (*Blackout.*)

Seven.

THE BEAST *in his apartment. His view of Lillian's apartment is now entirely obscured by a high-rise apartment building.* THE BEAST *stands next to the curtain, holding a handful of rose petals. One. Two. Three. He pulls back the curtain, revealing a spectacular dress made entirely out of paper snowflakes. The dress hangs on a hanger, ready to go. The beast sprinkles the dress with his home-made rosewater. Then, the rose petals, a flurry of petals, the finishing touch. He steps back, admires his work. He takes a quick breath, and rubs his hands together: Its time to get ready. Note: as he travels from preparation to preparation as described, he does a little jig more of an "I'm happy" skip. He may also improvise a little percussive ditty "ch ch ch cha!" as he moves between preparations. He does not, however, sing or skip as he performs each preparation. During those times, he must have total concentration: he doesn't want to fuck this one up. He is a somewhat anal-retentive beast, and so his routine should feel established, even if somewhat inefficient. For instance, his mirror is really far away from the bucket with his water and toiletries. But it all makes sense to him. OK. The beast skips to a small bucket, washes his hands and face. Pulls out a razor. Wets razor. Skips to mirror. Almost starts shaving, then, upon examination, realizes he doesn't really need to shave, except one tiny spot. He shaves that one tiny spot (one stroke). Skips back to bucket, pulls out a tooth brush. Brushes teeth. Pulls out a bottle of mouthwash. Gargles. Pulls out some dental floss. Skips back to mirror. Flosses teeth. Admires teeth. Makes sure there is no dental floss hanging out of his mouth. Skips back to bucket, drops off dental floss. Reaches for his cologne. It's not there. Where is it? He sees it over by the mirror. He slaps his forehead, he can't believe his giddiness has inspired such an absent mind. He skips to the mirror, puts on aftershave. Looks to his table (which he has repaired) his jacket, best hat and boutonniere have been laid out. Skips to table. He puts on his jacket. Very Nice. He puts on his best hat. Pats it in place. He picks up boutonniere, skips to mirror, pins boutonniere. Admires boutonniere. He pats his jacket pocket. Looks in pocket. He needs money. He skips to his money jar. He counts out lots of coins and several dollar bills. He puts the money in his pocket. Then he looks to the dress. Suddenly he gets nervous. Can he do this? He looks around the room, for a brief moment aware of the absurdity of his condition. But he quickly shuts it out. He skips towards the dress with great resolve. He pauses for a moment, bowing his head in prayer:*

THE BEAST. Soft Prairie, willow face

A word is a thief

Never one sigh to heal blisters

and never is the sound of why I wonder:

Holy Prairie

Covered in Sand

Blanket my aching bones

Now

Now

Now.

> *(He lifts up his head. He takes a breath. He carefully picks up the dress and slowly, slowly, slowly crosses to the door. This should take a long time, and should be both beautiful and excruciating to watch. He opens the door. He exits the door. He closes the door behind him. Simultaneously, with the click of the door, the lights blackout.)*

Eight.

LILLIAN DAVIS *sits on her couch with her tabby cat. She strokes its head and neck. A nearby table is set for dinner, food and all. Through the sliding glass doors we can see the entire grand cityscape, unobscured.*

LILLIAN. You are deserving of something very dense and valuable. You have striven for nothing in your life, and have expected nothing in return. I bet you can feel the hairs as they grow out of your back.

The day the oceans dry up, all the tabby cats in the world will laugh for joy. For though they seem lazy and dull in the here and now, they are filled with a Wisdom so perfect it is all they can do to sit still and purr. To do anything more would be a sacrilege.

(*She looks at the clock. She looks at the table set with food. She looks back at tabby.*)

Am I a trout? Am I a salad fork? Am I a parsnip?

Between you and me, tabby, I'm glad we've had these four days alone together. Swapping spells, admiring the view. Don't tell Ned.

(LILLIAN's *face reads: Well, That shouldn't be a problem. She half sings:*)

Towards the beginning of time, when the ocean dried up for the first time, at the bottom of the ocean, they found the bedraggled tabby cat. Is it dead they cried is it dead? No it is not dead they said. Its soul is living temporarily inside the body of a wise and sophisticated metropolitan housewife who indeed might he the Woman Who Sees All Things so do not desecrate the body of this tabby cat do not encase its five appendages in glass no leave the tabby cat there on the dried ocean bed until the tabby spirit returns to the tabby body and relates to us the Wisdom of the Woman Who Sees All Things place pillows of finest silk under its head and vases of exotic herbs around its four paws and tail no do not touch the tabby cat do not touch it if you feel you must touch it come on the designated day and you will be given the proper gloves and the proper hat and you will be allowed one touch in the proper place in addition we will build an emerald replica of the tabby cat that is slightly smaller than the real tabby cat and the devoted will be allowed to come and kiss the replica that's right kiss the replica — no don't be disgusted this is a very holy ritual consider yourself lucky — and so the people did all this and in addition small clusters of the devoted were sent on pilgrimages to seek out the Wise and Sophisticated Woman inside whose body the tabby cat was living the Sophisticated Woman Who Sees All Things now these small clusters of devoted pilgrims had very few funds and very few possessions and so in order to survive they formed the Cult of the Tabby Cat, attracting curious customers with their curious wares: they sold small pieces of jewelry wrought into the shape of the tabby cat they sold restorative ink enhanced with the oils extracted from the hairs of the tabby cat they sold handkerchiefs which held the impression of the tabby cats tail and in this way they made their way and in this way they also formed their long term plan for finding the Wise and Sophisticated Woman Who Sees All Things for they knew that their wares would one day from the natural and somewhat random progression of market trends become fashionable and therefore expensive so expensive that only Sophisticated Metropolitan Housewives could afford them in this way would they narrow down the field of possibilities in this way would they find the Wise and Sophisticated Woman Who Sees All Things the Unassuming Eye that holds the soul and secret of the Tabby Cat and so the pilgrims voyaged and sold their wares and the faithful at home tended to the body and surrounding altar of the tabby cat and made effigies of the tabby cat out of dirt, snow and sand and chanted the chants of the tabby cat and developed mystical numeric systems and ecstatic purrs based on numbers and purrs found in the tabby cat and one day—

(NED *enters. The spell is broken.* LILLIAN *stands.* NED *glowers. He takes off his coat, hangs it up. He loosens his tie. He walks over to the table. He places his napkin on his lap. He serves himself food. As he is about to eat,* LILLIAN *cries out.*)

LILLIAN. Dear—

(*But it is too late. The food is four days old.* NED *spits it out all over the table.*)

NED. That food is four days old!

LILLIAN. You are four days late!

NED. Why aren't you wearing shoes!

LILLIAN. Because I don't have any feet!

(NED *begins fucking up the table in whatever method seems appropriate, stageable and downright nasty.* LILLIAN *picks up the tabby cat and walks to the other side of the room. She whispers.*)

LILLIAN. I won't leave you with him, don't worry. I'll leave you to someone better.

(NED *stops fucking up the table.*)

NED. What was that!

LILLIAN. I wasn't talking to you.

(NED *starts again.* LILLIAN *pets the tabby cat. This petting and fucking up goes on for awhile. It seems like something else should happen. Then the lights blackout.*)

Nine.

LILLIAN *sits in her apartment. Her view is completely obscured by the next-door building. She has been alone for quite sometime. She sits on the couch. She makes some odd, grand movements, trying to look around to see if anyone is watching her, but she doesn't want anyone to know that she is looking around to see if someone is watching her. She reaches deep inside the cushions of the couch, searching for something. She pulls out her binoculars, which she has turned into a kind of grotesque, ramshackle viewfinder— mirrors, lenses and slides have been added to the original set of lenses. She puts them on and immediately starts to giggle. She giggles and gasps at whatever show is going on inside her glasses. The door to her apartment opens. It is THE BEAST. He takes baby steps, and treads carefully, as he is dressed in his jacket, his boutonniere, his best hat, and he is carrying the papersnowflake dress. LILLIAN stops giggling. Then:*

LILLIAN. Millicent? Millicent dear is that you? My dear I am so glad you are here you are the one who enters without knocking you are the one who I let in to all my fragile little dioramas. I am glad you are here Millicent for I have a suspicion I must tell you about a suspicion I fear no one else will give any credence to and here is that suspicion: There is a Beast who watches me. This beast, a bona fide beast, lives in an apartment several miles South of here. It is a crappy apartment with inadequate light, nothing like this apartment. He first started ogling me through a small window with a very expensive telescope that is the only thing of value that he owns. Everything else he owns is either crappy or not really his. From the very first time he started ogling me I could feel the lens of his telescope squeaking across my body like a greasy fingernail. He clings to that telescope even though the building next door makes it entirely impossible for him to locate me in the scope. Now that ogling from afar is not an option, I fear he is planning a visit. I fear that he is operating under the false assumption that he has figured out certain things that I want that I *myself* am not aware that I want. Ha! Ha! As though he has some divine right to assume such things! As though as a result of this knowledge he might bestow upon me the perfect gift, a delicate, intricate, handmade gift, a gift that will compel me to saw through my own sternum, extract my own cold, cruel heart and devour it whole. As if, after this grotesque act of auto-cannibalism the two of us will gaze into my sawed open ribcage and watch a new heart grow, a heart as tiny and fragrant as a primrose and as dear as an infant's palm, as though the two of us might then rejoice at my generating this sweet, beneficent new heart and stroll together, together down the primrose path through the new fallen snow, la la la pocket full of posies la la, as though by new heart might cajole me to look his into his wet, beastly eyes and call him "Jonathan" or even "Jonathan Keene." But you Millicent, you know that some hearts are genetically cold and cruel and unchangeable, and that I would never, ever, even in a thousand million eons accept any gift from a steaming, stinking, rotting *Beast.*

(PAUSE. Breathing from both THE BEAST and LILLIAN. LILLIAN knows it is the beast, but she hopes she has discouraged him. Indeed, she has discouraged him. He walks out, heartbroken, carefully holding the dress. He shuts the door.)

LILLIAN. Millicent? Oh Millicent?

(LILLIAN *takes off her glasses. She looks around to see if anyone is watching her, this time, not trying to hide the fact that she is doing so. She inserts the glasses back into the couch. She sits in the same fashion in which she sat at the beginning of the scene. She is stationary for a little too long— has the technician forgotten the blackout? Quickly, she places her hand on her heart and just as quickly the lights blackout.*)

Ten.

Outside the window it is snowing. LILLIAN's *view is partially obscured by the next door building—perhaps we see steel girders and other aspects of construction. Lillian enters the room, striding with great determination towards the coat rack. She is going out. She puts on her coat with great fervor. She does a little "buttoning up the coat" dance. She picks up a small box from beneath the coat rack. She opens the box, pulls open the soft wrapping paper inside, and extracts a new, beautiful headscarf. She swoops the headscarf over her head and ties it with a flourish. She is about to leave, when she notices it is snowing outside. She looks down at her respectable shoes. Will they be ruined if she wears them outside? Yes, they will be ruined if she wears them outside. She opens a closet door, or some other similar compartment. She roots and roots, throwing things out of the compartment as she roots. She finds one galosh. She roots and roots. She finds another galosh. She places the galoshes near the table and puts back all the other things she rooted out. She sits on the couch and pulls on one galosh with agonizing difficulty. She pulls on the second galosh with equal if not greater difficulty. She sits, tired. Now she's not sure if she wants to go out anymore, the world is such a difficult place, anyway. Oh don't be silly, Lillian. You should go out. Its the first snow of the season you should go out. The tip of your nose will tingle and you will be giddy like a girl. She stands. She straightens her scarf. She is about to leave when there is a knock on the door.* LILLIAN *opens the door. It is her daughter,* NORMA. *She is terribly pregnant.*

NORMA. Mother, don't say a word, I've decided there are things you must know.

LILLIAN. (*Surprised and delighted, as though the following revelation might save their mother/daughter relationship.*)

My goodness you're going to have a baby!

NORMA. Yes, and besides that, I want you to meet your twenty grandchildren.

(NORMA *introduces each child. Each child is represented by some inanimate object, objects which, for the most part, should be small and hand held.*)

This is number one, Reginold Rust, his father's only son and the sickliest of the bunch. She how he coughs as though he is hacking up the weight of the world? See the track marks on his arm from painful, long-term IV's? So many times Reginold begged us to let his life slip away but his father wouldn't hear of it, no his father insisted that he be kept alive and even whipped poor Reginold for whimpering about his fate.

These are Regina and Gina Rust, the first set of twins and the most giddy. Yesterday they were kicked out of pre-school for giggling it up during a lecture about Mummification. You would think they could keep their little mouths shut but when I asked them about it all they could say was Mummy please someone has to find the humor in the ritual I mean really liquefying the brain by injecting a serum through a straw shoved up the nostril? One day we will be canonized no *mummified* for our giddiness and they laugh and laugh they are difficult to tell apart but I think Gina has inherited your shallow breathing.

This is Regenerate Rust who assumed the shape of a brown cardboard box at an early age, becoming a living aberration of the phenomenon of natural selection

This is Reggie, Reggie and Reggie Rust, triplets whose names are distinguished but the increasing force with which you roll the "R" which initiates their name.

    (*Noticing* LILLIAN's *attire.*)

Were you getting ready to go out?

LILLIAN. No no no I was staying in.

NORMA. OK, then, I'll continue.

Next is Regingerbread Palm Rust (nickname Doom Palm Rust), a boring girl, actually, who undermines all the duplicitous potential of her name by sitting around waiting for the sun to hit just right so she trim her toenails in comfort.

Reginrummy Rust stinks of peaches and fancies herself a poet.

These are Ginny, Ginseng, Regensburg and Regent Rust, who have taken their Quadrupleness seriously and make every one of their mistakes four times each, so I have to deal with their mistakes 16 times each, and every single time they give me that blank, befuddled look that says Mom we don't know how this happened, it must be something in our genetic makeup, some fierce genetic mishap passed down from *your* mother, for we really have no Will of our own, and even if we exerted our non-existent Will we would do so four times each and then think of how much more miserable you would be.

Gingival Rust was born with lime green gums and spends her nights tormenting her sister Doom Palm by making up characters named Doom Palm who are far more interesting than the actual Doom Palm.

Gingersnap Rust oh fuck it she's so transparent you can figure her out for yourself.

GIN, Nig and Gin Rust are a triptych of sisters which, when they stand in the proper formation, tell the story of one of our forgotten family matriarchs, a matriarch who YOU NEVER TOLD ME ABOUT, MOTHER, a Madame Veronica Vanderlay Davis, who discovered Neon in the makeshift chemistry lab in the basement of her bungalow only to be swindled out of her discovery by a certain Samuel Lemkins, who convinced her that neon was not a rare, inert gaseous element but was actually quite common in Tadzikhistan and parts of the Orient. And when she realized that she had been swindled, when she realized that Samuel Lemkins was taking credit for her discovery did she weep or sigh or pluck out all her hairs? Did she exile herself to the top of a high rise apartment building? No she swallowed her pride and took to the streets as a roving instructor of young girls, and let her beard grow long and her wisdom grow thick and she is still to this day honored in certain countries as a Woman of Great Regard, unlike you, mother, and unlike me, your daughter and if you had told me earlier about Madame Veronica Vanderlay Davis perhaps I would have made a few different choices in my life, choices which would not have resulted in my bearing 20 children in 7 years, but, no, really I don't mean that because I am so so so grateful and thankful for GIN, Nig and Gin Rust who, through their birth from my womb, have introduced me to this family treasure and everything I might have been.

> (*PAUSE. NORMA is really exhausted and freaked out, but neither NORMA or LILLIAN can say anything. NORMA continues.*)

And these are the two Lillians Rust.

One has crystal blue eyes and the other emerald green.

Lillian the first likes to read Louisa May Alcott and Lillian the Second prefers Dickens.

They are each enrolled in cello lessons, and charmed the audience to the point of real tears at their last recital.

Lillian the first likes gymnastics.

Lillian the second likes bikes.

Which makes them a real human interest story, seeing as Lillian the first is missing her right foot and Lillian the second is missing her left.

And that's the whole lot.

And besides all that Napoleon has left me and filed for divorce.

LILLIAN. Oh, sweet Norma, please let me—

NORMA. Which means I need you to watch the kids while I go into labor for number 21.

> (NORMA *immediately goes into labor.*)

LILLIAN. Norma!

NORMA. Don't worry. The paramedics are already here.

(A paramedic enters, and guides NORMA *out of the room as she breathes and groans with the contractions.* LILLIAN *is alone with her 20 grandchildren. All is quiet, except for their snotty childish breathing.* LILLIAN *stands among them, still bundled up to go out. A lullaby:)*

The baby's made of sand
The sky's a paper painting
When it rains the baby sings
Huzzah the world is fine

The baby's made of water
The world's a ball of glass
When the ball cracks baby sighs
Sky sky sky

Tipsy topsy over
Flid Flad flood
Dry as a bone in summer
Mid mad mud

The baby in a bottle
The world's an open sea
When the wind blows baby sings
All this belongs to me

Tipsy topsy over
Flid fl ad flood
Dry as a bone in summer
Mid mad mud.

(LILLIAN *situates her 20 grandchildren, as though arranging them for a family portrait. She places herself in their midst. Pose.)*
(Blackout.)

Eleven.

THE BEAST *on a park bench on a city street outside* LILLIAN's *apartment building. He still wears his jacket and boutonniere. His best hat sits beside him, turned upside-down like a bowl. No dress.* THE BEAST *is depressed. It's cold out and he is lonely. He sips Thunderbird out of a paper bag.* THE BEAST *looks into his best hat. He takes out a single, tiny, piece of paper. He blows it into the wind. A barely audible cry:*

THE BEAST. Liiii–

(NED *walks by, whistling, on his way home from work.* NED *tips his hat to the beast.* THE BEAST *glowers. When* NED *is gone,* THE BEAST *raises his fists up to the sky, silently cursing the Gods. A slightly more audible cry:)*

THE BEAST. Liiiiii–

　(And the buildings echo back: Liiiiii. THE BEAST is surprised. He continues:)

THE BEAST. Leeee–

　(Echo: Le Le Le Le)

THE BEAST. Aaaaaan,

　(Echo: An An An An.)

THE BEAST. Li–

　(Echo: Li)

THE BEAST. Lee–

　(Echo: Lee)

THE BEAST. An!

　(Echo: An)

THE BEAST. Lillian!

　(Echo: Lillian Lillian Lillian)

THE BEAST. Lillian!

　(Echo: Lillian Lillian Lillian)

　(And so the sky is filled with the name of his beloved. And so the syllables cycle, over and around and over. And so this BEAST becomes enraged by his predicament. And so he raises his best hat, and tosses the contents into the sky: Hundreds upon thousands of pieces of paper: the remains of the papersnowflake dress. This painful reminder makes him more furious. He looks around. He stomps over to the façade of Lillian Davis' building. He leaps up. He falls. He leaps up. He finds a place to grab hold. THE BEAST begins to scale the building. THE BEAST belts out:)

THE BEAST. LILLIAN!

　(THE BEAST continues to climb with grunts and groans.)

　(Blackout.)

Twelve.

LILLIAN's *apartment. It is many, many years earlier. The view from her sliding glass doors is completely unobscured. It is morning and she is busying herself doing chores. We have never seen her so busy, dusting, straightening, etcetera. As she works, NED enters (no mask), also busy. He's dressed for work. He picks up his briefcase, pours himself a bowl of tea, which he downs in one gulp, plopping the bowl back on the table.*

LILLIAN. Be careful sweetie those are my nice bowls.

NED. Ah yes the bowls I brought you back from China.

LILLIAN. You wouldn't want to destroy them would you?

NED. Do the China bowls make you happy?

LILLIAN. They make me quite happy, Ned.

NED. Alright then, dear. See you tonight.

LILLIAN. Will I see you tonight?

NED. Of course, dear.

LILLIAN. It won't be four days, now, will it?

> (*Dry laughs from both of them.* NED *crosses to her. Kisses her forehead.*)

NED. That's my little trickster. See you tonight.

> (NED *crosses to the door. As he exits:*)

NED. Do consider the obelisks, dear.

> (*He exits.* LILLIAN *continues cleaning. For a second, she gets a sour look on he face.*)

LILLIAN. "Do consider the obelisks, dear."

> (*As soon as she says this line,* NORMA *enters. She too is busy, dressed for school, and running late, looking for all the things she needs to put in her schoolbag, basically wrecking everything her mom has just straightened.*)

LILLIAN. Now dear please I've asked you wake up just a few minutes no a few seconds earlier so that you wouldn't—put that down—wreck everything that I have put into place—

WATCH THE PRINTS WATCH THE PRINTS WATCH THE PRINTS!

> (NORMA *mouths the following lines with* LILLIAN:)

Honey, those are my Warpohl prints.

> (*And* NORMA *is off again, rooting and running.*)

Norma, you know that I am glad that you at least make the effort to go to school Millicent Hiccup's daughter often can't even get out of bed to put on her shoes apparently she sometimes lays there for days, fondling her geodes and so I am glad that you go to school but I do wish you would get up just a few OH MY GOD!

> (LILLIAN *has just had a vision that a building is obscuring her view. She sees it and turns her back to it, gasping and holding her head.* NORMA *stops, looks at her mother.*)

NORMA. What is it, mother?

LILLIAN. I just had the most horrible vision. A vision that someone built a building right next to our building and obscured my view entirely.

NORMA. It's just a vision, mother.

LILLIAN. But it was so real.

NORMA. Visions are fake. As are spells and wishes. It is a perfectly balmy day outside. You can almost see the Statue with your bare eyes.

LILLIAN. I'll take your word for it, my goodness what a scare.

(LILLIAN *goes back to cleaning.* NORMA *goes back to looking for things. She turns over chairs. She takes books off of bookshelves. She takes the cushions on the couch. There is something inside.*)

NORMA. Mother, what is this.

(NORMA *pulls a cello out of the couch.*)

LILLIAN. Oh its nothing, dear.

NORMA. You never told me that you played the cello.

LILLIAN. I don't play the cello.

NORMA. Then what is it doing inside the couch?

LILLIAN. Dear cellos are not something for little girls to be worried about now you just let mother worry about the cello and you go on to your school now go on go.

(NORMA *drops the cello back in the couch and picks up her last few things.* LILLIAN *puts the couch cushions back in place. As* NORMA *leaves.*)

LILLIAN. Norma.

(NORMA *turns to her.*)

LILLIAN. Did you, um, happen to, um, get the *note* I slipped under your pillow last night?

(NORMA *rolls her eyes.*)

NORMA. Yes, mother, and the note before that and the note before that. I'm only 16. I'm not going to run out and get married and/or get knocked up half a bazillion times, so please take a chill pill and stop worrying.

(NORMA *exits, closing the door.* LILLIAN *goes on cleaning for one or two minutes. Then, she looks around to see if anyone is in the room. Then, she opens the door and looks down the hall. Tabby cat slips in.*)

LILLIAN. Hello tabby cat yes you are welcome come in and have a seat.

(LILLIAN *closes the door. She crosses to the couch and takes the cushions off. She pulls out the cello. She puts the cushions back on the couch. She sits on the couch, and tabby sits beside her. She positions the cello between her legs.*)

LILLIAN. Ready tabby?

(*She announces.*)

"The Ballad of Jonathon Keene Archipelago Redbreast."

(LILLIAN *begins to play. As she plays, she sings.*)

LILLIAN. Jonathon Keen Archipelago Redbreast
Was a curious little chap
He was willed into being by a delicate girl
With fairytale skin and gold hair rolled in curls.
with a dark blob growing in her chest
with a dark blob growing in her chest

"Oh!" (she said)
"My available suitors leave me simply aghast
With their peonies and tarts
I need a chap rife with magic and fibs
His own festering blob growing under his ribs
Whose name is
Jon Keen Archipelago Redbreast
Jon Keen Archipelago Redbreast"

And poof! He appeared in the cleave of her breast
Jonathon Keene Archipelago Redbreast
Tiny suitor with impish grin
And sack of strange herbs tied under his chin
There to serve her every behest
There to serve her every behest.

And so they commenced their great havoc-ing session
In the streets and public squares
Planting Jonathon's herbs in ears of old women
They swug absinthe, Shot quail and indulged in nekkid swimmin'
Without a care or thought of a possession
Without a care or thought of a possession.

"Oh Jonathon Keene Archipelago Redbreast"
Sighed the girl as he lounged in her palm
"You know our time is short, and our love is long
This affair must soon end for we just don't belong
in the realm of dull suitors and coffins oblong
Society will shun us, wrench us twain with brass prongs
but we will be immortalized one day in a song
which tells the tale of our love and how we proved them wrong
For I have a plan Johnny Redbreast
A plan does have I."

And Jonathon's tiny eyes filled with giant's tears.
And as he crawled up to lie in the hollow of her collar bone, she began:

"Oh When I grow old with family and home
One day I am sure I must write my own will
And tucked into the lists of my very long will
Will be a mischievous mention of you.

And this line in my Will will cause a great stir.
My husband will cry: "Who the hell is this Redbreast"
My daughter: "Redbreast!?! I know of no Redbreast!"

And they will embark on an ill-fated search.

And they'll search in circles, search high and search low
And they will grow mad, grow obsessed, rank with rage
For they'll never find you, nor your magic sage
For you my Jon Redbreast will die here with me.
Jonathon Keene Archipelago Redbreast you will die with me."

       (LILLIAN *speaks*.)
And comforted, Jonathon dozed off in her warn skin
And for a moment her entire life flashed before her eyes
with all its predestined obligations and possessions
and the accompanying walls of delusion
And she might have cried, had not Jonathon's sweet breath brought her great
comfort in that perfect moment...

Oh I could play and play and play!
    (*She does.*)
    (*Blackout.*)

Thirteen.

THE BEAST is scaling LILLIAN's *building. He is at about the 20ᵗʰ floor.
He has a long way to go. He grunts and groans. He pauses. He's got to find a
way to take his mind off the pain. He takes a breath. Suddenly, he remembers
(or misremembers) an old chain-gang chant from the days of his troubled youth,
during which time, for a brief period, he was incarcerated. He begins to climb in
time to his sing-chanting.*

THE BEAST. Oh My Tell Tale Sally
Hole In Yer Pocket
Show Me The Gold

Oh my Tell Tale Sally
Blister on Yer Lip
Show Me The Gold

Show Me The Gold
Show Me the Gold
Show Me the Gold
Ima Poor Man

Oh My Tell Tale Sally
Will Ya Ever Marry
Show Me The Gold

Oh My Tell Tale Sally
Saw Ya In The Bible
Show Me The Gold

Show Me The Gold
Show Me The Gold
Show Me The Gold
Ima Poor Man

Jelly In My Head
Jelly In The Dark
Jelly In The Chest
With The Big Lock

Oh My Tell Tale Sally
I Still Hold Yer Best Pair of Shoes
Show Me The Gold.

> (THE BEAST *climbs.*)
> (*Blackout.*)

Fourteen.

LILLIAN *is setting up the tea bowls. The view from Lillian's window is entirely obscured.* LILLIAN *arranges the tea bowls into the appropriate fashion. When she is done,* MILLICENT *enters. She carries the tabby cat.*

MILLICENT. Look who I found crawling around the front door of that dear neighbor lady whats-her-name. Tabby's always visiting that dear neighbor lady which is fine of course but you should know that I have seen her sneaking Tabby secret looks and small plates of caviar which will not only spoil his appetite but cause him to favor HER over YOU and we wouldn't want that now would we.

> (MILLICENT *sits down. She makes a curious show of picking up the tea bowl, complete with a knowing smile for* LILLIAN. LILLIAN *casually pours* MILLICENT's *tea.* MILLICENT *begins.*)

MILLICENT. And so anyway June (not the month my daughter ha ha) phoned me the other day only to find to her surprise that I had installed an answering machine and so June said into the machine—

LILLIAN. We mustn't talk about our daughters today, Millicent.

> (MILLICENT *is completely floored.*)

MILLICENT. Why not?

LILLIAN. Because our daughters depress me.

MILLICENT. Oh. How long has it been since she has been in touch?

LILLIAN. She has moved to a city called RAINBOW!, a city which voted to officially include the exclamation point in its name. I can't imagine she is in touch with anything of substance.

MILLICENT. She's just trying to make her own way, Lillian.

(MILLICENT *fondles the tea bowl, trying to cheer* LILLIAN *up.*)

LILLIAN. I am out of spells.

MILLICENT. What on earth are you talking about, Lillian?

LILLIAN. I cannot be cheered up. And we cannot talk about our daughters.

MILLICENT. Well then, what do you want to do? I mean, really?

(*A knock at the door.* LILLIAN *crosses to the door, opens it.* NED *stands behind the door wearing a plastic mask.*)

NED. Hello. I heard there were ladies having tea in this apartment.

(LILLIAN *is befuddled. She suspects it might be Ned, but she can't imagine why he would go through this charade again.* MILLICENT *pipes up.*)

MILLICENT. Why yes, you heard right. There are ladies having tea in this apartment.

NED. Would the ladies like some gentlemen company.

MILLICENT. Why yes, why that would be lovely. Please, come in. Lillian invite the gentleman in.

(LILLIAN *steps aside.* NED *enters. He can't see very well in the mask. He trips over things.*)

NED. I apologize. It's my Glaucoma. Could you escort me?

MILLICENT. Why it would be my pleasure.

(*She escorts* NED *to a place on the couch.*)

MILLICENT. Lillian won't you join us?

(LILLIAN *goes to the window.* MILLICENT *pays attention to* NED.)

MILLICENT. And so, Mister...

NED. Helicopter. Mr. Helicopter.

MILLICENT. And so Mr. Helicopter, do you live in the building?

NED. No, no, no. I don't live on the island. I live on the mainland.

MILLICENT. Some of us feel the island *is* the mainland.

NED. And some of us don't. What do you do, Ms...

MILLICENT. Hiccup. Millicent Hiccup. What is it I do?

NED. Yes, Ms. Hiccup, what is it you do.

MILLICENT. Well, I have a daughter named June, like the month but she is not a month, of course, she is my daughter. And then there are the chores about the apartment. Oh, and once a week I have tea with Ms. Lillian Davis, who lives on the 26th floor of my building.

NED. I know. Here we are having tea in Ms. Davis' apartment on the 26th floor.

(MILLICENT *looks around.*)

MILLICENT. Yes. So we are.

What is it you do, Mr. Helicopter?

NED. I manufacture helicopters, of course.

MILLICENT. Oh how INTERESTING.

NED. I have a helicopter factory. We churn them out by the dozens. Dozens and dozens of helicopters.

MILLICENT. My, I had no idea there was such a demand for helicopters.

NED. Oh, let me tell you, the demand is high. A man came in the other day with an unrecognizable accent, and, claiming he was from the CIA, ordered 300.

MILLICENT. 300 HELICOPTERS!

NED. We filled the order in 3 days.

MILLICENT. 300 HELICOPTERS IN 3 DAYS!

(*Laughs. Pause.*)

NED. And you Ms. Hiccup, what do you do?

MILLICENT. You already asked me that.

NED. Oh, pardon me.

(*They laugh.*)

MILLICENT. More tea?

NED. Just a spot.

(MILLICENT *pours the tea.*)

MILLICENT. Lillian, come join us.

(LILLIAN *ignores them.*)

NED. And so Ms. Hiccup, what do you do?

(MILLICENT *looks perturbed, then:*)

MILLICENT. Sometimes I clean out the toilet bowls with an antiseptic brush. And sometimes my daughter June comes to visit.

NED. Really? How often?

MILLICENT. As often as she sees fit.

NED. Good answer. And how old is June?

MILLICENT. June is always 32.

NED. Ah. And where does June live?

MILLICENT. One floor below me.

NED. Ah. And how does June make her living?

MILLICENT. Why are you asking so many questions of me, Mr. Helicopter?

(NED *looks a little offended, then:*)

NED. I was hoping you and June would join me for a helicopter ride.

(MILLICENT *feels silly: she didn't realize that's where all this was going.*)

MILLICENT. Oh, my! I apologize for being so suspicious. It's just, you see, well, June and I would love to go on a helicopter ride with you, Mr. Helicopter, manufacturer of helicopters. Perhaps June will even don her Bona fide Rosewater Dress, Mr. Helicopter. My, my, my.

(MILLICENT *gives him a look, trying to feel him out. Then, she picks up a tea bowl and begins to fondle it, gently, secretly, to see what* MR. HELICOPTER's *reaction will be. At first he seems to respond favorably to her "advances." She fondles more overtly. Then, he looks away, clearing his throat.* MILLICENT *quickly puts down the tea bowl, knowing she's gone too far. During their next few lines they try to cover their shared embarrassment and shame surrounding* MILLICENT's *behavior.*)

MILLICENT. So Mr. Helicopter is it difficult to manufacture helicopters?

NED. Well, I am highly skilled and so the world "difficult" is not really fitting. Is it challenging? Yes.

MILLICENT. I see.

NED. It's in my blood, though. I whittled my first helicopter out of knotty pine when I was 6 years old.

MILLICENT. Knotty pine! Imagine that. Knotty pine. Lillian, did you hear that? He whittled a helicopter from knotty pine, Lillian, Knotty pine. Knotty, knotty pine. Knotty pine, pine. Knotty pine, knotty pine. Knotty, knotty, knotty pine.

(*She giggles nervously at* NED. *He giggles back.* LILLIAN *turns to them.*)

LILLIAN. Before your eyes, in This Realm, I am a housewife. But there is another Realm, a Realm at first imagined but eventually Real, called Realm of Clear Seeing. When Viewed from the Other Realm, I am not simply a bored and sophisticated metropolitan housewife, staring out of a window, contemplating a view, but something more like a Revered Eyeball, an Eyeball charged with observing the Way Things Really Are. And believe me I have observed. I have spent hours gazing out this window, entire days focusing on a single object, trying to look deep into its being, past the illusion of static, physical form, hoping that I might observe something that filters through me to the other realm, where the substantial things shimmer with a clarity that we will never know. Now in the midst of all this observing, my life has taken shape around me. I married you, Ned—

(MILLICENT *gasps, realizing* MR. HELICOPTER's *true identity for the first time. She puts her hand to her mouth, and stays this way for the rest of the speech.*)

We moved into this spacious, rent controlled apartment, we conceived, together, a daughter which we named Norma, which daughter I tried to love, and indeed did love, but somehow, perhaps because of my role as Observer, I failed to establish any sort of bond with her, and her life has gone on. And you Ned, present charade accepted, have tried in your honest yet flawed manner to love and honor me and make a life with me, you have sweet-talked me into pursuing activities that might cheer me up, such as sculpting the clay obelisks that remain, still in the closet. And I do appreciate your efforts, Ned, I do, but the problem remains that I have played the role of Eyeball for so many years now, that I can no longer distinguish the essential objects from the non-essential ones—a husband and ball of twine will often exist in the same category for me, for example—and since I can no longer qualify any of the objects, animal or mineral, which surround me, I can only conclude that I DO NOT EXIST, and therefore find it impossible, or at the very least absurd, to engage in interpersonal relationships, or to consider the issue of my "tangible personal property" much less the distribution thereof.

(*PAUSE.*)

MILLICENT. (*Whispers:*) Ned is that you?

(NED *takes off the mask. He is sweaty underneath it.* MILLICENT *screams for 10 seconds.*)

MILLICENT. And here I thought this was something you had PLANNED for US, Lillian, some EXTENSION of all your cryptic DIORAMAS. And EXTENSION of our THING. Do you find me a fool? Well, I never. I am never coming to tea here again. Do you hear me, Lillian? Never.

(MILLICENT *storms out of the room.* NED *stands, goes to* LILLIAN. LILLIAN *falls into his arms and bursts into ugly tears that make her cough and swell.* NED *doesn't know what to do.*)

NED. Now, Lillian, what's this?

LILLIAN. There is a beast.

NED. There's no beast, Lilly.

LILLIAN. There's a beast and it is building that building so it can get a better view. So it can see right through me.

NED. But Lillian, that building went up years ago.

(LILLIAN *cries harder.* NED *awkwardly takes* LILLIAN *in his arms, as would an anal-retentive camp counselor who suddenly had to comfort a child he didn't know very well. As* NED *says the following lines,* LILLIAN *begins to calm down.*)

NED. There is no such thing as a beast.

There is no such thing as a beast

There is no such thing as a beast

There is no such thing as a beast

(THE BEAST's *hand appears on the balcony railing.*)

NED. There is no such thing as a beast

There is no such thing as a beast

(THE BEAST *heaves himself up over the railing.*)

There is no such thing as a beast.

(NED *sees the beast. He tries to shoo the beast away, and hide* LILLIAN's *eyes.*)

There is no such thing as a beast

There is no such thing as a beast.

There is no such thing as a beast.

(NED *escorts* LILLIAN *offstage.* THE BEAST *stands, on the balcony, sweating, out of breath.*)

(*Blackout.*)

Fifteen.

THE BEAST *stands on the balcony, out of breath. The view is still completely obscured by the building next door.* LILLIAN *enters in her bathrobe: she has just woken up from sleeping off her minor-breakdown of the night before. She is bleary-eyed. She looks at* THE BEAST, *rubs eyes.* THE BEAST *raps on the glass.* LILLIAN *rubs her eyes.* THE BEAST *raps on the glass.* LILLIAN *crosses to the door and lets* THE BEAST *in.* THE BEAST *crosses to the couch, sits. Looks at the tea bowls. Pours some tea. Takes a sip. Spits tea out.*

LILLIAN. The tea is old and cold.

(THE BEAST *gives her a look: great, now you tell me.*)

LILLIAN. I know you are real. I know you hold a beauty more precise than one snowflake or a single grain of sand. I know you are not the one who built that building. But if I cannot believe in the objects that make me Lillian Davis, how can I give myself to anyone? How can I give anything away?

(*Heartbreakingly sad reaction from* THE BEAST. *It feels so sorry for her. For a moment, it is at a loss as to what to do. Then, it starts a game.* THE BEAST *sits like a lady, with its hands prim and proper in its lap.* LILLIAN *doesn't get it.* THE BEAST *repeats the gesture.* LILLIAN *mimics the gesture. He indicates that it is* LILLIAN's *turn. She doesn't get it. It is her turn to pick a pose. She giggles a fake girl-giggle, hand over her mouth.* THE BEAST *mimics her right away, his giggle over lapping hers. Then,* THE BEAST *sighs a sigh of lost love, which* LILLIAN *mimics.* LILLIAN *then*

shrugs it off—ah well—and makes a gesture in which she offers THE
BEAST *tea.* THE BEAST *mimics her gesture.* THE BEAST *picks up his
tea pot.* LILLIAN *picks up her tea pot.* THE BEAST *pours some tea into
his tea bowl.* LILLIAN *mirrors this action, simultaneously. They mirror each
other as they pick up their sugar bowls and each put two spoonfuls of sugar into
their tea. They stir and stir. They raise their tea bowls. They sip simultaneously,
and simultaneously they spit the tea out. They laugh and laugh. They stop
laughing, and look at each other. Then, together, in perfect, gentle time, looking
into each other's eyes as though they are recognizing each other for the first time,
they speak.)*

LILLIAN AND THE BEAST. The tea is old and cold.

(*Blackout.*)

Sixteen.

LILLIAN's *apartment. A period of time equivalent to the period of one year
has passed since* NORMA *dropped off the 20 Grandchildren.* LILLIAN *has
the Grandchildren gathered around the sliding glass door, the view from which is
obscured completely by the building next door.* LILLIAN *shows the children the
view.*

LILLIAN. See, Gina, there in the circle is the statue erected in honor of
Desdemona Oak, who dedicated her young life to opening homes for the
incurables throughout the city. In her left hand she holds the leaf of an Oak
tree, on which is a small cocoon, out of which a butterfly is emerging—

(GINA *says something to* LILLIAN.)

Yes, I agree, the symbolism is a bit obvious but don't you find it the least bit
quaint? Now Doom Palm. Doom Palm. DOOM PALM now is not the time
to tend your toenails. There, at the tippy-top of the Baron Bank Building is
the peacock weathervane I told you about now look doompalm look. It is
said if you look at the peacock when it happens to be looking at you, you will
be miraculously cleansed of all fear and filled with self-direction. Watch the
peacock, Doom Palm.

Nig stop flicking your sisters earlobe. Yes, Reggie I will point out the
mysterious slant of the roof of the Oboe Lodge once again. But you know
how that slant makes Reggie and Reggie queasy so don't point it out to them.

Yes, Ginseng it is your turn to sit on my shoulders. Tee tee, ta ta.

(*And* NORMA *bursts in with great panache. She wears big, round sunglasses,
lots of lipstick, an ugly looking white fur wrap, a skirt, stockings, white socks
and white walking shoes. She smokes a cigarette and carries a small branch
filled with ripe figs. She has not been to* LILLIAN's *house since she left the
kids there.*)

NORMA. Mother, I'm here for the kids.

LILLIAN. Norma?

NORMA. Yes, mother don't you recognize me? It's me, Norma.

LILLIAN. Forgive me if I thought you had dropped off the face of the earth. You haven't called nor written in what I imagine must be a year.

NORMA. Yes, well, I've been busy.

(*PAUSE.*)

LILLIAN. Busy?

NORMA. Yes, busy. OK, now kids let's get you all ready to go, let's see who is who my how you all have grown well luckily we can fit you all in the back of the extra-long deluxe Winnebago your father has purchased for us.

LILLIAN. Napoleon Rust has taken you back?

NORMA. No, mother, I am marrying a wealthy doctor who took a shine for me during my delivery of my 21st child, the child I call FIG.

(*She holds up the fig branch.*)

Isn't he darling? Finally, another boy. Anyway one of the doctors in the delivery room, a doctor named ART PLYWOOD took pity on me for I lied and told him I was a homeless single mother who planned to take my son Fig back to the refrigerator box under the overpass where I made my modest home. He took Fig and me home and allowed us to live in the garage of his house where he lived with his wife and two kids. Well it didn't take long to get *them* out of the picture and now that Art and I are to be married he has sold that house and we are moving, today, to a nice town called RAINBOW! up the river.

(*PAUSE.*)

LILLIAN. Rainbow?

NORMA. No, RAINBOW!

LILLIAN. Oh. Well, Norma I feel I must mention that I have grown attached to Reginold, Regina, Gina, Regenerate, Reggie, Reggie, Reggie, Doom Palm, Reginrummy, Ginny, Ginseng, Regensburg, Regent, Gingival, GIN, Nig, gin, the two Lillians and even the elusive Gingersnap. I'd be most heartbroken if you took them away.

NORMA. (*Touched.*) You know all their names.

LILLIAN. Of course. We've been having a grand time together. I've been showing them the view.

(*PAUSE.*)

NORMA. Mother, there is no view.

LILLIAN. (*Whispers.*) Shhh. They're only children.

NORMA. All right, let's load them up.

LILLIAN. Let me get their coats, at least.

(NORMA *starts to take a few by the hand. The children cling to* LILLIAN, *crying like frightened birds.*)

NORMA. DON'T YOU RECOGNIZE ME? I'M YOUR MOTHER. IT'S ME, I'M YOUR MOTHER AND THIS IS YOUR BROTHER FIG. THE WINNEBAGO IS WAITING.

LILLIAN. Norma dear, wait. Don't you think you could leave well enough alone? I mean you seem content with Fig and I with the twenty others. I mean these 20 children are quite a handful, perhaps you have forgotten. And to be honest the children are frightened because I told them you had been horribly disfigured in a freak accident involving a garbage disposal and that you were now an old hag with fangs and one long hair growing out of your chin—

(*The children echo her, it's a little ditty they sing: "One long hair growing out other chin"*)

Living in filth under the overpass in a refrigerator box—I know that's the ironic part— and that you were never coming back, and that if you did come back they should call 911 immediately and have you locked in the zoo—

(*The children: "911 and lock her in the zoo."*)

And so if they seem a little startled, well, that's why, and I think you should reconsider your plan.

(*PAUSE.*)

NORMA. The plan can not be reconsidered. The plan is the plan.

(NORMA *starts to peel the children from* LILLIAN.)

LILLIAN. How will we get them all down stairs?

(NORMA *looks around, spies some kind of gym bag.*)

NORMA. Here, we'll just chuck 'em in this bag.

(NORMA *begins chucking the children into the bag.* LILLIAN *is bewildered.*)

LILLIAN. Cant we…perhaps we could…

NORMA. Just chuck 'em in the bag, ma.

(LILLIAN *helps* NORMA *chuck the kids in the bag. The bag is very full, and the kids are trying to crawl out, scratching and clawing.* NORMA *and* LILLIAN *have to work together, with* LILLIAN *trying to hold the bag shut while* NORMA *zips it. This takes a few, stressful minutes, When the bag is finally shut, they breathe a sigh and wipe their brows. An eerie whine comes from the bag, like the moan of an angry cat.*)

LILLIAN. And this new husband of yours, he will treat you like a queen?

NORMA. He says mother he will buy me the choicest of pearls.

LILLIAN. And this new husband of yours will he brush out your hair?

NORMA. Oh yes, mother he will brush out and tie back my curls.

LILLIAN. There days you can't be too careful.

NORMA. These days you can't ask for much.

LILLIAN AND NORMA. Hey nonny, nonny hey nonny nonny hey nonny nonny hey.

NORMA. Dear mother, do men sleep with knives in their lap?

LILLIAN. Yes, dear, but we learn to avoid them.

NORMA. But mother, if Men were first, are we God's mishap?

LILLIAN. No dear, but we might be his mayhem.

NORMA. These days you can't be too careful.

LILLIAN. These days you can't ask for much.

LILLIAN AND NORMA. Hey nonny nonny hey nonny nonny hey nonny nonny hey.

Hey nonny nonny hey nonny—

(*A ships horn sounds.* NORMA *is startled.*)

NORMA. Oh, that's Art in the Winnebago.

(NORMA *picks up the bag of moaning children. She heads for the door, opens it.*)

LILLIAN. I fear I will be lonely, and you, miserable.

NORMA. I fear I will wake up with a nose on my face.

(*They look at each other as if to say: "and there it is."* LILLIAN *faces front.* NORMA *shuts the door, and simultaneously the lights blackout.*)

Seventeen.

LILLIAN's *apartment. Her view from her sliding glass door is completely obscured by the next door building.* LILLIAN DAVIS *stands in the middle of the room, knee deep in sand. Sand pours in a steady stream from the ceiling onto her head. She stands.* THE BEAST *enters in his best hat and jacket with boutonniere. He carries his modest bouquet of flowers. He stands before* LILLIAN.

LILLIAN. I, Lillian Davis, being of sound mind and memory, leave the following instructions regarding the distribution of my tangible personal property.

The set of hand painted china tea-bowls goes to Millicent T. Hiccup, who fondled them so discreetly during our many languid afternoons at tea.

My collection of handmade obelisks in the hall closet goes to my only daughter, Norma.

In addition, I leave to Norma my collection of antique jewelry with instructions that she sell it off and use the money to support herself and her twenty-one children upon the occasion of her second husband's desertion.

The mysterious wooden crate in the back of the walk-in freezer goes to my husband Ned, with strict instructions that it be disposed of, unopened.

To Ned I also leave my binoculars, with the request that they only be used *outside* of this apartment. Perhaps on a voyage, or a car trip, or a stroll.

The tabby cat goes to the dear neighbor lady oh dear what's her name…

The ten Randy Warpohl prints are to be divided, equally among my 21 grandchildren in any manner they see so fit. I have wracked my brain and cannot think of a fairer solution.

To Jonathon Keene Archipelago Redbreast: My cello.

(*The sand stops pouring on* LILLIAN DAVIS' *head. She reaches up and pats the top of her head. She looks up to the place from which the sand was pouring. She looks down at her feet. She steps out of the pile of sand. She looks at* THE BEAST. THE BEAST *holds out the bouquet of flowers.* LILLIAN *takes it.* THE BEAST *pulls a pair of shoes from his coat pocket. He shows them to* LILLIAN. *He puts them on the ground.* LILLIAN *slips her feet into them. She moves her feet around in them, trying them out. Perfect fit.* THE BEAST *offers* LILLIAN *his arm and* LILLIAN *takes it. They walk towards the sliding glass door. As they walk towards it, the landscape behind the door changes to something wonderful, something pastoral, perhaps the primrose path in the new fallen snow. The sun is shining and the winter birds are singing and the path from the sliding glass door leads straight through the roses and the trees which are heavy with ripe fruit, even in the frost.* THE BEAST *opens the sliding glass door.* LILLIAN *steps out.* THE BEAST *steps out, closes the sliding glass door and takes* LILLIAN's *arm. They disappear. All is quiet for about one minute. Then, suddenly, the door opens.* NED *is about to take off his hat and coat and call for* LILLIAN *when he notices the pile of sand in the middle of the room. He looks quickly to the sliding glass door, and back to the pile of sand. A look of shock and then panic passes over his face.*)

(*Blackout.*)

End of Play

INKY

by Rinne Groff

Required royalties must be paid every time this play is performed before any audience, whether or not it is presented for profit and whether or not admission is charged. To purchase acting editions of this play, or to obtain stock and amateur performance rights, you must contact:

> Playscripts, Inc.
> website: www.playscripts.com
> email: info@playscripts.com
> phone: 1-866-NEW-PLAY (639-7529)

Inquiries concerning all other rights should be addressed to the author's agent: Val Day, William Morris Agency, 1325 Avenue of the Americas, New York, NY 10019.

For more information about rights and permissions, see p. 10.

All production groups performing this play are required to include the following credits on the title page of every program:

> The World Premiere of *Inky* was produced in New York City in 2005 by The Women's Project (Loretta Greco, Producing Artistic Director; Jane Ann Crum, Managing Director).

> A previous version of the play was workshopped at Clubbed Thumb, and co-produced by Clubbed Thumb (Artistic Directors Maria Striar and Meg McCary) and Salt Theater (Artistic Director Emma Griffin).

> *Inky* was originally developed at NYU's Department of Dramatic Writing with the generous support of Rita and Burton Goldberg.

BIOGRAPHY

Rinne Groff is a playwright and performer. Her plays, including *Jimmy Carter was a Democrat, Orange Lemon Egg Canary, Inky, The Five Hysterical Girls Theorem,* and *The Ruby Sunrise*, have been produced by the Public Theater, Trinity Rep, Actors Theatre of Louisville, PS122, Target Margin, Clubbed Thumb, and Andy's Summer Playhouse, among others. Ms. Groff is a founding member of Elevator Repair Service Theater Company and has been a part of the writing, staging, and performing of their shows, both in the U.S. and on European tour, since the company's inception in 1991. A recipient of the Whiting Writers Award and a Guggenheim Fellowship, Ms. Groff was trained at Yale University and New York University's Tisch School of the Arts.

Other Clubbed Thumb credits: *Jimmy Carter Was a Democrat* (reading, Autumn '00, Summerworks '01); *What Then* (Commission and Boot Camp '03, Summerworks '04, Winter Production '06); Clubbed Thumb Affiliated Artist.

ACKNOWLEDGMENTS

The original version of *Inky* was produced by Clubbed Thumb as part of Summerworks 1999, and was co-produced by Clubbed Thumb and Salt Theater at Altered Stages in January 2000. It was directed by Emma Griffin with the following cast and staff:

Summerworks Cast:

INKY	Maria Striar
BARBARA	Maria Porter
CLAY	Mahlon Stewart
ALLISON	Kate Moser

Production Cast:

INKY	Maria Striar
BARBARA	Maria Porter
CLAY	Mahlon Stewart
ALLISON	Camilla Jones

Sets	Louisa Thompson
Lights	Mark Barton
Costumes	Janet Sussman, Meredith Palin
Sound	Noah Scalin

Inky was premiered by the Women's Project in New York City on March, 13 2005. It was directed by Loretta Greco with the following cast and staff:

INKY ....Jessi Campbell

BARBARA .... Marianne Hagan

GREG... Jason Pugatch

ALLISON .... Elizabeth Schweitzer

Artistic Director .... Loretta Greco

Managing Director...Jane Ann Crum

Production Stage Manager........................ Brian Westmoreland

Set ....Robert Brill

Lighting... Sarah Sidman

Costumes ....Valerie Marcus Ramshur

Original Music and Sound ....Robert Kaplowitz

CAST OF CHARACTERS
BARBARA, forties
GREG, thirties
ALLISON, nine
INKY, appears to be somewhere between 16 and 22, but it's hard to tell exactly

TIME
1986.

PLACE
A luxury high-rise apartment. There is a sofa and a coffee table, a window that opens, and a crib for a baby.

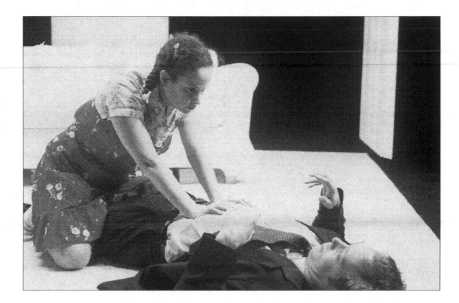

Maria Striar and Mahlon Stewart
in *Inky.*

Co-produced by Clubbed Thumb and Salt Theater at Altered Stages, 2000.
Photograph by Mark Barton

INKY

Scene 1

Ding. A boxing bell rings.

An isolated pool of light comes up on INKY, *a girl in her late teens. There is something vulnerable about her, undernourished.*

She has a peculiar accent, vaguely Slavic. It's not 100% clear if she knows what the following words mean, or if she learned them by rote.

INKY. "I will kill him. I'll tear his arm off. He doesn't stand a chance. I'm young. I'm pretty. I'm fast. I can't po... (*Struggling with the word.*) ...poss...possibly be beat.

I've got the height, the reach, the weight, the physique, the speed, the courage, the stamina, and the natural ability that's going to make me great. Putting it another way, to beat me you've got to be greater than great."

> (*The sound of a baby crying, somewhere in the distance.* INKY *doesn't respond to it.*)

INKY. "You tell this to your camera, your newspaper, your TV man, your radio man. You tell this to the world.

I will kill him. I'll tear his arm off. He doesn't stand a chance. I'm young. I'm pretty. I'm fast.

I can't possibly be beat."

> (*The baby's cries grow louder, more insistent.*)

INKY. "I'm king of the world.
I'm shaking up the world.
You must listen to me.
I'm the prettiest thing that ever lived.
I was born a champ in the crib.
I am the king.
I am the king.
I am the greatest."

> (*Ding.*)
>
> (*The crying stops.*)

Scene 2

Barbara and Greg's living room in a high-rise apartment building.

BARBARA, *[40s] a sophisticated, attractive woman in a bathrobe, stands over a frilly white baby crib. She stares into it. The baby, after screaming all day, is finally quiet.*

Ding.

The front door opens. GREG *[30s] enters, wearing a business suit.*

GREG. Hey.

(*He goes behind* BARBARA *and puts his arms around her. They both look down at the baby.*)

BARBARA. He's just like Allison.

GREG. Is he? Was she a good baby, too?

BARBARA. I mean how he can't look me in the eye either.

GREG. Ally's just going through a phase.

BARBARA. She hates me.

GREG. No one hates you.

BARBARA. Surely that can't be true.

GREG. I don't hate you. And Ally doesn't hate you.

BARBARA. How was work?

GREG. Brutal.

BARBARA. Brutal?

GREG. Fire in the hole and the entire mine shaft collapsed, but they got us out alive, even the canaries. (*Waiting for a reaction.*) Not even a smile? Men like it when you laugh at their jokes.

BARBARA. Then men should be funnier.

GREG. (*To the baby:*) Hey, champ. God, he's cute. How did you get to be so cute?

BARBARA. Did he look at you?

GREG. Would you stop with that? I told you at three weeks, they haven't developed the capacity to focus that far.

BARBARA. He did. He looked at you.

GREG. You've got to be eight to twelve inches.

BARBARA. He never looks at me.

GREG. Get closer.

(GREG *leans in toward the crib.*)

GREG. See? There he goes. He's got me locked in his sights. Look at that face. You are one powerful guy. You can do anything in this world, can't you? Oh yeah. He's so strong. Are you going to beat me up? You are, aren't you? A tough guy. (*To* BARBARA:) Where is Ally?

BARBARA. Girl Scout Cookies.

GREG. It's going to be dark soon.

BARBARA. Soon.

GREG. Should she be out there after dark?

BARBARA. She's having dinner with a little ole' gal pal of hers and then the mamma's going to drop her off.

GREG. Oh. Nice. What time are they coming?

BARBARA. Later.

GREG. Don't be sore.

BARBARA. I am sore.

GREG. Don't be. (*Beat.*) I've got some.

BARBARA. What?

GREG. I've got some.

BARBARA. You do?

GREG. Yes.

BARBARA. You did that?

GREG. I've done it a bunch of times. I was waiting for the right moment.

BARBARA. And this is the right moment?

GREG. Up to you, lady.

BARBARA. Good god.

GREG. Finally a smile.

BARBARA. What time is it?

GREG. Time enough.

BARBARA. I can't do much.

GREG. So we'll just…

> (*He trails off, letting the silence linger.*)

BARBARA. Dot Dot Dot.

GREG. Whatever you say.

BARBARA. I'm fat.

GREG. You're a knock-out.

BARBARA. It's been a long time.

GREG. I'm turning things around.

BARBARA. At work?

GREG. Let's not talk about work.

BARBARA. But things are moving forward? That's all I want to know. With these extra hours you're putting in.

GREG. Change gonna come.

BARBARA. The promotion?

GREG. Barbara, relax. Re-set. I've got some.

BARBARA. Oh man.

GREG. Right here on my person.

BARBARA. Do you now?

GREG. Try me.

(BARBARA *reaches into* GREG's *jacket pockets.*)

BARBARA. I don't feel anything.

GREG. Not there.

BARBARA. Not here?

(*She feels around in his pockets.*)

GREG. Not there.

BARBARA. Not here?

GREG. Nope.

(*She slides his jacket off his shoulders and lets it drop to the floor. She reaches into his pants pockets.*)

BARBARA. Not there?

GREG. Find anything?

BARBARA. You would know.

GREG. You didn't.

BARBARA. No, I didn't.

(BARBARA *unbuckles* GREG's *belt.*)

BARBARA. You're not playing with me, are you?

GREG. Barbara, how could you accuse me?

BARBARA. Because if you're playing with me...

GREG. Yeah, what then?

BARBARA. (*Struggling with the belt buckle.*) This fucking belt.

GREG. You bought it for me.

BARBARA. You are in big trouble.

(BARBARA *undoes the belt and undoes his pants.*)

GREG. Oh yeah?

BARBARA. You are in big big trouble.

(*She pats his shirt pocket. She smiles.*)

BARBARA. Oh my gosh.

(BARBARA *pulls a folded hundred dollar bill out of his pocket.*)

BARBARA. One hundred dollars.

(*She lets the money drop to the floor.*)

BARBARA. Is that all?

GREG. You tell me.

(*She feels around in his shirt pocket.*)

BARBARA. All right.

(*She unbuttons his shirt.*)

BARBARA. All right. I'll tell you.

(She kneels in front of him, sliding her hands down his legs.)

(She makes him stand on one foot to pull off his right shoe. She turns it over and shakes it.)

(A hundred dollar bill falls out.)

BARBARA. Oh my gosh.

(She removes his other shoe: another bill.)

(She reaches into his right sock. As she pulls it off, he falls to the ground.)

GREG. You're tickling me.

(She pulls out more money.)

BARBARA. Oh my gosh.

GREG. It tickles.

BARBARA. Oh my gosh. What else? What else have you got?

(She pulls off his other sock: more money.)

BARBARA. What else are you keeping from me?

(She reaches her hands inside his boxer shorts.)

BARBARA. Oh my gosh.

GREG. That's right.

(She pulls out another bill.)

BARBARA. Oh my gosh.

(Another bill.)

BARBARA. Oh my gosh.

(She puts her hands back into his shorts. She is on top of him. He reaches his arms around her.)

BARBARA. I missed you.

GREG. I've been right here.

BARBARA. Have you?

GREG. Trying.

(They kiss.)

(A knock at the front door.)

BARBARA. Shit, are they back already?

GREG. I thought they were having dinner.

BARBARA. People eat too fast. Lock the door.

GREG. Honey.

BARBARA. What honey?

(GREG rolls away from her and pulls his clothes together.)

GREG. Get yourself together.

BARBARA. Oh, I'm sorry, am I malingering? I need a second here.

GREG. We don't have a second. Pull your robe on.

BARBARA. So that's it? Game over.

GREG. We'll save it for later.

BARBARA. Do you have any cash for later?

GREG. Barbara.

BARBARA. What?

GREG. My daughter is standing in the hallway. I am opening the door now.

(BARBARA *grabs the bills off the floor and stuffs them in her robe pocket.*)

BARBARA. She's my daughter more.

GREG. Oh for crying out loud.

(*Another knock.*)

BARBARA. Just let me do it.

(*She moves past* GREG *and opens the door.*)

(INKY *stands in the doorway.*)

BARBARA. (*Confused:*) Hello?

GREG. Oh, shit. What's the date today?

BARBARA. Greg, who is this?

INKY. (*In well-rehearsed English.*) Hello. I am Inky.

(*Ding.*)

Scene 3

BARBARA *and* GREG *sit on sofa.* INKY *sits in a chair.*

Ding.

BARBARA. (*To* INKY:) Is that a problem?

(INKY *says nothing.*)

BARBARA. If it's a problem, say so now. As soon as we get the new place, of course, we'll have a private room for the nanny. And Greg keeps saying we'll move two months ago.

GREG. By the end of the year.

BARBARA. By the end of the fiscal year?

GREG. You know that's not what I meant.

BARBARA. Greg works long hours but still has trouble thinking in business terms.

INKY. (*Quiet voice:*) No problem.

BARBARA. What?

INKY. The room (*Indicating this room.*) is big. Is no a problem.

BARBARA. Do you swim?

INKY. In water?

BARBARA. In water: what a great idea. (*Explaining:*) We rent a lake house in the summer.

GREG. We'll see.

BARBARA. That's a "we'll see" now? *Your* daughter Allison is finally taking swimming lessons.

GREG. And she should learn to swim.

BARBARA. If she has nothing to look forward to but a pissed-in pool, what's the incentive?

GREG. I didn't say, no.

BARBARA. You said we'll see. (*To* INKY:) You want to know what "we'll see" means in Greg's English?

INKY. To see? I know "to see."

GREG. Barbara, enough.

BARBARA. Do you know how to swim?

INKY. I am born in a lake. House.

BARBARA. A lake house.

INKY. (*Nodding.*) I swim.

(GREG *rises.*)

GREG. I'm getting a beer. Anyone want something?

BARBARA. Hah.

GREG. Inky?

INKY. Hah?

BARBARA. Where did my husband find you?

GREG. (*Exiting.*) She's Joe and Ellen's nanny's sister. You know that.

(GREG *is gone.*)

BARBARA. But where do you come from?

INKY. The house builds on very small land, like a finger, between a two lakes.

BARBARA. And where is that?

INKY. That?

BARBARA. The two lakes.

INKY. Between.

BARBARA. Do the lakes have names?

INKY. Yes.

BARBARA. What are they?

INKY. In my language, names, different from English.

BARBARA. You don't say.

INKY. I do. I say, in English, I think, the Big Lake, and the Small. Lake. Or Two Lakes, people in English, I think.

BARBARA. And in your language?

INKY. For us, is also Big Lake, we say, for big. And for small, we say, Garabogazkol Aylagy which, from English, does no mean there is small, means there is no salt.

BARBARA. So there's salt in the Big Lake.

INKY. Yes.

BARBARA. Is the Big Lake by any chance an ocean?

> (*Pause.*)

INKY. You want something understand?

BARBARA. Excuse me?

INKY. I not have words, I think, to make you understanding where I came. From where came.

BARBARA. It's complicated, where you came from.

INKY. (*Nodding.*) Complicate. I not, can to not, to explain this.

BARBARA. But isn't this what I'm supposed to do: inquire about the pertinent info?

INKY. Your husband, he…

BARBARA. Yeah, I imagine he asked the opening questions. That's his strength.

INKY. "Strength" is like "strong." Husband strong?

BARBARA. He's good with the preliminaries.

INKY. Prell…?

> (GREG *enters with a beer.*)

BARBARA. Speak of the devil; and he appears with intoxicants. Give me a sip.

GREG. I'll get you a beer, honey.

BARBARA. I want a sip of yours, honey.

> (*He hands her his beer.*)

GREG. Shouldn't Ally be home by now?

INKY. Ali?

BARBARA. Not yet.

INKY. Muhammad Ali? Is here? In house?

BARBARA. (*Correcting Inky's pronunciation.*) Ally. That's my other child. Allison.

INKY. Allison. Is Ali.

GREG. Ally. Ally is my step-daughter. I told you about her.

INKY. (*Trying to say it just like Greg, but failing.*) Ali.

BARBARA. Ally is short for Allison.

INKY. My name is short.

GREG. Oh, what's your real name?

INKY. Inky is real.

BARBARA. What's it short for?

INKY. Very difficult for Americans. Everyone saying Inky.

BARBARA. But what is it?

INKY. You can no to say it.

BARBARA. But you can say it.

INKY. Yes.

BARBARA. So say it.

INKY. (*Mumbling:*) Irinjahtka.

GREG. I-ring-ya-ka?

INKY. Yes.

BARBARA. No. Ir-in-yah-ka.

INKY. Also.

BARBARA. With an "en" not an "ing."

INKY. Yes.

BARBARA. Yes?

INKY. Also.

BARBARA. Is it a "ing" or an "ennn?"

INKY. Yes.

BARBARA. You can't say yes. One of us has to be right.

GREG. Honey.

BARBARA. (*To* GREG:) What? (*To* INKY:) How do you spell it?

INKY. For you, it is, I think: (*With great difficulty and many hand gestures, spelling it out.*) I-N-K-Y.

    (*Pause.* BARBARA *waits.*)

BARBARA. That's Inky.

INKY. Yes.

    (*The baby starts crying.*)

    (*Without hesitation,* INKY *goes to the crib and sticks her finger into the baby's mouth. The crying stops.*)

INKY. Is fat.

BARBARA. It's the formula.

INKY. Is smooth. How he travel?

GREG. Excuse me?

    (INKY *turns to* BARBARA.)

INKY. No travel tunnel of you.

GREG. What do you mean?

BARBARA. I had a Cesarean.

INKY. Cutting out?

BARBARA. Yeah, they cut him out. No labor.

GREG. Is that what she meant?

INKY. (*Re: the baby.*) Very smooth.

GREG. How could you tell that?

INKY. You have luck.

GREG. We think so.

BARBARA. A bunch a lucky sons of guns.

(*Abruptly* INKY *bends down to the floor.*)

GREG. What is she doing?

BARBARA. What are you doing?

INKY. This is name, carpet?

BARBARA. Yes.

INKY. Yes.

(INKY *stands up.*)

INKY. May I, the bathroom?

GREG. First door on the right.

(INKY *goes.*)

BARBARA. Jesus Fuck.

GREG. Watch the language in front of the baby.

BARBARA. Good god damn.

GREG. What?

BARBARA. I born in lake.

GREG. She's very qualified.

BARBARA. To do what?

GREG. You wouldn't lift a finger to help find somebody.

BARBARA. Oh, is Poor Put-Upon Greg making his entrance?

GREG. I interviewed a lot of candidates, Barbara. At a time when I don't have a lot of time.

BARBARA. What are we paying her?

GREG. She's here and she gets to eat.

BARBARA. You've outdone yourself.

GREG. Not that money is the issue. She's going to care for our children.

BARBARA. At those prices, as long as she doesn't kill them, I guess we come out ahead.

GREG. Don't be disgusting.

BARBARA. I'm not the one who hired a bargain basement nanny. God, everything about us screams poverty…

GREG. Poverty?!

BARBARA. Our failures are screaming. It's a wonder the neighbors don't call and ask us to turn it down.

GREG. More money will come through as soon as…. (*He trails off.*)

BARBARA. Dot Dot Dot.

GREG. I am the only one in line for this promotion. And I've been promised the bonus either way.

BARBARA. Promises. I was promised that the second kid would be easier.

GREG. You talked about another child as much as I did.

BARBARA. I talked about how we couldn't afford it.

GREG. We can afford it. Everything will be all right.

BARBARA. "Everything will be all right, everything will be all right." It gets a little tiresome.

GREG. You don't know how tiresome. When I'm already busting my ass all day.

BARBARA. And me, I'm just lounging on the terrace every hour. Oh, that's right, we couldn't afford the place with the terrace, unless I go right back to work.

GREG. That's you who's insisting on that. You're the one who wants…

BARBARA. (*Interrupting.*) Yes, fine, okay, I'm the one who wants. Don't you ever want?

(INKY *returns.*)

INKY. Thank you.

GREG. Thank you, Inky. We can reach you at your sister's?

INKY. Reach?

GREG. By phone.

INKY. I write the numbers.

BARBARA. I'll remember. What is it?

(INKY *looks at her, hesitant.*)

BARBARA. What's the phone number?

(*Pause.*)

INKY. Is very easy for me to write.

BARBARA. Just tell me.

INKY. To write?

BARBARA. Do you know how to say numbers in English?

INKY. Please. I, to write.

(BARBARA *hands a pad and pen to* INKY *who sits next to her.*)

INKY. (*As she writes.*) May I, a beer, also?

GREG. Are you old enough to drink?

BARBARA. Make it two. (*Holding up two fingers to* INKY.) Two.

INKY. Yes.

(GREG *leaves.* INKY *watches him go. As soon as he is gone…*)

INKY. One, two, three, four, five, six, seven, eight, nine, zero. I know counting. I have reason I want sit very close. I go to baby, I find, on carpet, this.

(INKY *pulls a hundred dollar bill out of her pocket.*)

BARBARA. Oh. (*Touching her robe pocket.*) That's just…ummm…

INKY. I pick up. No one sees. No worry. I want know, if it is to you, your husband no steal it. (*Holding the money out.*) You take?

(*Ding.*)

Scene 4

BARBARA *at the crib. She wears a blouse, skirt, and heels. Dressed for work.*

BARBARA *stares into the crib. She tries to talk to the baby.*

BARBARA. Hello. Hello. Hello, baby. I'm your mother. Hello.

(*Ding.*)

(INKY *enters.*)

(BARBARA *moves away from the crib.*)

INKY. You want feed him?

BARBARA. No, it's okay.

INKY. I already feed him.

BARBARA. No, that's good.

INKY. You want coffee?

BARBARA. I'll get at the office.

INKY. You nervous?

BARBARA. Petrified, like my daughter.

INKY. Pet…?

BARBARA. Nervous, yeah, nervous.

INKY. Your parents make you going?

BARBARA. My parents?

INKY. They force you work?

BARBARA. Sort of. They force me to impress them when they visit. They compare my lifestyle to my little sister's.

INKY. Linda.

BARBARA. How did you know that?

INKY. I listen. Sister has old fat husband, no divorce, four quiet children, and a terrace. Your mother bless her "Lucky Lindy." (*Beat.*) What time you home tonight?

BARBARA. I don't know.

INKY. For eating dinner?

BARBARA. I have no control over that.

> (INKY *begins to gather the folded sheets and pillow that are stacked on the sofa.*)

BARBARA. You don't have to be so meticulous.

INKY. Metic...?

BARBARA. Cleaning up all the time. I'm not going to send you back to Siberia.

INKY. I no come from Siberia.

BARBARA. Right, the lake house.

INKY. Baby is big screamer.

BARBARA. This morning?

INKY. Yesterday. At doctor office, also. Much screams.

BARBARA. Screams?

INKY. For immunization.

BARBARA. Thank you for doing that. Yesterday just got so crazy.

INKY. Crazy.

BARBARA. I should probably get going.

INKY. Ali, also, to get going.

BARBARA. I know, but Greg's still on the phone.

INKY. Phone from four and thirty ringing.

BARBARA. Was it four thirty in the morning? I hate it when he's working in other people's time zones.

INKY. Time *zones*?

BARBARA. Overseas clients.

INKY. You work same from Greg, or no?

BARBARA. Similar. They just pay me less.

INKY. Why?

BARBARA. It's a joke.

INKY. Fun joke.

BARBARA. Greg, get off the phone.

INKY. He still taking Ali school?

BARBARA. The most blessed part of his day.

INKY. How come you no talk Greg good?

BARBARA. What do you mean, talk Greg?

INKY. Always talking bad. He no make enough money, even though your joke. He never winning racquetball. Soon you no talk him at all.

BARBARA. No talk who? (*Correcting her grammar.*) Not talk to whom? What are you talking about?

INKY. Also, father of Ali.

BARBARA. No, I don't talk to Allison's father. Is she done with breakfast? She has to brush her hair still.

INKY. I brush. Shiny.

BARBARA. Allison let you brush her hair?

INKY. Many knots. From crying last night.

BARBARA. Yeah. Why was she crying?

INKY. She is a girl.

BARBARA. What does that mean?

INKY. All she is crying is a girl.

> (GREG *enters in a business suit.*)

GREG. Morning.

BARBARA. Good morning. Did you get any sleep?

GREG. I'm all right. Just in a hurry.

BARBARA. Allison's finishing up breakfast. Inky will get her going.

GREG. I can't do it this morning.

BARBARA. Can't do what?

GREG. They needed me ten minutes ago. I'm headed down.

BARBARA. Down where?

GREG. I'm at the downtown office today.

BARBARA. But you'll drop Allison off first.

GREG. I can't; that's what I'm saying.

INKY. I tell Ali it time leave?

BARBARA. Yes.

GREG. No.

BARBARA. Greg.

GREG. Just this once, you're going to have to do it.

BARBARA. I'm back at work today.

GREG. You don't have to be in 'til nine, right? You might enjoy it.

BARBARA. *She* won't enjoy it.

GREG. She'll love it. It's almost all Moms in the morning. She'll show you off.

BARBARA. Moms? Oh god, am I expected to be a Moms?

GREG. You're expected to… (*He trails off.*)

BARBARA. Dot Dot Dot.

INKY. I get carriage. I and baby, together, take Ali.

    (INKY *exits.*)

GREG. They're not going to beat you up in the school yard, you know.

    (GREG *turns to the door.*)

BARBARA. Who were you talking to on the phone?

GREG. Darling, I have got to go.

BARBARA. You lower your voice when I come in the room. Who the fuck were you talking to?

GREG. Would you watch your language in front of the baby?

BARBARA. He doesn't speak English, Greg.

GREG. It's inappropriate.

BARBARA. What is going on at work? Why haven't you heard about the promotion? You want me to talk to Mark Spencer?

GREG. Don't talk to Spencer.

BARBARA. So you didn't get it. Who'd they promote?

GREG. I've got more eggs in the basket.

BARBARA. Too bad we don't have room for more eggs in this crappy little cubby hole.

GREG. The maintenance on this "cubby hole" is running close to two thousand a month.

BARBARA. Our nanny sleeps on the god damn sofa.

GREG. That girl has slept in worse places, believe me.

BARBARA. Is that an excuse?

GREG. I am doing the best I can.

BARBARA. That's exactly what disgusts me.

    (INKY *enters.*)

INKY. Ali asking, it is safe to come through now?

    (*Pause.*)

GREG. Why do you do this, Barbara? Do you ever ask yourself that?

BARBARA. Constantly.

    (GREG *walks to the front door and out.*)

BARBARA. Step. Step. Step. Open the door. Step. Step. And he's gone. It would be just as easy out the god damn window. Do you ever think about that? How you could just open the window and step out. So easy.

INKY. I never so much high before. I no need think it.

BARBARA. Well, I need think it. All my married life on the thirtieth floor and I think about it all the fucking time. Oops. I shouldn't let the kiddies hear me swear.

INKY. You have lines. Around your eyes.

BARBARA. Are we going to discuss my wrinkles now?

INKY. Not wrinkle. Pretty. Like birds. We say, you have the feet of birds. It means is why you want to fly.

BARBARA. Open the window, step, step, step?

INKY. Human people no fly like that.

BARBARA. How do you know? You ever tried?

INKY. My sister tried.

BARBARA. I thought your sister worked for Joe and Ellen.

INKY. Five girls. Four. Then three.

BARBARA. Two of your sisters jumped out windows?

INKY. No. No, Nadya killed when baby. Greg no have birds. He never have, not future also.

BARBARA. Great.

INKY. My father also. Some men never. (*Indicating around her eyes.*) Here, always smooth on some men.

BARBARA. And what does that mean?

INKY. That?

BARBARA. How some men don't have wrinkles?

INKY. Not so much. No one saying much what it mean. Mean only…like you say when too much bigger than words, when truth more than what you brave for.

BARBARA. What do I say?

INKY. Dot Dot Dot.

> (*Ding.*)

INKY. I to get Ali now.

Scene 5

> INKY *is on stage, near the crib.*
> *Ding.*
> *She empties a whole bunch of coins out of her pockets onto the floor.*

INKY. "I don't just want to be champion of the world, I'm gonna be champion of the universe. After I win this round, I'm gonna whup those little green men from Mars. And looking at them won't scare me none because they can't be no uglier than the folks I beat so far."

(*From under the sofa, she pulls out a shoe box. She counts the pile of change on the floor and then dumps it in the shoe box. She pushes the shoe box back under the sofa.*)

(*Still talking…*)

INKY. "I'm the boldest, the prettiest, the most superior, the most scientific, the most skillfullest fighter in the ring today. When I'm fighting, everyday is Christmas."

(INKY *stops still and listens.*)

(*She exits.*)

INKY. (*From off-stage.*) "Champions aren't made in gyms. Champions are made from something they have deep inside them: a desire, a dream, a vision. They have to have the skill and the will. But the will must be stronger than the skill."

(*She returns with a bottle of formula.*)

INKY. "I'm so fast that last night I turned off the light switch in my hotel room and was in bed before the room was dark."

(*Just before she gets to the crib, the baby begins to cry.*)

INKY. I listen you.

(*She gives the baby formula. He quiets.*)

INKY. I find money today. Nickels, quarters, fourteen pennies. No worry, baby. I listen.

(*Ding.*)

Scene 6

GREG *sits on the sofa. He holds his head in his hands.*
INKY *enters from the bedrooms.*
Ding.

INKY. I make you eating.

(GREG *looks up.*)

GREG. What?

INKY. I make you eating. Now.

GREG. What are you saying?

INKY. Sandwich?

GREG. No. No sandwich. Is she okay?

INKY. Ali sleep now.

GREG. I told Barbara it wasn't safe.

INKY. Her cuts, no more bleeding.

GREG. Who would mug a Girl Scout?

INKY. "Mug" means to take?

GREG. They'd better catch those punks.

INKY. You know who is it?

GREG. Some teenage hoodlums. They see a little girl alone in an elevator. Not that she should be alone in an elevator. She's nine for chrissakes.

INKY. "Mug" means more than finding on ground? Means not allowed for taking?

GREG. No, it's not allowed. They're going to throw those motherfuckers in jail.

(*He looks at* INKY *who stopped still when he raised his voice.*)

GREG. What do they do in your country if someone steals? Cut off their hands?

INKY. They cut hands here?

GREG. Her chin was bleeding. How could anybody hit a little girl?

INKY. In my country, there is building. You say, Girl Building, I think.

GREG. Inky, I never know what the hell you're talking about.

INKY. (*Correcting herself.*) Museum. Girl Museum.

GREG. A museum is a place for paintings.

INKY. No.

GREG. Yes, Inky, that's what museum means.

INKY. No for painting. Also museum to say, this what we are. History. Also this, museum.

GREG. A Natural History Museum?

INKY. In museum, bones, over and over, same bone, this bone, (*Running her hand up and down her thigh.*) over and over. It from, if a virgin, if very good, they take her, the bone from her here, (*Stroking the thigh.*) and put up over house and in this house, no more babies are sick.

GREG. That's barbaric.

INKY. Bar...?

GREG. They cut out the girl's bone?

INKY. Yes.

GREG. They cripple some poor girl for the rest of her life?

INKY. No. No is cripple.

GREG. Oh, really? How does a person walk without a femur bone?

INKY. The cutting out, this ends rest of life. She dead now.

(*Pause.*)

GREG. Why are you telling me this?

INKY. I think I tell something what that happen to girls. I understand history of girls. Museum. (*Pause.*) I make you eating.

(*She heads toward the kitchen. GREG stops her by the arm.*)

GREG. It's not necessary.

INKY. Eating?

GREG. No.

INKY. Sandwich?

GREG. No. (*Beat.*) You're good to Ally.

INKY. She sleep now.

GREG. You're good to all of us. Your arms are so strong.

INKY. Yes.

GREG. (*Joking:*) Have you been working out?

INKY. You have no lines in face. Even when you old man, no birds.

GREG. You think I'm old?

INKY. Eyes are smooth.

GREG. Yours, too. Smooth eyes. God, I can't believe how strong you are. You wouldn't know it to look at you, you know. But you're so strong. Ally's sleeping now?

INKY. She sleep.

GREG. So we can just sit here for a while?

INKY. To sit?

GREG. Is that so awful: to have to sit with me for five minutes?

(INKY *sits.*)

GREG. I told Barbara it wasn't right for Ally to be running around at night, even in the building. Didn't I tell her? I told her more than once. You know, Barbara is a lot of amazing things—she talked me through asking for my first raise; she's the only woman I've ever trusted to help me pick out a tie, or a sweater, a car; a house.

(GREG *looks over at* INKY, *sitting not too far away from him on the couch.*)

GREG. I'm probably boring you.

(*Ding.*)

INKY. I sit with you.

Scene 7

INKY *stands still. The room is silent.*
A long moment passes.
Ding.

BARBARA *enters through the front door.*
She carries a shopping bag.

BARBARA. Inky.

(INKY *doesn't respond.*)

BARBARA. What are you doing?

INKY. I listen.

BARBARA. To what?

INKY. Baby.

(BARBARA *goes over and looks in the crib.*)

BARBARA. He's sleeping.

INKY. Yes.

BARBARA. Look what I bought.

(*She removes a little girl's bathing suit from the bag.*)

BARBARA. Girls always need.

(INKY *looks up.*)

INKY. Pretty.

BARBARA. What do you say, would it inspire you to take the plunge?

INKY. It too big, for her.

BARBARA. I can never tell when I'm standing in the store. But it's cute, right? Sporty?

(INKY *takes the bathing suit from* BARBARA.)

INKY. Pretty. She grows. Three months, it hold her.

(INKY *lays the suit on the sofa.*)

INKY. Listen.

BARBARA. What?

INKY. You hear?

BARBARA. Hear what?

INKY. He breathe.

BARBARA. What are you talking about?

INKY. About the breathe of him.

BARBARA. Breath.

INKY. The breath of him?

BARBARA. Yeah. His breath. He *breathes*, but his *breath*.

INKY. You hear?

BARBARA. Do I hear his breath?

INKY. Yes, I do.

BARBARA. I don't hear anything.

(BARBARA *tries to listen.*)

BARBARA. There's nothing to hear, Inky. He's sleeping.

INKY. You listen?

BARBARA. I'm listening, but I don't hear any breathing exactly.

INKY. He breathe.

BARBARA. Of course, he does. People tend to. But I can't even hear me breathing, and I'm standing right here.

INKY. You not hear you breathing?

BARBARA. No.

INKY. You breathing.

BARBARA. I *am* breathing. I know I *am* breathing. And that he *is* breathing. Am, are, is…

INKY. Listen. (*She describes the sound of breathing. As she inhales, she says…*) Free. (*As she exhales…*) Ham. (*As she inhales…*) Free. (*As she exhales…*) Ham.

BARBARA. Free ham?

INKY. You hear?

BARBARA. Hear what?

INKY. His breath.

BARBARA. I'm afraid I can't hear his breath.

INKY. Do you want?

BARBARA. Do I…?

INKY. So then maybe you feel he look at you. Maybe if first you must to listen. (*With the breath.*) Free ham.

(*Pause. BARBARA is listening.*)

BARBARA. It's quiet to me.

INKY. (*Concurring.*) Quiet.

(*Long pause. BARBARA tries again.*)

BARBARA. I don't…

INKY. There. There. In black time, it is a only one thing you know. I tell Ali, too. More than any piece you own, more even than a body, you have that. There. There. There.

(*Ding.*)

(*They continue to listen together for a long moment.*)

Scene 8

The baby is sleeping inside the crib. No one else is on stage.
Ding.

BARBARA. (*From offstage.*) Greg, it's for you.

(BARBARA *enters from the kitchen with a picnic basket. She sets it near the door.*)

BARBARA. (*Calling to the bedroom.*) Greg.

GREG. (*Offstage.*) What?

BARBARA. Phone.

GREG. (*Sticking his head in.*) I'll take it in the bedroom.

BARBARA. We're leaving in three minutes, baby. Have you packed?

GREG. (*Offstage.*) What?

BARBARA. Are you ready to go?

(BARBARA *returns to the kitchen.*)

GREG. I said I'd take it in here.

(INKY *enters from the bedrooms with a beach ball and some towels. She puts the stuff by the door.*)

GREG. (*Offstage.*) Okay. Okay, Barbara, I've got it. Barbara, would you hang up please?

(INKY *heads to the kitchen.*)

(BARBARA *enters, bumping into* INKY.)

BARBARA. Where's Allison?

INKY. Down.

GREG. (*Offstage.*) Okay, I've got it.

BARBARA. (*Calling back to him.*) Okay. (*To* INKY:) What's his problem? Has he even packed?

GREG. (*Offstage.*) Could you hang up the phone, Barbara?

BARBARA. Oh. Sorry, Greg.

INKY. I hang it.

(INKY *goes to the kitchen.*)

GREG. (*Offstage.*) Would you hang up the…. Thank you.

(INKY *returns.*)

INKY. We going swim?

BARBARA. Our week has come. Is she nervous?

INKY. Petrified.

BARBARA. Go find her. She might try running away.

INKY. She learn to swim this day. We do it.

BARBARA. If we even get her into a bathing suit, I'll be happy. That suit's still too big, huh?

INKY. She have different suit, have what she need. We see the lake. We splash. She learn.

BARBARA. Yeah, we'll splash.

INKY. I take this.

(INKY *begins to load up with the stuff by the door.*)

BARBARA. You can't carry all that.

INKY. Yes.

BARBARA. You can. You don't have to.

INKY. I not have to?

BARBARA. Find Allison. I'll pack the boys up and we'll be down in a second.

(INKY *takes the stuff and goes out the front door.*)

(BARBARA *looks toward the crib. Pause. She takes a step closer and listens.*)

BARBARA. Free ham. Free ham.

(BARBARA *approaches the bedrooms. She listens.*)

BARBARA. Free ham.

(GREG *enters from the bedrooms, nearly smacking into her.*)

GREG. Were you eavesdropping?

BARBARA. No. I was practicing listening.

GREG. That's called eavesdropping.

BARBARA. Don't worry: I'm still no good at it. So who was it this time?

GREG. A client.

BARBARA. He wouldn't give his name.

GREG. It's a complicated loan situation.

BARBARA. Why do people call you here? Why do you give out this number?

GREG. You can't have it both ways.

BARBARA. What both?

GREG. You want me to make more money or free up the phone line?

BARBARA. I'm only saying it's our family phone.

GREG. And I'm only using it to serve our family.

BARBARA. Allison was crying again last night.

GREG. I know that, Barbara.

BARBARA. Inky goes in to her.

GREG. I heard the crying stop.

BARBARA. How does she know what to do?

GREG. Ally likes her. And it's her job to help.

BARBARA. Inky never hesitates. Have you noticed that? She just marches in there and... I don't know what she does.

GREG. She does what we pay her for.

BARBARA. We don't pay her.

GREG. So now you want me to give the nanny a raise?

BARBARA. Yes, I think we should.

GREG. Can you get off my back? I will come through with the money, without the promotion, without the bonus. We will move. If it kills me, I'll get you that new house.

BARBARA. All right, I don't want to fight. I don't want to wreck this for Allison. Are you ready to go?

GREG. Go where?

BARBARA. The Lake.

GREG. The Lake?

BARBARA. House. It's our week off. Didn't you pack before you left this morning?

GREG. I told you we couldn't do it.

BARBARA. It's our week.

GREG. Not this year.

BARBARA. This is absurd. I sent the check.

GREG. I got our deposit back. I told you that.

BARBARA. You didn't.

GREG. I did. We don't have the cash right now. I am using that cash.

BARBARA. What?

GREG. To get the deal with Spencer through.

BARBARA. You're using our money?

GREG. For like five days. It's no big thing.

BARBARA. You cancelled our vacation: that is a big thing.

GREG. Rescheduled.

BARBARA. But this is our week. It's our week.

GREG. We'll go in August.

BARBARA. But it's our week.

GREG. Yeah, keep repeating that because I'm beginning to see your point. Two hundred more times and I'm sure I'll get it.

BARBARA. How many? No, how many times before you get it? One, our week? Two, our week? Three, our week? Four, five? What did you say two hundred?

GREG. Barbara, cut it out.

BARBARA. Because I want you to get it. Six. Seven. Eight. Nine. I mean, what the fuck are we doing here? Ten. Eleven. Twelve.

(INKY *enters.*)

BARBARA. Inky. Inky, you know counting. Help Greg out. Thirteen. Fourteen. Fifteen. Sixteen. Come on; don't play dumb. Seventeen. Eighteen. Nineteen.

(INKY *joins in.*)

BARBARA and **INKY.** Twenty. Twenty-one. Twenty-two. Twenty-three. Twenty-four. Twenty-five. Twenty-six.

GREG. You're acting like a child.

BARBARA and **INKY.** Twenty-seven. Twenty-eight. Twenty-nine. Thirty. Thirty-one.

GREG. I'm going back to the office.

(GREG *walks out.*)

(BARBARA *watches him go.* INKY *keeps counting.*)

INKY. Thirty-two. Thirty-three. Thirty-four. Thirty-five. Thirty-six. How much you need?

BARBARA. Don't stop.

INKY. Thirty-seven. Thirty-eight. Thirty-nine. Forty. Forty-one. Forty-two. Forty-three. Forty-four. Forty-five.

BARBARA. (*Overlapping.*) Please, don't stop.

INKY. Forty-six. Forty-seven. Forty-eight. Forty-nine. Fifty. Fifty-one. Fifty-two. Fifty-three. Fifty-four. Fifty-five. Fifty-six. Fifty-seven.

(*Ding.*)

Scene 9

The baby cries.

INKY *sits on the sofa, nibbling on Girl Scout cookies. She counts a fairly big wad of dollar bills, unfolding them and placing them in a shoe box as she goes. Ding.*

As GREG *enters through the front door,* Inky *dumps the money, closes the box, and slides it under the sofa.*

He looks at her sitting on the couch. He looks at the baby wailing in the crib.

GREG. (*Speaking loud over the crying.*) What's going on?

INKY. I listen.

GREG. What? (*Crossing to the crib.*) What's wrong with him?

INKY. He cries.

GREG. I hear that.

INKY. (*Offering.*) Cookie?

GREG. Barbara'll kill you if you get crumbs on the couch.

INKY. I, meticulous.

GREG. What?

INKY. I, cleaning up all the time.

GREG. Ally's still selling those things?

INKY. We have business.

GREG. Cookie business?

INKY. (*Offering again.*) You want? Special price.

GREG. No, I'm fine. Are you sure he's okay?

INKY. Yes.

GREG. Shouldn't someone pick him up?

INKY. He already eat. Now he want sleep.

GREG. Are you sure?

INKY. Yes.

GREG. It's a little unnerving.

INKY. It come soon.

> (*The baby continues to cry.*)

GREG. Is Ally home?

INKY. When you home from work, I get her from swim house.

GREG. She's still going to the lessons?

INKY. But she no jump in. Afraid of drowning.

GREG. Anyway, I'm home now.

INKY. When you suppose be home, that when I get her.

GREG. Suppose*d* with a "d."

> (*The baby's cries subside into silence.*)

GREG. (*Re: the baby.*) You were right.

INKY. Something I know.

GREG. Something you know?

INKY. I know some thing.

GREG. Yeah. I need to talk to you about one of those things you know. About what you taught Ally.

INKY. About swim.

GREG. Not swim.

INKY. I teach her the stroke. She strokes.

GREG. Not swimming. She showed me her fist.

INKY. Oh. She punch.

GREG. How long have you been teaching her to do that?

INKY. Yes.

GREG. I asked you a question.

INKY. From when teenage hoodlums push her down in elevator.

GREG. That was over a month ago.

INKY. I show her hand a fist. She like it.

GREG. *I* don't like it.

INKY. She hit you?

GREG. I don't think you should be teaching her that.

INKY. She hit hard?

GREG. It's not appropriate.

INKY. Appro…?

GREG. Not what should be happening.

INKY. Like when you home in day's middle: not what should be happening.

GREG. It's not as if I'm not working. I was at the office until three last night.

INKY. Working overseas.

GREG. The bottom line is I'm doing what has to be done if we're going to make a new down payment. Some of these places want thirty percent up front.

INKY. Yes, you very busy man. No taking Ali to school.

GREG. Did she say something to you about that?

INKY. I take her school now. You can no to do it. No can to pick her up also. For me, is no a problem.

GREG. I offered to take her yesterday.

INKY. Oh, yesterday, you offer.

GREG. She didn't want me. She wanted you.

INKY. We take care of business.

GREG. I could do it tomorrow.

INKY. Tomorrow no is school, for Saturday. What time zone you in?

GREG. I need your help with this, Inky. I need some help.

> (INKY *kisses him.*)
>
> (GREG *pulls back.*)

GREG. Don't do that.

INKY. You do that.

GREG. No, I don't do that. And I won't do that ever again.

INKY. You do it again.

GREG. No more. Just because I did something once, when I was very angry at Barbara…

INKY. (*Interrupting.*) You do once, twice, three times. They have English for three times?

GREG. I was in a very difficult situation. If you're just filling a gap…

INKY. You mean about money problem now?

GREG. I'm mean about all these god damn stresses I'm under.

INKY. Poor Greg. He put-upon.

GREG. Stop it.

INKY. I give help.

(*She kisses him.*)

GREG. Inky, don't do this.

INKY. My strong arms, you say. You grow up, no money like me. We understand the other.

GREG. I am trying to do the right thing here. I'm trying to...

INKY. Dot Dot Dot.

(GREG *grabs her.*)

GREG. Don't say that.

(INKY *touches his face, near his eyes.*)

INKY. I tell Barbara you have no lines in face. It is only one thing I tell her.

(*She kisses him.*)

(*Ding.*)

Scene 10

It is the middle of the night. The lights are dim.

INKY *stands over the crib. She speaks very quietly.*

INKY. "You are a bear. You, bear. Look at you, you big, ugly bear. You can't do nothing right. Come on. Come on, sucker. What's the matter with you, you big, ugly bear? What's the matter? Can't hit me? Come on. Here I am. Come and get me, sucker. Hit me. You can't even hit me."

(*Ding.*)

(BARBARA *enters wearing a robe.*)

BARBARA. Inky.

(INKY *backs up from the crib.*)

BARBARA. Has he been keeping you up?

INKY. Not him.

BARBARA. I couldn't sleep either. (*Beat.*) What's the matter? Look at me. What happened to your hands?

(INKY *hides her hands away.*)

BARBARA. Let me see.

INKY. No.

BARBARA. Don't tell me no.

(INKY *holds out her hands.*)

BARBARA. Your knuckles are swollen. Did you fall?

(INKY *doesn't answer.*)

BARBARA. I'll get you some ice.

(BARBARA *exits to the kitchen.*)

(INKY *looks at her hands.*)

INKY. Maybe I fall. "But I don't got a scratch on me. I whupped him so bad he has to go to the hospital, and I'm still pretty. Not a scratch on me. What do you have to say about that, huh?"

BARBARA. (*Entering, overlapping.*) What are you saying?

(INKY *looks at her, silent.*)

BARBARA. Give me your hands.

(BARBARA *places a bag of ice on* INKY's *hands.*)

INKY. Burns.

BARBARA. It's good for you.

INKY. Do you like fighting?

BARBARA. Fighting?

INKY. I like fighting also.

BARBARA. You?

INKY. Yes.

BARBARA. You don't look like much of a fighter to me.

INKY. "If that bum beats me, I'll give up fighting. I'll crawl across the ring and cut off my hair. But that's not going to happen because I'm the greatest fighter in the world."

BARBARA. Who taught you that?

INKY. I teach myself.

BARBARA. Boxing?

INKY. They think only boys want see. My father take my brothers to watch on the screen. But I follow. I am nine, even six, I follow. The room dark. On white screen, two men, both angry, like heroes angry. And no one say, how wrong, no angry, men. We cheer. After one man falls, other man—he my favorite one, pretty face, pretty smile—he talk very good.

(INKY *sets down the ice. She shadow-boxes and struts to* BARBARA's *amusement.*)

INKY. "Float like a butterfly.
Sting like a bee.
His hands can't hit what his eyes can't see."

(BARBARA *laughs.* INKY *punches the wall, the sofa, the coffee table.*)

INKY. "Now you see me, now you don't.
He thinks he will, but I know he won't."

BARBARA. (*Still laughing.*) Inky, stop.

(INKY *keeps punching, harder.*)

INKY. "I done wrassled with an alligator.

I done toussled with a whale.

Only last week, I murdered a rock.

Injured a stone.

Hospitalized a brick."

BARBARA. I'm serious. You'll hurt yourself.

INKY. (*Still punching.*) "I'm so mean…"

(BARBARA *grabs* INKY's *arms to stop her.*)

BARBARA. And you'll wake the baby up. Then we'll really have a fight on our hands.

(INKY *stops.*)

INKY. Like heroes angry.

BARBARA. You like to watch boxing?

INKY. I like to watch my favorite. He is the Greatest.

BARBARA. Muhammad Ali?

INKY. He buy house for mother. Jewels, pretty jewels. He have many children. He make everything good when he fights.

BARBARA. Have you ever seen a boxing match where somebody got killed?

INKY. Only with accident.

BARBARA. That's what comes from people slugging each other's brains out.

INKY. They learn never stop. They see blackness, but no stop.

BARBARA. Animals.

INKY. No. Animals run. Surviving. Animals stop. Only people do beyond that.

BARBARA. Even when the blackness comes?

INKY. They to fighting. To keep fighting.

(*Pause.*)

(INKY *pulls a hundred dollar bill from under the sofa.*)

INKY. I find this one hundred dollars. (*Holding it out.*) I know what oh my gosh means.

(BARBARA *takes the bill and puts it in her robe pocket.*)

BARBARA. Are you going to ice those hands?

(INKY *puts out her fists, and* BARBARA *places the ice bag on them.*)

BARBARA. You were listening to us in the bedroom?

INKY. You start in living room.

BARBARA. We made too much noise?

INKY. Good ears.

BARBARA. Free ham.

INKY. More than breath.

BARBARA. It upset you?

INKY. Is that what it sounds to love?

BARBARA. What are you asking?

INKY. If you to love him?

    (*Beat.*)

BARBARA. Have you ever had sex?

INKY. I not so young.

BARBARA. Sometimes that comes very young.

INKY. Sometime.

BARBARA. On the banks of the Garabogazkol Aylagy.

INKY. What?

BARBARA. The Small Lake. Where you're from.

INKY. Garabogazkol Aylagy.

BARBARA. That's what I said.

INKY. Also.

BARBARA. Did you love him?

INKY. Who?

BARBARA. The boy from your home?

INKY. No, there is no boy. A man. He ugly. I am too young for what he take. (*Beat.*) We say, two kinds of men. One man, he touch you, you feel is he want eat you, take until you gone. That his desire. Other man, different. His touch tell he want hold you, up, hold you up. How a strong stick hold a weak house. That his touch. A woman choose because of touch.

BARBARA. I suppose that means there are two kinds of women, too.

INKY. No, many kinds of women.

BARBARA. I mean, one who likes the one kind of touch and one who likes the other.

INKY. There are many kinds of women.

BARBARA. What about you?

INKY. I no choose. I tell you, that man take from me.

BARBARA. But what kind of woman are you? Of the many kinds. You're maternal, I know that.

INKY. Mat…?

BARBARA. Like a mother.

INKY. I not like my mother.

BARBARA. Do you want children to call your own one day?

INKY. Do you?

BARBARA. I asked you first. Can you picture yourself giving birth?

INKY. Not birth.

BARBARA. Not...?

INKY. Death.

BARBARA. Oh.

INKY. From this, you not want birth. You glad they come out of you dead, from this.

>   (*Pause.*)

BARBARA. How old are you?

INKY. I see, have seen, many things.

BARBARA. I'm sorry.

INKY. Not you.

BARBARA. But I'm sorry you had to see all those things.

INKY. "Had to see"?

BARBARA. What?

INKY. Not "have seen"?

BARBARA. Also. I mean, you said it right before: You have seen many things.

INKY. I say it right.

BARBARA. You do. Will you tell me the poem again?

INKY. What poem?

BARBARA. After the butterfly part, everyone knows that part.

INKY. Is not poem. Is true. Muhammad Ali find million of dollars after he hits. He has luck.

BARBARA. Not all fighters have luck.

INKY. All the ones we know.

BARBARA. Teach it to me.

>   (INKY *stands up. She begins to shadow box.*)

INKY. "I done wrassled with an alligator.
I done toussled with a whale.
Only last week, I murdered a rock.
Injured a stone. Hospitalized a brick.
I'm so mean, I make medicine sick."

>   (*Ding.*)

Scene 11

No one in the apartment but the baby.

Ding.

The baby cries. It goes on for a little too long.

INKY *enters through the front door. Out of breath.*

She empties a whole bunch of crumpled bills of varying denominations and coins out of her pockets onto the floor.

From under the sofa, she pulls out a shoe box. She carefully unfolds each bill and places it in the box.

She pulls out another shoe box. She counts the pile of change on the floor and then dumps it in the shoe box. She pushes both boxes back under the sofa.

She goes to the kitchen.

She returns with a bag of ice, lies down on the sofa, and ices her hands. Her eyes close.

INKY. I listen. I listen. No worry, baby. I have dollars and dollars and nickels. More than what we find on ground. I come home with dollars.

(*Ding.*)

(*But the crying continues.*)

INKY. Please, no worry. No worry.

Scene 12

BARBARA *stands over the crib, looking in. The baby is quiet.*

Ding.

GREG *enters.*

GREG. I met with the Scout Master.

BARBARA. Today? There wasn't a meeting.

GREG. They're kicking Ally out. She's on probation.

BARBARA. From the Girl Scouts?

GREG. It's serious. There are some serious charges.

BARBARA. Charges? What, did they call a tribunal?

GREG. The rest of the girls stopped selling cookies a month ago. We were supposed to hand in all the forms a month ago.

BARBARA. I don't even remember signing the forms. Do I have them?

GREG. I have them now. Barbara. Ally refuses to hand in the money from her cookie sales. (*Pause.*) It's not funny. She told the den mother that she and Inky worked very hard for that money, and they're not going to just give it away. It's not funny.

BARBARA. She has an argument from the capitalist standpoint.

GREG. It's stealing. We're going to have to talk to her.

BARBARA. Why didn't you just write the old bag a check?

GREG. Because it doesn't work that way. They don't accept a payback after they catch you red-handed.

BARBARA. What are you getting so excited about? We can always visit her in the gulag.

GREG. Where is she?

BARBARA. Selling cookies.

GREG. That's impossible.

BARBARA. Inky went with her.

GREG. I'm going to find them.

BARBARA. And do what?

GREG. We have to do something.

BARBARA. And we will. But if we run around tracking them down, we won't be here when they get back.

GREG. I'm so fucking angry. This is Inky's fault.

BARBARA. Greg. Look at this.

GREG. What?

BARBARA. Come here.

GREG. The baby?

BARBARA. Yes.

GREG. Is something wrong?

BARBARA. Look.

GREG. Everything's fine?

BARBARA. I think so.

(GREG *comes up behind her and looks down at the baby.*)

GREG. Uhhhh, he kills me.

BARBARA. I know.

GREG. Why is he so beautiful?

BARBARA. Because he's so clear.

GREG. Clear of guilt.

BARBARA. Clear of pretension. He doesn't feign competence.

GREG. That's beautiful?

BARBARA. Evidently. Can you hear it?

GREG. Hear what?

BARBARA. Me either. I wish I could hear it.

GREG. I'm going to get out of this suit.

BARBARA. Have you ever hit someone?

GREG. What?

BARBARA. As hard as you could?

GREG. Of course not. I hope you're not suggesting we spank Ally.

BARBARA. No, god no.

(GREG *moves to exit, but* BARBARA *stops him.*)

BARBARA. Have you ever been punched? Been on the other side? A fist in the face.

GREG. Barbara, cut it out.

BARBARA. You know Inky lets Allison hit her.

GREG. What are you talking about?

BARBARA. She's teaching her boxing.

GREG. I asked her to stop that.

BARBARA. That's how Inky gets all those bruises. She says she doesn't mind. She says it's just a body; people can do what they want to it.

GREG. It's not just a body.

BARBARA. What is it then?

GREG. We're not animals.

BARBARA. No, I know. We don't know when to stop.

GREG. Stop what?

BARBARA. Hitting. That's what they say in boxing: if you have "heart," that means you keep on, keep on punching punching punching, no matter what you feel. You never go down until you die. They call that "heart." I don't know. I was never even punished as a child, not in that way, so I don't know.

GREG. Know what? You're not making any sense.

BARBARA. Know anything. Anything beyond these walls, this building. Don't you sometimes feel like you want to know something beyond all this privilege?

GREG. Now you think we're too privileged? It's a little late for a change of opinion.

BARBARA. Why is it too late?

GREG. There's no way of pleasing you.

BARBARA. It's not about pleasing.

GREG. What is it then? I don't know what you want.

BARBARA. I want Dot Dot Dot.

GREG. That's helpful.

BARBARA. I want you to hit me.

GREG. What?

BARBARA. Haven't you ever wanted to? Here's your chance.

GREG. Barbara.

BARBARA. You don't even have to do it as hard as you can. Just enough to be real.

GREG. You cannot be serious.

BARBARA. I won't tell anyone.

GREG. I'm going to go change my clothes.

BARBARA. Just once, to see what's on the other side.

GREG. I'm going to change.

BARBARA. Just a little bit of real. Just one good solid slug.

(*He exits to the bedrooms.*)

(*Ding.*)

(BARBARA, *alone, walks toward the window. She looks out.*)

Scene 13

INKY *shadow-boxes.*

Ding.

INKY. "After he loses that zip in the 12th round, I'll start pounding him. Whop. Whop. Bop. I'll keep shaking him up. Pop. Pop. After I laid him flat, when he's lying there, flat, I'm going to stick a carrot in his mouth, a carrot with some green on it. Nibble on it, Rabbit, I'll tell him. Don't you think that will make him give up? Don't you think that will make him leave the country?"

(GREG *enters.*)

GREG. I told you to stop that.

INKY. Ali no punch you more.

GREG. It's not only the punching; the talk is just as bad. I don't ever want to hear her saying that stuff again.

INKY. Whop. Whop. Bop.

GREG. I said I don't want to hear it.

INKY. Pop. Pop.

GREG. Not from you either.

INKY. Is words.

GREG. Words that I don't want to hear.

INKY. You like Barbara strong. You like Inky strong. Why you not want Ali strong, too?

GREG. Because she's a little girl. Let her be a little girl.

INKY. Strong little girl. Strength.

GREG. You are not the father here.

INKY. You either. Step-father.

GREG. Do not push me.

INKY. Step step step; maybe you open the window and jump out.

GREG. I said, shut the fuck up. (*Beat.*) Why do you do that? Why do you make me be a person I'm not?

INKY. *I* making you? I hear *you* making.

GREG. "I making, hear you making:" don't you think it's about time you learned to speak English properly?

INKY. (*Slowly:*) I have many times heard you on the telephone.

GREG. What are you talking about?

INKY. Barbara is not knowing about investigation.

GREG. It's hardly an investigation. (*Catching himself.*) Wh… Who told you that?

INKY. I listen you when you lie. You tell money in account, you tell them that money came from father of you. You no have father. It come from other accounts, not to you. You do this more than once, more than to fill a gap. You make gap bigger. You take more, lies more and more. But they notice: how number in this column is not like that number there. That's investigation.

GREG. I didn't do anything wrong, or even unusual. Everything that I did… I'm not going to explain this to you. There's nothing to worry about.

INKY. I not worried. The man on the phone…

GREG. Enough.

INKY. He worried.

GREG. The man on the phone is a friend of mine. He's going to help me work this misunderstanding out. And that's the end of the problem.

INKY. Money is no yours to give. You can no take us to new home.

GREG. I'm handling the interest already on everything I re-allocated, and I'll pay back every account in full.

INKY. They have jails.

GREG. I need one deal to come through. One out of several I have going.

INKY. Also they cut hands.

GREG. If everyone wasn't breathing down my neck all the time…

INKY. The man on the phone.

GREG. No.

INKY. He take everything away.

GREG. I'll put it all back.

INKY. You have nothing.

GREG. No.

INKY. You have none.

(INKY *reaches into* GREG's *clothes.*)

INKY. I don't feel anything.

GREG. Stop it. What are you doing?

INKY. I don't feel anything.

GREG. There's nothing there.

INKY. Not there?

GREG. I don't have any money.

> (GREG *pushes her away, but she keeps on, pulling at his clothes.*)

INKY. You make up this game. Now you must to keep playing.

GREG. What do you know about our game?

INKY. Is how you win our Barbara. She never fuck you other way. Now me no either.

GREG. I'm not playing. Not with you.

INKY. (*Suggestively:*) You're not playing with me, are you?

GREG. Stop it.

INKY. Because if you're playing with me.

> (*Her actions grow more aggressive. She pushes him to the ground and digs inside his pants.*)
>
> (*At first,* GREG *struggles underneath her, but less and less as* INKY *rips at him.*)

INKY. Am I tickle you? Say this.

GREG. You're tickling me.

INKY. What else? What else have you got?

GREG. Nothing.

INKY. Oh my gosh. Oh my gosh. You can no stop. Oh my gosh.

> (*Ding.*)

INKY. You bring me money, now.

Scene 14

> INKY *alone.*
>
> *Ding.*
>
> BARBARA *enters from the bedrooms, still in her robe.*

BARBARA. Did Greg leave already? I hardly saw him last night.

INKY. Greg gone. You stay at home today. Tell them on phone; say how you are sick.

BARBARA. Inky, I can't. We can't.

INKY. We can. Close your eyes.

BARBARA. What?

INKY. We can. (*Beat.*) Closed.

(INKY *covers* BARBARA's *eyes and leads her to the sofa.*)

BARBARA. Did you make me something?

INKY. I make something you. Feel.

(INKY *takes* BARBARA's *hand and guides it under the sofa to pull out one shoe box, then another, then another, then another.*)

INKY. Open.

(Inky *uncovers* BARBARA's *eyes.*)

BARBARA. They're open.

INKY. Lift up top.

(BARBARA *takes the cover off the box.*)

BARBARA. It's a bunch of coins.

INKY. Next.

(BARBARA *opens another.*)

BARBARA. There's a lot of change in here. How did you get all this?

INKY. Next.

(BARBARA *opens another. She removes a stack of bills.*)

BARBARA. Inky.

INKY. You proud of me?

BARBARA. Where did this come from? There must be...

INKY. Nine hundred fifteen and three three of it. One nine seven papers and two zero zero six coins. I know is no enough. But it make a start.

BARBARA. This money isn't for me.

INKY. Yes. I want be provider in this house.

BARBARA. Inky, you could do something with this. You could buy something.

INKY. No, it is you, for you.

BARBARA. Me?

INKY. For your unhappy. It takes, will take you to new home.

BARBARA. What are you talking about?

INKY. The way new home, bigger home, always talk you, like a ghost. New home, it not exist, like ghost, but it talk you. It no will come. You say with money, it come. With money, it stop talking and come.

BARBARA. I know I talk a lot about a bigger apartment, but this won't help with that.

INKY. But is all I can so far. With Ali. How we start. Now we three do together. Three woman.

BARBARA. Three women?

INKY. Barbara, Inky, Ali. And we take baby, too.

BARBARA. Are you kidding me?

INKY. This is money for new start.

BARBARA. It's money, Inky, but…

INKY. Your poverty stop screaming and you find happy.

BARBARA. You need to keep this. One day, you're going to leave here, and you could use this.

INKY. No.

BARBARA. This doesn't help me.

INKY. This is money. This is money.

(*She hits the box of money to the floor, dollars spilling out.*)

INKY. Why you say I have to leave? I bring this you, to you. I do it. No more Greg.

BARBARA. What about Greg?

INKY. He gone. *I* make change gonna come.

BARBARA. Greg went to work. He'll be back.

INKY. He is not work. He need leaving, not me leaving. He have to give back what he take.

BARBARA. Is this the Girl Scout money?

INKY. Some from cookie. Some… You say, more, always more.

BARBARA. Where did you get it?

INKY. Greg can no give you the more.

BARBARA. Inky, tell me how you got this money.

INKY. Boys at Ali school. They bad boys. Not like our baby. Mean boys. We wait. I say, "You give me that dollars or we punch." We say, "You no tell your mother or we punch." We punch hard.

BARBARA. You and Allison?

INKY. I hit. Hard I can. If I hit hard I can, then money come.

BARBARA. You hit her schoolmates?

INKY. We good girls, for you, your girls.

BARBARA. You stole this for me.

INKY. No, I mug.

BARBARA. Who taught you that?

INKY. I listen the words.

BARBARA. Not the words. Who taught you (*Re: the whole situation.*) this?

INKY. To listen. To listen. Why you not want my present? Why you throw me out?

BARBARA. No one's talking about throwing you out.

INKY. You want more? I have more.

(INKY *reaches into her underwear and pulls out seven folded hundred dollar bills.*)

INKY. I have this. Seven of this one hundred dollars.

BARBARA. One hundred dollars.

INKY. I take oh my gosh from Greg, for you.

BARBARA. From Greg.

INKY. So that never how you do with Ali father, never you cut me off.

(*Silence.*)

(BARBARA *looks at the money, shocked.* INKY *sees that* BARBARA *is not pleased, but still she tries.*)

INKY. You take?

(INKY *holds out the money to* Barbara.)

(BARBARA *does not move.*)

INKY. Greg is eater. Only. Please to take.

(INKY *goes to put the money in* Barbara'*s hand.*)

(BARBARA *pushes her away.*)

(INKY *moves* BARBARA'*s hands down and tries again.*)

(BARBARA *gets her hands free and hits* INKY *in the face.*)

(INKY *instinctively responds with a hard punch right in* BARBARA'*s gut.*)

(BARBARA *reels backwards.*)

(INKY *cries out. She didn't mean to do that.*)

BARBARA. Do that again.

INKY. No.

(BARBARA *swings at* Inky, *landing a hit on her body.*)

(INKY *is about to strike back, but stops herself.*)

(BARBARA *hits* INKY *again. And again.*)

BARBARA. Do it again. Fight with me.

INKY. No.

BARBARA. I trusted you.

INKY. Not fight.

BARBARA. In my house. Hit back.

(BARBARA *is hitting at* INKY, *but* INKY *is not hitting back.*)

INKY. No.

BARBARA. That punch. You have a good punch. Like Muhammad Ali.

INKY. Not ever again.

BARBARA. Like you did it to get the money.

INKY. Not you.

BARBARA. Pretend I'm a child. You like hitting children. Little boys.

(BARBARA *hits* INKY *in the face.*)

INKY. Sweet birds you have.

BARBARA. Pretend I don't. Pretend I'm smooth like glass. I break.

INKY. Please to no.

(BARBARA *keeps on hitting, landing some decent punches.* INKY *hardly moves to avoid them.*)

BARBARA. Pretend I'm the ugly man. You were too small then to fight him off. Or your mother. Did she throw you out of the house? Send you packing once those dead things started coming out of you?

(*Finally* INKY *hits back. Whop whop bop. With a few hard hits, she knocks* BARBARA *down.* BARBARA *is laid out.*)

BARBARA. (*From the floor.*) Don't stop. Don't. I want to feel it.

INKY. I stop now.

BARBARA. Animal.

INKY. Yes, I surviving. So many times I am surviving.

(*Ding.*)

(INKY *sinks down to the floor. She cries softly.*)

(*A long moment passes.*)

(*Finally* BARBARA *struggles to sit up.*)

BARBARA. Man. That really hurts.

(INKY *and* BARBARA *are together on the floor.*)

BARBARA. Oh, Inky. Don't cry. Or cry. Go ahead. I think I'm crying, too. Blow your nose. (*Getting a sleeve or a tissue.*) Here. You're all snotty. Blow.

INKY. I only wanted to take care of you. You need…

BARBARA. No more. No more.

(*Long pause. Quiet.*)

BARBARA. Do you hear that? What's that sound?

(BARBARA *listens to the soft breathing coming from the crib.*)

BARBARA. There. What is that?

INKY. Normal.

BARBARA. It sounds so strenuous.

INKY. Stren…?

BARBARA. Hard.

INKY. Yes. Is hard.

(BARBARA *listens.*)

BARBARA. There. There. It's so hard. There.

(*She rises and goes to the crib to pick up the baby.*)

Scene 15

BARBARA *and* GREG *in the living room.* BARBARA *is still in her robe. It is late afternoon.*

Ding.

GREG. Inky doesn't even know what most words mean.

BARBARA. She seems to know what "internal audit" means. "Pending involvement of the state attorney." It was only when she got to this idea of recognizing yourself to the FBI, that the language barrier finally got the better of her. (*Waiting for a response.*) Not even a smile?

GREG. It's not funny.

BARBARA. No, it's not.

GREG. I did it for you.

BARBARA. And did you touch Inky for me? Is that why you touched her?

(BARBARA *takes the seven hundred dollar bills out of her robe pocket.*)

(*Silence.*)

BARBARA. It's just money. But it kind of silenced me, too.

(*She throws the money in the air. It lands with the other bills already on the floor.*)

BARBARA. We're rich, we're rich.

GREG. Stop it.

(*She bends down and picks up as much of the cash as she can.*)

BARBARA. This is what we've earned. This is it.

(BARBARA *crosses to the window, taking the money with her.*)

BARBARA. If only we had a terrace. (*Opening the window.*) A terrace on the thirtieth floor. Step step step.

GREG. (*Grabbing her.*) Stop.

BARBARA. And out the window. Out.

(BARBARA *throws the money out the window. The wind blows most of it right back inside.*)

BARBARA. It's going to be harder than I thought.

(GREG *is still holding on to her.*)

GREG. (*Noticing for the first time.*) What happened to you? Did you get hit?

BARBARA. Does it show already?

GREG. Oh god, someone hit you?

BARBARA. Someone hit me very hard.

(*There is a knock at the door.*)

GREG. Fuck. If it's someone from the office, I'm not here.

BARBARA. You can't do that.

GREG. Just tell them I'm not here.

BARBARA. You have to be here; here is where we are.

GREG. There's money all over the floor.

BARBARA. Yes, there is. Open the door, Greg.

> (*He crosses to the door and opens it.*)
>
> (ALLISON *stands there.*)
>
> (*She is wrapped in a big beach towel. She is breathing very hard as if she ran all the way here. She doesn't speak.*)

GREG. Ally.

BARBARA. Ally, what's wrong?

> (*But* ALLISON *doesn't come inside.*)
>
> (*Pause.*)
>
> (*Then* INKY *comes into view, in the doorway with* ALLISON.)

INKY. She wants to tell you something.

> (ALLISON *still doesn't speak.*)

INKY. Today she do it. She jumped in.

> (INKY *leads* ALLISON *inside the apartment. She unwraps her towel.* ALLISON *is wearing the bathing suit from Scene 7.* ALLISON's *still a little afraid, but* INKY *gives her a nod of encouragement.*)

INKY. She wants to tell you. (*To* ALLY:) Like you tell me. Tell them.

ALLISON. "I don't just want to be champion of the world, I'm gonna be champion of the universe. After I win this round, I'm gonna whup those little green men from Mars. And looking at them won't scare me none because they can't be no uglier than the folks I beat so far."

> (ALLISON *looks to her parents, tentative.*)

BARBARA. You swam.

> (*Ding.*)
>
> (*Beat.*)

ALLISON. I did.

BARBARA. Look at me. (ALLISON *looks at her.*) Look at you.

> (INKY *is near the doorway, as if she might just slip away.*)
>
> (*The wind is blowing in the window.*)

BARBARA. Look at you.

> (*The baby wakes up and begins to cry.*)

End of Play

DEAREST EUGENIA HAGGIS

by Ann Marie Healy

BIOGRAPHY

Ann Marie Healy's play *Dearest Eugenia Haggis* received a workshop production with Clubbed Thumb's Summerworks 2005 as well as a development reading with The Cape Cod Theater Project and the LAByrinth Theater Summer Intensive. Her two latest plays (*When He Gets That Way* and *Have You Seen Steve Steven* were recently developed through the support of Soho Rep and MCC's Playwrights Coalition. *Now That's What I Call A Storm* was produced by Edge Theater Company last spring. *Somewhere Someplace Else* was produced with Frontera/Hyde Park in Austin (winner of two 2002-2003 Austin Critics Table Awards).

Her writing is published through Playscripts Inc., Samuel French, in various Smith & Kraus anthologies, and in *The Kenyon Review*. She is a five-time finalist for Actors Theater of Louisville's Heideman Short Play Award and a finalist for The Perishable Theater's International Women's Playwriting Festival. She is an affiliated artist with Clubbed Thumb; a member of MCC's Playwrights Coalition; a member of 13P; a former member of the Soho Rep Writer/Director Lab and a writing fellow at New River Dramatists in North Carolina. She was recently awarded a 2006 NYSCA commission.

Other Clubbed Thumb credits: *Beach* (Summerworks '00); *Summer-a-gogo* (reading, Summerworks '01); *Somewhere Someplace Else* (Summerworks '03); *Common Decency: A Parable* (Commission '06); Clubbed Thumb Affiliated Artist.

ACKNOWLEDGEMENTS

Dearest Eugenia Haggis was originally produced by Clubbed Thumb as part of Summerworks 2005 at The Ohio Theatre in New York City. It was directed by Melissa Kievman with the following cast and staff:

MISS PAULINE KHENGIS .... Caitlin Miller
MISTER BLIND JOHNNY KNOLL .... Matthew Cowles
MISS EUGENIA HAGGIS .... Mara Stephens

Sets .... Raul Abrega
Lights .... Josh Epstein
Costumes .... Anne Kenney
Sound .... Shane Rettig
Props .... Pete Sarafin

Special thanks to all of my wonderful collaborators in the original Clubbed Thumb production as well as the amazing development support from the LAByrinth Theater cast, The Cape Cod Theater Project and New River Dramatists.

CAST OF CHARACTERS

MISS PAULINE KHENGHIS (PK), A young lady
MISS EUGENIA HAGGIS (EH), An old maid
MISTER BLIND JOHNNY KNOLL (MBJK), An old blind man
THE VOICE (VOICE), The Voice of John-O Sanagret

SETTING

Someplace very far away from many things, almost everything
Most definitely the furthest outskirts of a little tiny copper town called
Calumet in the Upper Peninsula of Michigan

TIME

A long time ago or maybe far far in the future
Most certainly the dead of winter

Caitlin Miller
in *Dearest Eugenia Haggis.*

Produced by Clubbed Thumb at The Ohio Theatre, 2005.
Photograph by Anne Kenney

DEAREST EUGENIA HAGGIS

Prologue
The Way Things Were In The Beginning

A dining room table with piles of old papers on top and a set of stiff mahogany chairs. Perhaps there is an empire sofa in the corner of the room? If so, it is hidden under a dust cover covered with dust. There are most certainly small sets of leaden glass windows that look out onto a frozen lake. Through the windows: no other homes, no other sign of life. A pale light of a winter afternoon sun is turning purple. The weak sun makes it look inviting outside but the snow is, in fact, frozen in glittering mounds. PAULINE KHENGHIS sits with MISTER BLIND JOHNNY KNOLL. She holds a small notebook and they look out on the lake as they speak. Suddenly, the light disappears and it is night.

MBJK. Well she was beautiful.

PK. (*She writes this down and then adds to it.*) And she was rich.

MBJK. She was beautiful and she was rich.

PK. She was…careless. (*She writes this down.*)

MBJK. Yes. She was careless.

PK. But she was only careless because she could be. (*She writes this down as well.*)

MBJK. You mean, she could be careless with me?

PK. (*Continuing to write.*) She could be careless with you because she had so many other men to choose from.

MBJK. …She did. I forgot she had so many other men to choose from.

PK. (*Looking up to speak to* MBJK.) But that's why you're special Mister Blind Johnny Knoll.

MBJK. …Remind me again. Why am I special?

PK. You're special because you have experienced. Love.

MBJK. I have experienced. Love.

PK. Not everyone feels like we feel.

MBJK. No. No. It's true. Those lucky people.

PK. We feel more deeply than other people Mister Blind Johnny Knoll. And that is why we must protect ourselves.

MBJK. Are you writing all this down?

PK. Yes. Yes. Of course.

MBJK. Read it back to me. Please.

(PK *begins to read.*)

PK. In the beginning there was. *Ferdinand.* Filled with the sensation of longing—

MBJK. Wait a minute. You're naming me *Ferdinand* in the novel? I thought you were using my real name.

PK. I can't use your real name Mister Blind Johnny Knoll.

MBJK. Why not?

PK. Mister Blind *Johnny Knoll?* It sounds so…Dull.

MBJK. Okay. But. *Ferdinand?*

PK. Ferdinand has a real "ring." It sounds like the name of a real. Protagonist.

MBJK. *Ferdinand?*…Fine. Keep going.

PK. (*Mumbling aloud some of the earlier sections before finding a place to begin:*) Ferdinand walked onto the grounds of her estate and he was immediately consumed by the sensation of longing. Everything around him, everything in *her* life was beyond his reach. *She* was beyond his reach. The very notion of becoming worthy of her consumed him

MBJK. Well now it doesn't consume me. I have. I have other things in my life Miss Khenghis.

PK. Like what?

MBJK. (MBJK *tries to think of something.*) Well. You know. Like…Okay fine. *Consume.*

PK. (*Continuing to read.*) The very notion of becoming worthy of her consumed him. He did everything he could to make himself. *Fascinating.* If only he were fascinating, he might finally be worthy of her gaze. It was this great desire, the potency of his longing for…Charm…That confirmed his experience of. Love.

MBJK. Love. Yes. Love.

PK. Should I keep reading Mister Knoll?

MBJK. Some people get served up all of the love Miss Khenghis. The rest of us pick from the scraps.

PK. Oh Mister Blind Johnny Knoll! I'll write that down!

(*She speaks it out loud as she writes it down.*)

Some people get served up all of the love. The rest of us pick from the scraps.

MBJK. Doomed. I am…

PK. (*She begins to write.*) Ferdinand cried out: *Doomed! I am doomed!*

(*A series of snow toboggans race by the window. PK moves to the window and offers them her profile through the reflection while she continues her conversation with* MBJK.)

MBJK. (*Perhaps more to himself.*) Fascinating. Yep. Fascinating. (*Speaking again to* PK.) All right then. Put it away now Miss Khenghis.

PK. But I haven't even finished the end of the first chapter.

MBJK. No. No. It's… Please stop.

PK. Mister Blind Johnny Knoll. We haven't even gotten to the part where she breaks your heart in the letter…

MBJK. The letter. (*I forgot about that letter.*) So that's how it ends then.

PK. Oh no. No no. You write her back and you tell her that no matter what happens, no matter her response, you will always feel this. Love… You're too courageous to let go of it.

MBJK. Please Miss Khenghis. Let's stop for tonight.

PK. We'll have to move faster if I'm going to finish it this winter.

MBJK. Who. Who is ever going to read this?

PK. Oh Mister Blind Johnny Knoll. People just like *us*…Once I finish it, I'll get it published and then…Who knows. Who knows what will happen.

MBJK. Who knows who knows…

(MBJK *gets up and paces around the room while* PK *goes back to scribbling on the paper.*)

MBJK. Are you hungry?

PK. Hmmm… I am.

MBJK. Me too. Maybe we could. Warm something up?

PK. …Hmmm…Yes. Maybe. That's a good idea. (PK *goes back to scribbling while* MBJK *sits back down.*) Maybe later.

MBJK. Wouldn't it be nice if a steaming hot bowl of stew just…landed on the table?

PK. (*Scribbling away in her notebook.*) What's that? Oh yes. Steaming hot stew. Mmm…That would be nice.

MBJK. And maybe a loaf of warm buttered bread.

PK. Warm bread Mister Blind Johnny Knoll? No. No. Gratuitously hot buttered bread! Or. Or. Pineapple juice and champagne!

MBJK. Hmmm…Yep. Whatever you say.

PK. (*Returns to her scribbling and she speaks out loud.*) Ferdinand sat down at *her* table set for a supper of pineapple juice and champagne.

MBJK. *Ferdinand.* Some people get served up all of the love and Ferdinand picks from the scraps. (*He listens to* PK *writing.*) Oh Miss Khenghis. I will look forward to the day that Ferdinand dies for love. It's. It's too heavy. His broken heart.

(PK *continues her scribbling.* MBJK *sets his head down on the chair and begins to fall asleep.*)

Wull as long as there's no supper…I'll just. Maybe I'll just check the back of my eyelids for a moment.

PK. Goodnight Mister Blind Johnny Knoll.

MBJK. Goodnight Miss Pauline Khenghis.

(PK *begins to write again as* MBJK *falls asleep and starts snoring. The snow toboggans fly by in the dark of the night.* PK *goes to the window and takes in their presence. She goes to a mirror and fluffs her hair gently before going to the window and offering the unseen snow toboggans another glimpse of her profile. She returns to her notebook and begins to write more but her head droops with fatigue. She pulls a blanket from off to the side and she falls asleep in her clothes alongside the snoring* MBJK. *The pages of her notebook fly out from under her and dance magically in the air, as if guided by an unseen hand. They crash suddenly on the floor, forming a chaotic bundle at her feet.*)

Scene 1
Set Down Your Hat And Call It Home

The next afternoon. PK *wakes up on the couch.* MBJK *is no longer asleep in his chair. The sound of* MISS EUGENIA HAGGIS *coming in from the other room.*

EH. (*Voice from offstage:*) Well then you say then that you don't need someone to keep house in this house...

(EH *comes bustling into the dining room carrying a hard, square suitcase. She does a quick decisive assessment of the disheveled room.*)

But I'm afraid I beg to differ Mister Blind Johnny Knoll.

(MBJK *follows* EH *into the room.* PK *hides herself in some slightly absurd spot in the room so she can eavesdrop on the ensuing conversation.*)

MBJK. Miss...Miss?

EH. Name's Haggis. Miss Eugenia Haggis.

MBJK. Yes then Miss Eugenia Haggis. I will have to say it again. I'm not looking to hire anyone.

EH. *Anyone!* (*She sniffs.*) You'd be lucky to find *anyone* much less me.

MBJK. Much less you?...Wull. Where else have you worked in town...?

EH. I've worked in the homes of (*She searches for the word:*) eccentrics before and I've met some pretty eccentric people. I have also worked for some pretty important people (not that I tend to care too much about that sort of thing but pretty prestigious types). I think you'll find that I do my job well and I've got a good hearty soul for the winters. I'm strong enough to clean out the coal shed and I've never had a hitch getting the heat up. I'd rather do just about anything than sit around and twiddle my thumbs so if you don't have any sense of the chores, I can always make you some shanks and beets for the supper. (Folks at Miss Willet's were too fancy for my shanks and beets...)

(*Pause.*)

MBJK. ...Miss Willet's...

EH. I held a position there for over two years. Just left.

MBJK. ...You left...Her,,,?

EH. She wanted me to stay. Begged in fact. HA! I just picked up my suitcase and walked right out her door. Right out her door and came right here.

MBJK. You must have. Surprised her. Hurt her. Feelings. Perhaps?

EH. (*She sniffs.*) Well now Mister Blind Johnny Knoll. I will tell you the straight up truth because I don't believe in anything that comes out crooked. That woman, Miss Willet, is straight up stuffed full of herself.

> (*Pause.*)

Now I suppose I have offended you but I had to tell you the straight up truth about the matter.

> (*Pause.*)

I can see that I put my foot in my mouth so I'll just take my suitcase and be off. I'm sorry that our new arrangement didn't take but I don't think I have it in me to work for anyone attached to a *puff pastry* like Miss Willet.

> (*Pause.* MBJK *starts laughing. He laughs and laughs. It comes as a surprise to both of them.*)

MBJK. (*Speaking while laughing:*) A...Puff pastry.

EH. (*She does not laugh with* MBJK. *She delivers only the "straight up" truth.*) Yep. A puff pastry. With a dollop of sugared crème on top.

MBJK. HA! I've never. I've never heard her described that way.

EH. So you are familiar with the ways of Miss Willett?

MBJK. Yes. I am. She...I knew her. A long time ago.

EH. Then you are familiar with her puff pastry ways. Just like all the people from her fancy set in Houghton County. None of them ever took to me much and maybe that's more my own fault than anyone else's. I'm not so frivolous to dwell on that matter. I guess I just figured I'd try boarding out here because I heard folks out here were less... Full of themselves.

MBJK. Well. I'm not. Interesting enough to be full of myself. HA!

EH. Oh ya? Me neither. HA!

MBJK. My life wouldn't even make a meal. (*ha*)

EH. Nope. Nope. Mine neither. Oh well.

MBJK. Someone wrote something like that to me once...In a letter.

EH. Oh ya? Wull. Wull I've never even got a letter ever...So there! HA!

MBJK. It was. Not just someone. Someone specific. Someone like. Oh I don't know...Miss Willet.

EH. Oh. Huh. Well. By the looks of it, the two of us are already off to a better start than I ever had with Miss Willet.

MBJK. Miss Willet wrote something like that to me once. (*He pretends he has forgotten.*) Something like: "Johnny Knoll. Your life would be more interesting if you were a more interesting person." (*He laughs. He stops.*) Or. Something like that.

EH. What's that supposed to mean?

MBJK. It was supposed to mean that… She thought I was boring.

EH. People come up with words like that because (*She tries to articulate a gem of wisdom but nothing comes to her.*) You seem interesting enough to me. You're blind, for one. That's gotta be pretty interesting.

MBJK. Well now it is. It is. Though this person, Miss Willet, wrote this particular thing. When she wrote it, I wasn't blind. I was. Much younger. Almost attractive even. (*ha*) But the fact is, she wrote it because. Her house was full of more interesting people and parties and…My house…

EH. (*Interrupting* MBJK's *line:*) Her house was full of gossip…

MBJK. …Maybe in God's eye—

EH. Eh?

MBJK. Do you think…Miss Haggis…Do you think that in God's eye, we are all. Equal. Even. Fascinating?

EH. Fascinating. HA! It doesn't much matter to me. I haven't expected anything fascinating for my life since I was…

>   (*Out of habit,* EH *begins to tidy up some of* PK's *notebook papers lying around the house.*)

MBJK. Er. Just out of curiosity. What do you think of the name *Ferdinand?*

EH. Ferdinand? Huh. Ferdinand? Wull. Sounds like the kind of name Miss Willet would give a poodle.

MBJK. Oh Miss Haggis. It does, doesn't it? A (*He finds the words that suit the description:*) …Yappy. Little poodle…

EH. Papers here and there. You've got these papers flying everywhere. To tell you the straight-up truth Mister Blind Johnny Knoll, (EH *begins to bustle around to help pick up the extra notebook papers.*) I'd be happy with a nice quiet winter. Decent lakeside folks shouldn't expect more than a nice quiet winter on a nice quiet…(*She opens the door to take out a collection of the papers and there is the sound of the snow toboggan revving up the distance for the nightly ride.* EH *quickly shuts the door and steps back inside.*)

MBJK. Miss Haggis? Are you all right Miss Haggis?

EH. I know that sound…That's the sound of the Sanagret boys… (*Her voice lapses into ominous silence.*)

MBJK. Oh the Sanagret boys. Decent lakeside folks. Their mother, at least. (They lost her to The Fever when all nine of them were babies…)

EH. They're…animals.

MBJK. Now now Miss Haggis. Just decent lakeside folks fending off the graces of domestication…

EH. ...What would happen if they rode those...snow toboggans...around here by your house?

MBJK. Well they wouldn't Miss Haggis because my house is my property.

EH. But what would happen if they went out boozing out on that lake and they rode those snow toboggans right up to your door?

MBJK. What would happen? You would be safe Miss Haggis. That's what would happen.

EH. (*She turns to look at* MBJK *as though he can see her.*) How do you know?

MBJK. You'd be safe because you'd be safe here inside this house. (*With me*)...And. And. Nothing interesting ever happens to me. Remember? HA!

(*Pause.* EH *considers this fact and concedes.*)

EH. Oh ya. HA! I fergot. ha. (*She sniffs.*) Folks down at Macauley's told me that the Sanagrets haven't worn socks in months. Folks at Macauley's said they've got the *chilblains*...(*She sniffs again and looks around.*) So how do you feel about shanks and beets?

MBJK. Shanks and beets...

EH. For the suppers.

MBJK. Wull Miss Haggis! *Unlike the folks in town*, this folk would be happy to sup on some shanks and beets.

EH. Wull then. Wull then. Glad to hear it. I think you'll find that this house could really use someone to keep house in this house. Yup.

MBJK. ...I think you might be right.

EH. I'll go put on some shanks and beets for the simmering and we'll have something for this week's sup.

MBJK. Oh no. Get yourself settled first. Take the room at the top of the stairs and take the white oak wardrobe to hold your things.

(EH *picks up her suitcase and begins to exit.*)

Be sure to slide a hot brick in the bed for some warm-up in the evenings!

(EH *continues to exit out of the room until she is almost offstage.*)

Oh and watch yourself in the washroom because you'll share it with the other girl.

(*Pause.* EH *reappears in full sight on stage.*)

EH. ...The other girl...

MBJK. Oh yes. The other girl. You didn't know there was another girl?

EH. No. I didn't know there was another girl.

MBJK. She's a young writer. Boarding out here until she finishes her novel.

EH. Another girl. (*She sniffs.*) Knowing the way most other girls are, she'll be downright distraught about sharing that washroom. Wull tell her that I don't bother much with primping. Tell her I'm not one to primp my days away in the vanity glass.

MBJK. Oh I think the two of you will be just…Well. Enough said.

EH. I'll have a breakfast of corn meal mush and coffee ready for all of us at six. Six on the dime.

MBJK. I haven't eaten at six on the dime since…What did you call her again?

EH. Who?

MBJK. Miss Willet?

EH. Oh. You mean the puff pastry.

MBJK. HA! *Puff Pastry.* That's just. That's just exactly what she is Miss Haggis. Miss. Eugenia. Haggis.

> (MBJK *looks at* EH *as if he is seeing her. She stands and waits for a dismissal. When none arrives, she initiates her own exit by picking up her suitcase and walking offstage.*)

EH. I'll show myself to my room now Mister Blind Johnny Knoll. (*Calling from the furthest corners of the house.*) Glad to hear that you folks are just decent lakeside folks like me! (*Perhaps her voice even fades out on this next line.*) Just decent lakeside folks like meeeee…

> (MBJK *stands at the window. Pause. There are sounds of a "snow toboggan" sputtering away eerily outside the window, crossing through the frozen landscape. Tiny slits of headlights come into the room. They shoot away into the darkness.*)

MBJK. Good evening Miss Khenghis.

PK. (*Coming out of hiding and running to the door to retrieve her papers.*) Why did you let that Macauley's woman throw away my notes…!

> (*She throws open the door and stares out into the absolute stillness of the winter night. The papers are nowhere to be seen.*)

MBJK. Good riddance to bad garbage Miss Khenghis.

PK. But that was our story.

MBJK. My story Miss Khenghis. Mine.

PK. (*Staring out into the night and delivering the next line with a bit of theatricality:*) The beautiful story of your broken heart…

> (*The snow toboggans inch along outside. Perhaps she gives them a little pose before shutting the door against the cold.*)

It's gone. All of it…Gone. How could you Mister Blind Johnny Knoll?

MBJK. We have Miss Haggis to thank. She's got an eye for the beauty of the straight up truth.

PK. Miss Haggis?! Miss Haggis wouldn't recognize beauty if it. If it. Had her name written all over it.

MBJK. That's because she's not… vain.

PK. She's one of the *Macauley's people.* How could she be vain?

MBJK. It just occurred to me: Vanity is the cause of great unhappiness.

PK. (*She gives up on trying to collect any of the papers in the room.*) I know lots of vain people. They all seem perfectly happy to me...

MBJK. I think you'll feel differently when you get a gander of Miss Haggis. She's. She's. Something else.

> (*The putter of the snow toboggan continues, both fantastical and dull. It is monotonous in a foreboding way.*)

PK. Cheers to Miss Haggis! (*With a bit of despondent dramatic flair.*) Fetch me some arsenic on ice Maestro! (*She turns back to the unseen bartender.*) Make it a double. (*She flops back against the couch and stares out the window.*) I don't think I'm going to make it through this winter. HA!

MBJK. Miss Khenghis. Take my word for it: Your life would be more interesting if you were a more interesting person. Better to leave those indulgences to the fancy folks and get on with the living.

> (MBJK *exits the room.* PK *is stunned by his reprimand. It is as if she has been slapped in the face.*)

PK. But it was... Beautiful. Your story... The *straight up truth.* (*Calling out to* MBJK:) There's nothing interesting about the *straight up truth!*

> (*The motor toboggans pass by again accompanied by loud whoops and hollers. Eventually the sounds fade away and a tiny speck of a light appears in the distance. It is an ice fishing shack sitting on top of the frozen water. She opens the window to the chill of the air and the distant hum of activity carries right over the lake.* EH *walks in.*)

EH. They're gunna keep us up all night huh?

PK. I suppose.

EH. Don't mind sharing the washroom with me do you? Name's Miss Eugenia Haggis.

PK. No. No. Don't mind a bit...

EH. Me neither. I don't mind a bit neither.

> (*Pause.*)

I've never shared a washroom with anyone before. Don't know why that is. Wull it's probably because there's never been anyone there to share it with. That's probably why...HA!

> (*Pause.*)

EH. I was just joking with ya.

PK. I know you were joking.

EH. I've got such a funny way of saying things. Sometimes people don't know that I'm joking.

PK. I knew that you were joking...

> (*Pause.*)

EH. So it's not a problem then. The washroom.

PK. No. No problem.

EH. Wull Mister Blind Johnny Knoll has told me a lot about the house and the chores and it sounds like the two of us will be getting on together almost every night. As long as we can get on together I don't suspect there will be a problem. Do you?

PK. Did you have a problem when you worked for Miss Willet?

EH. You know I worked at Miss Willet's? Well. No. No problems. Except. I have to say, I was stuck at Miss Willet's for more than two years and none of those folks ever said a word to me. I mid' as well have been nothing in their eyes. Sometimes I would say things that were the right things to say but they must have sounded funny to all of them. I would say "mush" instead of "mash" when I was stirring up the yams. Something like that. Something that didn't matter. Alls I know is that they all started laughing at me and saying: "She said mush instead of mash"... And I would laugh with them just to make it easier but I know that they were making fun of me...

PK. Mush instead of mash. Huh. That is funny. That is a funny way of saying it.

> (*Pause.*)

EH. I just had a feeling I'd have better luck *out here*. Had a feeling that the people working out here would want to say goodbye to all that. Nonsense.

PK. Oh I'm sure the people working out here would. But. I don't work out here for him...

EH. What do you do if you don't work out here for him?

PK. I work out here for him. But I don't keep house. I take care of him. I'm his assistant.

EH. So you work out here for him.

PK. Not like a hired person.

EH. Did he hire you?

PK. Yes.

EH. Well then...

PK. But it feels more like I live here...

EH. Like family?

PK. Yes. Like family.

EH. But he pays you?

PK. ...Yes.

EH. HA! Some family.

PK. He feels like family...

EH. Wull. I didn't have to hire my family but. (*She sniffs.*) I don't take up much time in the washroom. I'm not one of those mirror hogs and I'm proud of that. So...I also do all my own baking. The cookies will look like they're bought from town but they're not. Just means I know how to make 'em look like they're from the store but I make everything homemade.

PK. All right.

EH. 'Spose you are...

PK. What's that?

EH. One of those mirror hogs?

PK. I take my time in the washroom. If that's what you mean...

    (*Pause.*)

EH. I've seen you before. You're the daughter of that...

PK. Probably not.

EH. No. The daughter of that man who used to work in the back of Macauley's.

PK. You must be thinking of someone else.

EH. Nope. That was you. The daughter of Old Man Khenghis. You used to come in when you were just a little kid. Your father used to brag about you 'cause you wrote some story...Some story about us folks in the back of Macauley's...The story about the windbags...That was. You.

PK. Maybe so...

EH. Wasn't it called "The Story About the Windbags"?

PK. Actually. It was called. "A Story About the Windbags" and it was. It was...

EH. Yep. Yep. (*Perhaps more to herself.*) Pauline Khenghis.

PK. It was. Almost accepted to be published in. Calumet's *Daily Delights*. I imagine they'll publish my novel just as soon. Just as soon as I...Finish.

EH. "A Story About the Windbags." Yep. Yep. Figures. Just figures I'd go from Miss Willet's to... Never mind.

    (*The toboggans start up again and snake by the window in the dark. The loud motors and overwhelming shouting shake the room.*)

EH. Goddamn Sanagrets! Nobody ever tells those Sanagrets off. For Pete's sake, somebody outta just tell them off and put them in their place. They're not. Gods! They're just...Animals!

    (*She opens up the window and stands in the freezing cold in her nightgown. She calls out in the fake voice of a man.*)

EH. GODDAMN SANAGRETS! KEEP THOSE GODDAMN FANCY PANTS SLEDS OFF MY PROPERTY!

    (*The sounds stop suddenly. There is an eerie silence.*)

VOICE FROM DARKNESS. IS THAT EUGENIA HAGGIS?

    (*EH quickly closes the windows. She turns out the light so they can no longer see her.*)

EH. Damn Sanagret boys. I didn't think they'd see me...I don't care. They were trespassing on Mister Knoll's property. Don't you think? Don't you think that was right of me to tell them to get off our property...?

PK. It's not exactly your property Miss Haggis.

(*Pause.*)

EH. Well then. Actually. No skin off my back suits me fine... Goodnight Miss Khenghis.

PK. Goodnight Miss Haggis...

(EH *begins to exit but she turns around to deliver one last remark.*)

EH. Funny thing is your father used to brag and brag about you writing that story. But you never once went to the back of Macauley's to spend time with him the way the other kids did...So when I asked him about you, when I asked him about your story, your father told *me* that you were sort of (*She emphasizes these words with cruelty:*) A cold fish. Yep. Those are the words he used to describe you.

(EH *exits.* PK *is left standing at the window. She opens the window and she stares out. She can see her reflection in one of the windowpanes.*)

PK. A cold fish. A. Cold. Fish.

(PK *shudders. She goes back to her notebook and tries to write something. She waits. Nothing comes. She wanders back over to the window and blows fog onto the glass. She begins to write with her finger in the mist.*)

THE-BEAUTIFUL-STORY-OF...

(*Her finger draws a heart and then trails down the pane of glass in dissatisfaction.*) Love.

(*Suddenly, a motor toboggan light shines directly in her face. It is close enough to touch. She jumps back.*)

VOICE. (*Terrifyingly Close:*) Give me your hand Miss Eugenia Haggis...I think you're pretty...

PK. (*Whispering:*) I'm not. I'm not...Eugenia Haggis.

VOICE. Tell Miss Eugenia Haggis to give me her hand. Tell her I'll be waiting all winter. Right here on the lake...

PK. I'll...I'll tell her...

VOICE. Who are you?

PK. ...I'm...I'm...Nobody.

VOICE. Give me your hand Nobody.

(PK *puts her hand out the window and she screams. When she pulls her hand back in, there is a piece of delicate stationery and an envelope in it. The motor revs up again and the toboggan slides away into the darkness. It is still and black.* PK *is motionless until the sound of the snowmobiles fades.*)

PK. I'll...I'll tell her...

Scene 2
'Scuse Me Miss...You're Stepping On My Heart

PK writes her letter by the soft light of a candle. Perhaps she reads the letter out loud as she writes? Perhaps there is some kind of voiceover? Maybe it is done in the voice of PAULINE as she "pretends" to be Mister Alfred Sonneville?

Dear Miss Eugenia Haggis,

Please don't think me a forward man. The truth is that I find you a very comely woman. I know your looks are not to everyone's liking but I find them very much to my liking. Just in the way that a cook must spice his stew for every different diner, I like my stew spiced just to my taste. I believe that God has spiced you to be a stew to my liking and that gives me the satisfied feeling of a diner enjoying a long and sumptuous meal.

Miss Eugenia Haggis, I was wondering if you would send me a photograph of yourself. I think about you often but I live outside the borders of Houghton County and it's not often that I can catch a glimpse. If you find me worthy of a correspondence, please send your letters to my post office box in town. I will guard the secret of my identity behind my designated "pen name" until the blossom of passion's flower begs for a harvest.

Yours so ever truly,

Mister Alfred Sonneville

P.S. I do not want to trouble you with particularities about the photograph but I would appreciate something small and square (i.e. a pocket-size gravure for ease of carry).

> (PK *seals the letter. She inspects the outside of it and smudges a post office stamp with some ink. She looks at it one final time. She blows out the candle.*)

Scene 3
Boy Ho Boy Things Are Really Cookin' Now

The next day. MBJK *at the door with the letter in his hands.*

PK. ...Is that a letter?

MBJK. Seems to be. A real letter.

PK. A real letter. And who is it for...?

MBJK. (*Pretending, perhaps wishing, he is in possession of the power to find out:*) Well it is a letter that arrived by post so. It is larger than most and smells. Fresh. Like the outdoors. Must be for. Let's see.

PK. (*Taking the letter:*) It says here: Miss Eugenia Haggis.

MBJK. Miss Eugenia Haggis.

PK. Miss Eugenia Haggis.

EH. (*Calling out from offstage:*) Mister Blind Johnny Knoll! The coal shed's cleaned out and we can start loading in the new now for the winter…

(*There is a pause between* PK *and* MBJK.)

MBJK. Who knew she was a woman of the world. Receiving news of the world…

PK. You received a letter once didn't you? Remember that one time that you received a letter Mister Blind Johnny Knoll.

MBJK. Well. I did receive a letter. Once…She sent me a letter and she told me that my life would have been more interesting if I had been a more interesting person…

PK. Miss Willet?

MBJK. Oh no. No. Just a woman I knew…Why did I bring this up? (*Calling out to* EH:) Miss Haggis! Miss Haggis! You have a piece of correspondence from… (*He pretends he can read the letter.*) Someone very important! Please come in here to pick up your correspondence.

(EH *appears from the coal shed. She is covered with marks of coal on her face and dress. From the looks of it, she is a "mess."*)

EH. What's that Mister Blind Johnny Knoll…?

MBJK. A piece of correspondence just arrived for you in the post.

EH. The post. That's funny. The post…I (*She looks at the return address.*) Well I'll be…

MBJK. Do you have a special friend in town Miss Haggis? (*he he*) I certainly hope not.

(EH *does not hear* MBJK *because she is already wandering over to a corner of the room. She opens the letter to read it.* PK *watches her through the reflection in the glass of the windows. It is growing dark with purple light outside.*)

PK. I do believe I just saw Miss Haggis blush a touch of crimson…

MBJK. Crimson…What for crimson?

PK. I do believe she…

MBJK. She what? She what? What does she look like now Miss Khenghis? What does she look like now?!

PK. Well. She is taking the letter in her hands and she is looking once, twice at the return address and she is looking at her name and now she is opening it and she is reading it Mister Blind Johnny Knoll. She is reading it rapturously Mister Blind Johnny Knoll. She is turning crimson because the letter enraptures her…

MBJK. And now? And now?

PK. And now…

MBJK. And now what? And now is she blushing a touch of crimson…?

PK. Well now. Now she is…She is…Oh well…

(PK *will not take her eyes off the reflection of* EH *in the window.*)

I'm afraid it is impossible to explain Mister Blind Johnny Knoll. If only I could…It really was something to see.

(MBJK *laughs in a sad pathetic way.*)

MBJK. I'm sure. I'm sure. I could tell that it was. Something.

(EH *must sit down in the corner after reading her letter. She begins to read it again and again and again.*)

PK. (*Speaking more to herself as she watches* EH *with rapt attention in the window's reflection:*) Winter Winter Everywhere
And not a drop to drink…

MBJK. What is that…?

PK. It's a joke. Just a little joke with myself.

MBJK. Oh yes. I get it. I get the joke. (*he he*) Winter Winter Everywhere…

PK. (*Transfixed by the sight of* EH *in the window.*) Mister Blind Johnny Knoll. I do believe you were right about Miss Haggis. When you can catch a gander of her, she really is… Something.

MBJK. Isn't she though? She's the kind of woman who. Well. She's the kind of woman who is really. (*He can't think of anything.*) Something.

PK. There will be something quite…Tragic. About her…

MBJK. There will?

PK. In my novel.

MBJK. Oh. That novel. You're still gunna make it a tragedy Miss Khenghis.

PK. Of course it's a tragedy. It's a love story.

MBJK. Wull. I wouldn't mind something a bit. Oh. I don't know. Something a bit happier.

PK. (*Turning away from the window to speak to* MBJK.) What do you mean?

MBJK. Like a story about. How 'bout you write a story about a nice quiet winter on a nice quiet lake.

PK. …A nice quiet winter on a nice quiet lake…Who's going to be interested in that story.

MBJK. Oh. Wull. I s'pose you're right. No one wants to hear about someone…Boring…(*Perhaps more to himself:*) But then again…(*Calling out to* MISS HAGGIS:) Miss Haggis! Miss Haggis! When you are finished with your letter, I would love to get a moment with you! We can start making plans to load in the coal shed and get those pantry floors cleaned for the food store. Nothin' like getting' ready for a long cozy winter!

(EH *does not look up from her letter.*)

PK. She's not listening to you Mister Blind Johnny Knoll.

MBJK. No. No. She's not. Well I'll tell her as soon as she's done with her letter…

PK. What? What will you tell her?

MBJK. I'll tell her…I don't know. I don't know what I'll tell her but I'll tell her. Wull. Ya know. If I could say one thing, I would say…

PK. What? What would you say?

MBJK. I would say. I would say… "I stopped expecting fascinating for my life too."

(*It is only dusk outside, perhaps four o'clock. PK looks at EH smiling and rereading the letter. She closes the curtains suddenly and turns around to* MBJK.)

PK. Too late. Night's long since fallen…Time for bed. Hup! Hup!

MBJK. Already…?!

PK. You know winter…

MBJK. Winter winter everywhere and not a drop to drink…?

PK. It gets dark so early now…

MBJK. So early now…

PK. So early now so…

MBJK. Morning into Evening. So quickly! But I get nothing done between the sleeping.

PK. You're the one who wanted a nice quiet winter.

MBJK. But I was hoping to. Get in a word with Miss Haggis.

PK. You don't want to *get in a word with her*. You want to walk over and *woo* her Mister Blind Johnny Knoll. Walk over and place your arms around her waist and whisper the words: "I find you comely." Ladies love that Mister Blind Johnny Knoll. Ladies love a man who is forward.

(MBJK *stands and contemplates action.* EH *continues to read her letter.*)

MBJK. Yes then. I can be forward. I can tell her she's "comely." One need only be a forward man to make these simple things move forward.

(*Pause.*)

But don't be ridiculous Miss Khenghis. I—I…I'm just not entirely sure how I would go about it so…Better to wait until…Until…

PK. Goodnight Mister Blind Johnny Knoll.

MBJK. Yes then. Better just to say goodnight. For now. Much better. Goodnight Miss Khenghis.

(MBJK *pads away up the stairs.* PK *looks after him and then opens the curtains for the last gasp of day.* EH *is back from the far corners of the room.*)

PK. Any news. From your correspondent?

EH. Hmm. Oh no.

PK. Funny. I almost thought. Well. Never mind. It's not my place.

EH. What's that Miss Khenghis…?

PK. I almost thought for a moment that your letter was from a suitor...

EH. Hmmm. A suitor? Me?

PK. Just for a moment. The way your cheeks turned a touch of crimson...

EH. Oh no. Miss Khenghis. No suitors for me. Just a cousin with a post box in town.

PK. Hmmm. And what's the news from town. I'm always curious about the folks at Macauley's.

EH. But you're not...Miss Khenghis.

PK. Excuse me.

EH. You're not curious about the news from the folks at Macauley's. When was the last time you went to see your father?

PK. ...I couldn't say...

EH. Curious huh? You want to hear what it says in my letter?

PK. Very much.

> *(Pause.)*

EH. I didn't want to be the one to tell you then Miss Khenghis but since you asked. The news in my letter, news from town, is that your father is dying of The Fever. He's been sick with The Fever for some months now. It's not getting any better. Dizzy Spells. Delusions. My cousin said you haven't been in once to see him.

PK. That's the news in your letter. From your cousin in town.

EH. You should go into town and stay with him Miss Khenghis. Take a day or two. He doesn't even have a nursemaid. He hasn't got anything and he's all alone in that *dirty wood shack* where you grew up.

> *(Pause.)*

PK. Thank you for the news Miss Haggis. It's a real shame what can happen to a working man with The Fever.

EH. Isn't it though. A real darn shame...

> *(MBJK calls out.)*

MBJK. Miss Haggis! Miss Haggis!

> *(He appears in his long johns peeking around the corner.)*

MBJK. Excuse me for appearing in these indecent undergarments. I just wanted to tell you something...I wanted to say...

> *(EH and PK turn to look at MBJK while he stands in an uncomfortable growing panic.)*

I wanted to say...Nothing. Nothing. Never mind...Miss Khenghis: I am having a devil of a time getting myself to sleep. I would greatly appreciate a nip from the flask? Just because of this sleeping disease that has overcome me...

PK. Just a nip for tonight Mister Blind Johnny Knoll.

(PK *goes to a drawer. She pulls out a silver flask and hands it to* MBJK. *He takes a quick nip and hands it back to* PK. *She puts it away.*)

MBJK. It's ah. Miss Haggis. Miss Haggis?

EH. Yes Mister Blind Johnny Knoll?

MBJK. It's ah. Getting harder and harder to find the sweet land of Nod these days…HA! (*An awkward little pause.*) Er. Never mind. I mean. Goodnight.

    (*He is gone.*)

EH. Goodnight Mister Blind Johnny Knoll! (*She turns back to* PK.) It's only coming around dusk Miss Khenghis.

PK. That it is.

EH. And Mister Blind Johnny Knoll is going to bed…?

PK. He told me he was tired.

EH. He can't just sleep the day away.

PK. No. No. But. He's old. He just wants a nip, that's all.

EH. (*She sniffs.*) You shouldn't indulge him like that. You shouldn't let an old man sleep the day away. Pretty soon he'll have no life except sleep and dreams.

    (PK *wanders over to the window.*)

PK. Let him have some pleasure.

EH. Doesn't sound like pleasure to me.

PK. Let an old man live out his last days in ignorance. Sounds like bliss to me.

EH. You're one to talk about ignorance Miss Khenghis. The way your own father sits and waits for you with The Fever.

PK. Yep. Yep. Just like you said. (*She blows more fog into the windowpane and she writes and speaks the following words: Dizzy Spells! Delusions! My father and The Fever!*) Do be sure to tell me when you get more news on him. Miss. Haggis.

    (EH *goes to a special chest or drawer set she has in the room and pulls out her own set of stationery for correspondence. It is nothing fancy, the simplest of writing sheets and paper.*)

EH. Well then I will. I'll write my cousin right now and I will find out just exactly what is happening with Old Man Khenghis and all the other…What was the word you used in that showboat story? Oh yep. Yep. "Windbags." I'll ask my cousin about all of the windbags.

    (PK *walks to a chair and she begins to knit something as she watches* EH *out of the corner of her eye. A look of great joy is quietly passing over* EH's *face. It is growing dark outside. The revving up of the Sanagret's "toboggan motor" is beginning.*)

Scene 4
A Winter Ain't A Winter With A Letter From The Likes Of You
MISS HAGGIS *responds.*

EH is in a small pool of light. Perhaps PK is still visible in the background. It is even more likely that the sound of PK's knitting needles is still audible.

Dear Mister Alfred Sonneville,

Your letter took me by great surprise. I don't often receive letters of courtship from people I don't know. (*A little pause.*) But I am happy to be your personally spiced bowl of stew. I can't say that so many other people have found me to be the right taste but that doesn't bother me so much. So many people in this life are just consumed with their own happenings. Sometimes I wish everyone would just look around and see outside those petty vanities.

Listen to me now. I am sure you will see that I have strong opinions about the likes of things and I hope that doesn't bother you. I can't say that so many people have taken to me. That's all right I s'pose. Most people develop charm so they can get out of their chores. I don't mind doing my chores so much. I work hard and for that I deserve to be as upright and uppity as I want to be.

I wonder where you live in Houghton County. Sometime in the future I will buy meat for Mister Knoll at the butcher down on Orchard and I wonder if maybe you will see me there. Sometimes I wonder if you are the butcher. Maybe you are the man who makes the leather saddles at Boomers? You're prol'y not the Marquette butcher…

I think you'll find me fairly easy to get on with because I'm no delicate flower. I don't expect fancy hats and candies like the girls at the Creever's Formals. I just wanted to feel comfortable writing to you, just the way I do. I imagined things working out for me in this way and I can't help but feel that, because I imagined it, the Lord on high has made it come true. The eye of the Lord can turn a hearty imagination into a whole load of happy luck.

Yours in fondness,

Miss Eugenia Haggis

(*She pulls an old photograph of herself out of the box. She stares at it for a moment. She returns to the paper.*)

P.S. I do not have a photograph of myself so I will have to leave you with the memories of me. I prol'y look better in your mind than I do in any photograph. HA!

(*She looks over that last joke. She decides it is too bold. She takes it out by crumpling that sheet.*)

P.S. Maybe you are the Marquette butcher…

(It is now dark outside. She seals the letter. PK's knitting clicks away in the shadows. Blackout.)

Scene 5
Oh I Know The Way This Feels This Feels Like Winter

The snowmobiles are out in full force and they are sputtering away on the lake, getting ready for their nightly ride. PK presses her hand against the chilly glass of the window.

EH *holds a large white letter.*

EH. I'm…I'm just gunna bring this letter out to the box…

PK. Don't take that letter outside now…

EH. I've got to get this letter out to the box tonight.

PK. It's almost dark out there Miss Haggis. It's almost dark and—

EH. Wull I'll just take a lantern to make it down the lane.

PK. But Miss Haggis. Miss Haggis…

EH. Yes Miss Khenghis?

PK. Remind me again…Why did your correspondent write to you?

EH. Oh. She just. Hears some news from time to time and she keeps a post box in town…

PK. Your. Cousin.

EH. My. Cousin.

> *(The two women look at each other for a moment. EH breaks the stare and calls out to* MBJK *in the kitchen.)*

Now I'm just gunna go and put this letter in the box. Don't even go dipping your finger in that stew Mister Blind Johnny Knoll. It needs to simmer for a touch before we can even go about dipping our fingers in.

MBJK. *(Entering the room:)* Thank you Miss Haggis.

> *(EH goes to put on a wool coat and a thick wool hat and she makes her way out the door, stopping for some galoshes. When she opens the door, the rev of the snowmobiles begins. She is gone for a moment.)*

MBJK. Dear Miss Haggis…I wonder what Miss Haggis would think of the thaw. I wonder what she would do with those blocks of ice from the thaw. Miss Khenghis? Don't you wonder?

PK. *(Staring after* EH *in the window:)* Yep. I wonder that all the time.

MBJK. She would enjoy the spring so much more than the winter. Considering how handy she can be with the coal shed, imagine what she would do with the spring bloom. Can you imagine what she might do with some of those seedlings from the spring bloom?

PK. *(Still looking after* EH:*)* Hmm…Spring seedlings…Fascinating.

MBJK. I should really ask Miss Haggis to stay on and board past the winter.

PK. *(Jolted out of looking out the window.)* What?!

MBJK. Miss Haggis. Stayin' on past the winter.

PK. But I can stay on and board as well Mister Blind Johnny Knoll.

MBJK. You? You'll finish your novel and move on...

PK. Well sure. *(Maybe.)* But until then. I can stay on and board here.

MBJK. No. No. No. You'll write your way to fame and fortune. Someday maybe you'll write the real story of my life on the lake. Write that story but give me the funny lines...Lines like...Oh well. I can't think of anything. Never mind. You'll write and you'll live and you'll go where your fate takes you...

PK. ...My fate...

(Outside, there is a sharp rev of the snowmobile disappearing into the night. It is suddenly extremely silent. EH comes back inside the front door. She has been running and she is breathless and red with cold. She shuts the door and she begins to weep.)

EH. I'm...Oh boy...Oh boy...I'm sorry to be...I really don't feel comfortable causing such a stir like this...

(MBJK stands frozen and speechless, incapable of offering comfort to EH.)

It's just that they were following me and they...They told me they wanted to marry me...Those Sanagret boys...And it's not that I could care a rat's tail...What they say doesn't bother me any more than anyone else but they...They wanted to hurt me...

(MBJK attempts a gesture of comfort to EH.)

MBJK. But Miss Haggis...I—I

EH. *(She begins to regain some strength and anger.)* Cause I knew John-O Sanagret from the grade school in town and he's just about the meanest slice of sin I ever met. He's just a mean old slice of sin and his brothers are no good either and they used to tease me back then...Said I was an eyesore...But...But...Good Lord on high...They really wanted to hurt me...For no good reason at all...Just...Bored...They might have killed me. Dead.

MBJK. You're—you're...Miss Haggis. You're—

EH. Yessir Mister Blind Johnny Knoll. My apologies for the outburst and the display and all. I just. I was just taken by surprise. But they won't stop me. I'll just go about my chores the way I always have. I can't imagine that they'll keep this up. After all, it is me. HA! Sooner or later I'll just bore them to death...

PK. You. You. You were just consumed. By turmoil. Miss Haggis.

EH. Turmoil huh? I guess. Turmoil.

PK. What will you do next?

EH. Wull. (*Pause.*) I think I'll see about living with my cousin. The cousin with the post office box in town. Maybe.

(EH *still holds the letter in her hands.*)

PK. Oh Miss Haggis! Why don't you let me mail your letters from now on? Those Sanagret boys don't even see me. I'm practically invisible.

EH. You can mail this for me tonight?

PK. The sooner you give it to me, the sooner I can mail it.

EH. …All right then. Miss Khenghis. That's. Nice of you. She's. My older cousin. She's waiting on word and she'll be…Anxious.

PK. Sure. Sure. Old ladies are always anxious for word. To be honest, I'm anxious for word, too…About my father.

EH. Thank you Miss Khenghis…I shouldn'ta yelled out at them. Got too big for my britches. But still.

PK. It sounds like you have a place to go if it gets too dangerous out there…

EH. I. Do. I really do.

(EH *hands* PK *the big white letter. Perhaps a spotlight appears to accentuate the scrawl of the cursive spelling out the letters: "A. Sonneville.")*

MBJK. But. But you're not. You're not really leaving us Miss Haggis. Are you?

EH. The only thing I'm doing right now is serving you up some shanks and beets Mister Blind Johnny Knoll.

MBJK. Exactly. Let's. Let's get more shanks and beets on the stove. Let's do that. As soon as possible Miss Haggis. I've got something I need to say to you. And it is. It is. (*Pause. Panic. Pause.*) I want to say that I'm hungry! And I. I. I don't appreciate it when you keep me waiting for supper.

(MBJK *begins to exit towards his room in an awkward huff.*)

EH. (*Calling after him:*) I'll just. Get my nerves in order here. Need to just serve you up some shanks and beets and scrub down the pantry and (*Her voice fades away as she heads to the kitchen area offstage.*) But I do have a place to go…

(PK *is left alone on stage. She holds the big, white envelope in her hands. She puts on her "winter" clothing and pretends to get ready to go out.*)

PK. MISS HAGGIS! I'M GOING DOWN THE LANE NOW! I'M GOING DOWN THE LANE NOW TO PUT YOUR LETTER IN THE BOX.

EH. THANK YOU MISS KHENGHIS…THANKS A WHOLE LOAD!

(PK *opens the door to the cold. She considers the outside world. She shuts it and stands perfectly still with the letter in her hand. The bright silent light from the unseen snowmobile shines directly in her face. She lets out a startled, almost silent scream of surprise. She opens the windows and snow begins to blow in around her. The voice calls out to her from the snowmobile.)*

VOICE. Is that nobody…

PK. Yes…

VOICE. Are you from the *back of Macauley's* Miss Nobody?

PK. …No.

VOICE. Why don't you come outside and mail that letter…Come outside…

PK. …Not tonight…

VOICE. You are from the back of Macauley's aren't you Miss Nobody…

PK. No. No. I'm not.

> (*Pause.*)

VOICE. I have one more question for you, Nobody…

PK. All right…

VOICE. *Who do you think you are…?*

> (*The lights go out immediately and the snow toboggan groans away in the dark. There is the sound of a spoon scraping against a bowl as* MBJK *finishes his shanks and beets somewhere in another room.* EH's *scrub brush and water splash and swish against the floor of the pantry even further away.* PK *is left standing at the open window. She looks at the letter. She opens it.*)

Scene 6
Don't Matter Much Where I Look For You.
Feels To Me Like I'm Always Alone.

MISS KHENGHIS *responds.*

PK *writes a letter by candlelight.*

Dear Miss Eugenia Haggis,

I imagine you consumed by a passionate turmoil.

> (*A strange moment for* PAULINE. *She looks at this phrase. She scratches it out and begins again.*)

I have a father but I am failing him. I do not have a big enough heart to love him without…shame. I am so greatly afear'd that my connections in the world will all blow away like pieces of laundry whipped away in the wind…I have…Not wanted to be close to anyone who remembers the person I used to be. The person I used to be was. …Despicable…

…This courtship has taken on the momentum of a new pony. I never intend to tell you the things that I tell you but they come out like this. I need to tell you that you will not be anyone's old maid, Miss Eugenia Haggis. I need you to know that, no matter what fears are in your heart, you will not slip away from me in the bone cold wind. We will go on and on like this until our courtship flowers into something strange like spring.

Always,

Alfred

> (*She seals the letters and smudges the postmark. She writes "Miss Eugenia Haggis" on the front in the same loving cursive. She blows out the candle.*)

Scene 7
Yep. Yep. It's Just That Way You Said It Was Going To Be.

The dead of winter, as always. It is growing dark, again the dusk hour of three or four. MBJK enters from the outdoors carrying the second letter.

PK. Is that another letter Mister Blind Johnny Knoll?

MBJK. Oh dear. It. Seems to be. *Another* letter.

PK. *Another* letter. (*She takes it from him.*) For Miss Haggis. (*Calling out:*) Miss Haggis! Miss Haggis! You received another letter!

> (*EH enters eagerly.*)

EH. Oh! Oh! Thank you Miss Khenghis.

> (*She tries to take the letter from PK but there is some resistance.*)

PK. Maybe you can. Read it out loud with us?

EH. Please. Give it to me Miss Khenghis.

PK. Don't you want to. Share it with *me?*

EH. With *you* Miss Khenghis?! You don't even know how to share the washroom. (*Grabbing the letter out of her hands.*) And I'd appreciate it if you wouldn't get your pasty little hands all over my things.

> (*EH exits somewhere to read her letter.*)

MBJK. Another letter. If she received another letter, I better...I better...

PK. (I know how to...share.)

> (*MBJK takes out a lockbox of money and begins to count out bills. PK stares after EH and then picks up her notebook. She attempts to write something but her mind wanders off in the direction of EH.*)

MBJK. Two. Three. Four. Five.

PK. (*Staring at her notebook without writing.*) Do you have to count out loud Mister Blind Johnny Knoll?

MBJK. Twelve, Eleven, Ten...

PK. I can't concentrate when you count out loud.

MBJK. Nineteen, Seventeen, Fifteen...

PK. Oh! It's useless! (*She looks down at her notebook and starts to tear it apart.*) ...Without her...It's just...

> (*MBJK continues to pull out the coins from the bottom of the box. PK turns her attention to him.*)

You have too many bills saved. You know that, don't you Mister Blind Johnny Knoll.

MBJK. This money is going towards the two-lb bags of seedling that they sell in the back of Macauley's.

PK. The back of Macauley's? Since when do you shop at the back of the Macauley's?

MBJK. I think she'd like some of the spring shipment from the back of Macauley's…Like those 5-lb bags of the corn meal mush?

PK. But you could do something. Beautiful. With that money. You could buy her a beautiful set of pink pearls. Like the kind that come in the dainty velvet sacks on the top shelf of Creevers. (*She tries to write the following down in her notebook.*) "A-dainty-velvet-sack-of-pearls."

MBJK. Miss Khenghis. Decent lakeside folks don't require all that hoopla.

PK. *Decent lakeside folks.* (*She shudders and turns quickly to* MBJK.) Well! Look at that moon! Time for one decent lakeside folk to head to bed Mister Blind Johnny Knoll.

MBJK. Up the stairs to stardom?

PK. Up the stairs to stardom.

MBJK. But I need to. There's still. Oh well…Up the stairs to stardom. Up the stairs to stardom. Goodnight Miss Khenghis.

> (MBJK *exits.* PK *sits alone in the room.*)

PK. (*To herself:*) Goodnight Mister Blind Johnny Knoll.

> (EH *reenters carrying her opened letter.*)

EH. Ah. Miss Khenghis.

PK. Yes?

EH. I. I. I need to ask you for a favor.

PK. …All right.

EH. If you're busy with your. Daydreaming. We can just. We don't have to do it now.

PK. No. I'm not doing anything. At all.

EH. Well. The other day. You said a word: *Bliss.*

PK. …Bliss.

EH. Yes. That word. Well. What did you say about it?

PK. I said. *Sounds like bliss to me.*

EH. What do you mean. Oh. Never mind…

> (EH *exits in an awkward huff.* PK *goes back to her notebook. She keeps attempting to put words to paper.*)

PK. (*Writing as she speaks:*) She was overcome with bliss upon receiving the dainty velvet sack of pearls. Her bliss was a feeling that could only be described as...*Relief after dismay*...(*She looks this over. She says the words out loud with some reservation about their accuracy:*) *Relief after dismay*...?

    (MBJK *enters.*)

MBJK. Miss Khenghis?...Is it morning yet?

PK. Nope...It's the dead of the night.

MBJK. I'm. Ah...Er. I wouldn't mind a few nips from the flask before I actually face. Miss Haggis.

PK. (*Pulling out the flask.*)...Take as many as you need Mister Knoll...

MBJK. Really?

PK. Really. (PK *looks down at what she has just written and she takes a long swig of the flask before handing it to* MBJK.) If we take quite a few, we'll sleep right through our dreams.

MBJK. Thank you once again for the nips Miss Khenghis. Thank you ever so much...

    (MBJK *exits.* PK *returns to her notebook to look over the last phrase.* EH *comes in with a new sense of determination.*)

EH. Okay then. Okay. Here goes: What do you mean exactly when you say bliss?

PK. Surely you know bliss?

EH. Of course I know bliss but I mean...As a writer. How do you. Describe it.

PK. ...*Relief after dismay.*

EH. Oh. Huh. Okay.

PK. Do you know dismay? Miss Haggis?

EH. ...Yes.

PK. What do you know of dismay Miss Haggis?

EH. I know...Something of it.

PK. Now think of the moment after dismay. The moment the dismay disappears.

EH. ...Well now. All right. But then. That's right now. That's... (*She starts laughing.*) Right now. And now! And now! HA!

PK. Are you...In a state of bliss Miss Haggis?

EH. Well no. But then. It's with me. Something was with me and now something new is with me. Miss Khenghis.

PK. Yes?

EH. Will you. How does one. Write this. Feeling. In a letter?

PK. (*Looking again with even more doubt at her notebook:*) Bliss? Well—

EH. HA!...Bliss. Yes. HA!...But how does one. Tell this to someone. This? Right now. I would like to say something. I would like to say something like...Now I know what the people were talking about when they talked about...Life. HA! People always said "That's life"...And now I know what they mean. Because. It's...

PK. ...It's what?...Miss Haggis.

EH. How do I write. I want to write someone and I want to tell them that they have made me. Happy. How do I do that?

> (*Pause.*)

PK. I don't know Miss Haggis...You tell me.

> (*It is growing dark outside. The revving up of the Sanagret's "toboggan motor" begins.*)

Scene 8
The Snow And The Ice And It's Still Getting Dark

MISS HAGGIS *responds.*

Perhaps EH*'s bun is let down from her hair and a long, thick braid hangs down the side of her white cotton nightgown? She writes by the light of a lantern. The scratching sound of calligraphy pen against paper is remarkable.*

Dear Alfred,

Truth be told, I've never had much family myself. I don't know that you need them. Or, least, I didn't. I think it's a big ole waste of time to worry about the things that might have been. Alls I know is that (*Pause.*) I feel real relief after dismay when I write to you. I felt relief after dismay all day.

> (*She looks that over. It is dissatisfying to her. She crosses it out. She tries again.*)

All's I know is that writing to you is the way it must feel for those thirsty folks who fall down deep in the Houghton County well. They fall down deep with water enough to last a whole lifetime.

Yours in fondness,

> (*She pauses and rewrites.*)

My one true love.

Eugenia.

Scene 9
You See Me You Know Me

PK *is in the room reading* EH*'s letter by the window.*

PK. My. One. True. Love...

> (MBJK *begins to call out.* PK *hides in the room and eavesdrops on the conversation that ensues between* EH *and* MBJK. *She grips the letter the entire time.*)

MBJK. Miss Khenghis? Miss Khenghis?

EH. Say there Mister Blind Johnny Knoll.

MBJK. Oh dear. Excuse me. I was just...I was just having a difficult time sleeping. I was going to ask Miss—

> (*Pause.*)

EH. Is there something I can do for you Mister Blind Johnny Knoll?

MBJK. No. Yes. I. I. I'm just...So happy it's you.

EH. Oh. Wull. All right then.

MBJK. I've been. Thinking of things to say to you. All winter.

EH. Really? What kinds of things?

MBJK. Well...Like...I forgot.

> (*He starts laughing. She looks at him and laughs as well.*)

EH. Sounds like a pretty interesting conversation.

MBJK. Oh dear yes. I'm afraid that's all I'm good for...

EH. What's that?

MBJK. ...(*A pathetic little joke.*) I forgot!

> (*They both laugh again. This time they laugh at the same time. There is a little pause.*)

EH. Wull...

MBJK. Yep?

EH. Is that what you were going to say?

MBJK. Oh. Yep well. Never mind.

> (MBJK *stumbles away. He stops. He turns around and speaks quickly.*)

I-stopped-expecting-fascinating-for-my-life-too.

EH. Oh. Huh...I wonder why Mister Blind Johnny Knoll...

MBJK. ...Oh. Wull then...So do I...Miss Eugenia Haggis.

> (*Pause.*)

EH. Get yerself back to your bed now Mister Blind Johnny Knoll.

MBJK. Oh good. Yes then. Very good. All right.

EH. Yer gunna catch a chill in those *indecent undergarments*! HA!

MBJK. HA! Yep. HA! ...I was planning to ask Miss Khenghis for the flask but I...I don't think I want it anymore.

> (MBJK *gives a gallant little tip of the hat to* EH *as he exits to his room. She laughs and watches him. She heads back to the kitchen.* PK *watches them disappear from the room. She looks down at the letter in her hands. She goes to her notebook and she stares at it. She opens the window and throws it out into the dark night sky with a sense of great freedom and relief. The papers dance as if choreographed and float away in the night.*)

> (PK *races for her own hard, square travel suitcase. She makes hasty preparations to leave; perhaps she throws some disheveled things in the suitcase*

quickly. She puts on her winter gear with a growing sense of urgency. She is about to open the door when the lights from the toboggan shine on her from outside.)

VOICE. I know you. You're *Cold Fish Khenghis.* From the back of Macauley's. *Pauline Cold Fish Khenghis.* (*The* VOICE *starts laughing.*)

PK. I'm not…I'm not…A cold fish…Anymore.

VOICE. Why don't you tell that to your father *Cold Fish Khenghis?*

PK. I—I—I— will…

VOICE. Why don't you tell him about *love?*

PK. I WILL! I WANT TO! I WILL I WILL I WILL!

VOICE. Come outside *Cold Fish Khenghis*…

PK. …Not yet.

VOICE. …Come outside…

PK. …I want to…

VOICE. I have a present for you if you come outside.

PK. …You can give it to me right here.

VOICE. Be careful. This is a present just for you.

> (*A giant hand in a thick leather mitten appears through the window. It is holding a ridiculously dainty white envelope. PK takes the letter.*)

VOICE. A letter addressed to *you* Miss Pauline Khenghis.

> (*The light of the snow toboggan suddenly turns off and there is only silence and darkness outside. She waits for the rev of the motor to sound. There is nothing. She waits. Nothing.*)

PK. PLEASE!

VOICE. (*Too close for comfort:*) Please what Miss Khenghis…

PK. PLEASE GOD! …DON'T LET IT BE TOO LATE…!

VOICE. My condolences. Pauline.

> (*She stares down at the dainty envelope in her hands. EH enters and she sees the envelope.*)

EH. Miss Khenghis! Give me my letter.

PK. I just…

EH. Give it to me!

PK. Oh Miss Haggis. Please. Please tell me how to. How do I. I want you to tell me how to. I'm! Miss Haggis! I'm! I want to go home and I want to tell him—

Please how do I say: I'm sorry? Tell me how to say I'm sorry. So that it sounds real.

EH. Sorry? Say sorry for what?

PK. Everything. Everything is my fault. Everything that happens to everyone…Is my fault.

EH. You think that everything that happens to everyone is *your* fault?

PK. Yes I do.

EH. (*Taking the letter out of her hands.*) *Who do you think you are?*

> (*She begins to walk away with the letter. She stops in her tracks when she looks down at the address.*)

EH. (*Reading the name:*) Miss. Pauline. Khenghis.

> (EH *returns the letter to* PK. *She opens it and pulls out a small, gold embossed stationary card.*)

PK. "Dear Miss Khenghis. We regret to inform you that your father, Arthur Khenghis, passed away last night at 3 a.m. He had been suffering from delusions and dizzy spells associated with The Fever for a number of months. We were not able to contact you so we asked members of the Sanagret Family to deliver this letter to you across the lake. Please let us know how we can assist you in this time of need. Sincerely, Members of the Town Council and Ladies of the Junior League."

> (*Pause.*)

EH. Wull then…(*She tries to give* PK *a little tap on the shoulder.*) My heart is with you Miss Khenghis…

PK. He's…Gone?

EH. I did try to warn you…

PK. … All this time…?

EH. You didn't never once go to visit…

PK. …But I was…I was going to…Say…

EH. I'm real sorry…It's a…It's a real loss…

PK. Get…away…

> (*Pause.*)

EH. Gladly…Miss Khenghis…

> (PK *watches* EH *exit before she begins crying. She opens her suitcase and begins to throw her clothing out onto the floor in a chaotic mess. Her frenzied tantrum grows more powerful as she undoes all of* EH's *tidying and straightening in the house. The dining room is now even more disheveled than it was at the opening.* PK *sits down to write the last letter.*)

Scene 10
The Darkest Day

MISS KHENGHIS *responds.*

Greetings to you Miss Haggis,

> (*She looks at this for a long moment. She begins again.*)

Dearest Eugenia Haggis,

(PK *stops. Pause. She begins to write again without any artifice.*)

The straight up truth is: I'm just real lonely. My life just goes on by like this and I am so lonely...I don't have a thing to say to anyone anymore but you...I try to talk but...You. Are my only. Comfort. In this world...

(*Pause.*)

I want to change my devilish ways. I want to change these habits of daydreaming dramatics. I would like to be a different person. I want you to make me different. I want you to make me. Happy.

(*Pause. PK gets up and walks over to MBJK's lockbox of money. She takes it out and empties it of all its contents. She gathers the bills together in a bundle and slides them in the envelope.*)

Please be my wife please and make me different. I am including some money for the train fare to the station near my homestead #RR34 Crossing (and a little extra for a wedding trousseau!) My cousin is a preacher and he can align us for eternity just as soon as you get here. If you take the Thursday train, we can be joined in holy matrimony by midnight.

Together forever thanks to imagination and the eye of the Lord,

Most Sincerely.

Me

Scene 11
Everywhere I Go It's Just As Cold As Bones

EH is standing in the room with her hard suitcase and a traveling coat. She hands PK a list. As the scene continues, it grows dark outside.

EH. I believe that's everything...Mister Knoll will be able to bring in someone new after the lake ice melts..."Til then you two should make it through the winter with the supplies in the pantry and the salted meat stored in the cellar...Means you're in charge of the house now Miss Khenghis...Means you better wash down that pantry...Don't let the water freeze!...Time to get down to work Miss Khenghis! Time to put in some elbow grease! You told me you wanted to change and one way to be different is to get your chores done. No use pondering the universe if your pantry floor is dirty...Let's see. Let's see...Shanks on the stove...Should last at least three days...That is, if Mister Blind Johnny Knoll doesn't ask for seconds. He will ask for seconds but I just say no. Lately, I'll give him half of the first for firsts and then I'll give him the second half of the firsts for seconds...He doesn't know any better...

PK. (*Looking at the list:*) And the coal...?

EH. The coal. I wrote something down about the coal didn't I?

PK. No. Nothing about the coal...

EH. Well (*She sniffs.*) You'll just have to do it yourself then. I don't have time to be down there demonstrating the coal shed...

PK. No. You don't...

EH. You're gunna get all up in arms about it I'm sure but. That's just the way it is...

PK. No. No. I understand the way it is...

EH. But I'm sure you're ready to fight me on it tooth and nail...

PK. No. No. We'll manage. Last thing you need to worry about right now is the coal...

> (*Pause.*)

EH. Well. Thank you Miss Khenghis. That's real nice of you. I just. I just sewed this new dress and I'd be a fool to wear it down in the coal shed...

> (EH *takes her winter cloak off and she is, indeed, wearing a brown velvet dress. It is flattering.*)

PK. It's really lovely Miss Haggis. It's really very lovely and pretty on you.

EH. Oh now. I'm too smart to hear words like "lovely" and "pretty." I'll tell you what it is: It is a good solid dress and I look good and solid inside it.

PK. Yes. But. You should know Miss Haggis. It's. It's more than that because the brown really does make your eyes look. Your eyes look quite beautiful in that dress. They look rich and dark and...Your eyes look like velvet.

> (EH *considers this. She walks to a mirror. She inspects.*)

EH. Normally I wouldn't even bother to check but...

PK. They really do look like velvet. Your...cousin will be so happy to see you.

> (*Pause.*)

EH. It's not my cousin. Today. Today...It's my wedding dress Miss Khenghis.

PK. Oh! Miss Haggis...!

EH. Now why did I just say that out loud. I didn't mean to say that out loud.

PK. But that's wonderful.

EH. Oh now. Well yes. It is. I didn't mean to tell *you* about it but...

PK. That's really wonderful...How. Did the two of you meet?

EH. We met at. He ran into me up in Calumet while I was running some errands and then he...We kept up a correspondence and...Like that...I feel silly I even brought it up seeing as it hasn't happened yet and...Bad luck and all...

PK. There's no bad luck! There is only...Imagination and the eye of the Lord.

EH. Well of course but (EH *considers PK for the briefest of all brief moments.*)

Miss Khenghis. Miss Khenghis have you been reading my letters?

PK. ...No...Yes.

EH. *Miss Pauline Khenghis.*

PK. And I want you to know. He really loves you. He really really loves you. In a way. I just. I just didn't know existed before I met you.

(*EH takes in this information.*)

EH. But there's always the little fear. What if I get there and we. We're like strangers to each other...?

PK. I feel. Fear in the important things too.

EH. But. You're about the last person who would get on a train for a wedding on some strange man's homestead...You must think I'm about the biggest (*She starts laughing.*) I just realized I have no idea what you think. Well your father and now...I'm real sorry about the hand you're holding these days Miss Khenghis. Can't say I understand it but I'm sorry for it...Too bad we never...Oh well. Jes' don't say anything to anyone. Please.

PK. ...I won't...

EH. Don't say anything until I'm really gone. More than gone.

(*Pause.*)

PK. But you're not really going...Are you?

EH. Wull sure...The train leaves at six.

PK. You can't walk to the station in the dark...

EH. I'm gunna have to...

PK. You can't Miss Haggis...You have to walk across the lake...

EH. If it's not the Sanagrets, it's something else...If it's not one thing, it's another...

PK. They'll see you Miss Haggis...You know they'll see you...

EH. Don't much matter Miss Khenghis. For the first time in my life, the Lord is really on my side. Out of the blue, the Lord sends me (*She speaks his name carefully.*) Alfred and I feel that the Lord is on my side.

PK. Alfred...You think that the Lord is on your side because of Alfred.

EH. ...I know it.

(*Pause.*)

PK. Your love. Miss Haggis. Your love story is. Beautiful.

EH. (*Another moment of consideration that ends before it begins.*) Maybe a love is waiting for you too, Miss Khenghis...Who knows Who knows?

PK. Who knows...

(*EH picks up her travel suitcase and puts her coat back on. She opens the door to the cold cold night.*)

EH. Now just remember Miss Khenghis.

PK. Yes?

EH. Just remember. Only half a shank for firsts. Half a shank for seconds…Ignorance is bliss. HA!

> (*She heads out the door. A flurry of icy winds comes into the house. It stops the minute she shuts the door. PK stands in the silence. The sound of EH's boots crunching against the hard packed snow. PK goes to the dark window and watches. The sound of the boots continues. A faint song? EH singing in the night? Suddenly the crunching of the boots stops. There is a bright flash of the snow toboggan light.*)

PK. (*Whispering:*) Eugenia…!

> (*The scene ends quickly in blackout.*)

Scene 12
This Is Not The Last Cold Night On Earth

It is later on the same evening. PK is staring out into the night. Outside it is dark and dead still. MBJK is sitting in a dark corner pretending to read a book. The title is upside down. They are both occupied with their activities for a moment before MBJK calls out.

MBJK. Miss Haggis! (*He waits a moment.*) There will be shanks…Yes? Miss Haggis…Shanks and beets?

> (*He waits another moment.*)

Miss Haggis?

> (*Pause.*)

PK. Miss Haggis is no longer with us…

MBJK. What?

PK. Miss Haggis has gone away…

MBJK. Where. Where did she go?

PK. I don't know. She's gone away…

MBJK. People always say that. But then they end up coming back. She'll be back yes?

PK. No. She's never coming back. She will never ever come back here.

MBJK. …Why?

PK. Miss Haggis found…Love.

MBJK. Love? Who loves her?

PK. Mister Alfred Sonneville. She left with her suitcase to marry him. She said she was taking the train to his homestead…

MBJK. …But she wouldn't have been safe…

PK. You might have stopped her but you must have been sleeping…

MBJK. …I guess so…Risking her life to meet some man she's never met…

PK. ...Yep...

MBJK. She must have told you something. She must have given you some kind of explanation...

PK. Mister Blind Johnny Knoll. Do I need to tell you what it's like to find love...?

MBJK. Of course not. But. Why not. Yes do. Please.

PK. She must have thought it was worth risking her life for him. And such a feeling must be. Love.

MBJK. I guess. Some people feel this way. Some lucky people...Good Lord. Good Lord Bless Our Miss Haggis.

(*Pause. They are quiet again. The silence outside is eerie and ominous.*)

I always. I always had it in the back of my mind to. Marry her myself.

PK. Why didn't you?

MBJK. I just. I kept meaning to and then. I don't know. She was a tidy woman. I was...fond of her.

PK. And now. She's *gone*...

MBJK. But I really. I meant to ask her to marry me. Miss Eugenia Haggis. I meant...Oh! Please! Please don't make me go to sleep yet...Just a few more minutes. I just want to get to the end of this chapter...

PK. Go right ahead Mister Blind Johnny Knoll...You want to stay up, you stay up. It doesn't matter anymore anyway.

MBJK. Oh thank you. Thank you Miss Khenghis. (MBJK *returns to his book for a moment. A pause. He looks up.*) It won't make me different though will it...

PK. What?

MBJK. Even if I do stay up. It won't change the fact that I would have been a flop with Miss Haggis and the spring thaw...I would have been a fool when I handed her those seedlings...I would have...Bought all the wrong bags...I would have planted every row wrong. I would have been...Yep. Yep. It would have been just as it has always been.

(MBJK *goes back to reading the upside down book.* PK *stares at him for a long time. She stays perfectly still. She calls out as if she has just found something important.*)

PK. It can't be...It cannot be...!

MBJK. What's that...?

PK. I just...I just found a letter addressed to you from Miss Haggis...It's a letter from...(*Saying her name with a new intimacy:*) Eugenia.

MBJK. Where?

PK. It just slid out from under the rug. It's just peeking out and I'm holding it in my hands now.

MBJK. Addressed to me...

PK. Addressed to you...I should read it. Yes?

MBJK. Well then. Yes. Yes. I suppose you should.

PK. (*Using a piece of paper to fabricate the sound of a letter opening, she begins to read a letter out loud. She does not ever pause or give any indication that the letter is fake.*)

Dear Mister Blind Johnny Knoll,

It is difficult to say good-bye to these desperately sad days. I understand you and, at some level, I do care for you but. Something strange has happened. Something strange and. Beautiful. I have finally allowed myself to reach out to another and, at this moment, I can finally experience the truth depths of...

     (*Pause.*)

Love.

     (*Pause.*)

Now I am risking everything I have to find him because, if I don't...If I don't...I will be forced to accept the fact that I am not courageous enough to ever truly love. Anyone.

     (*Pause.*)

Sincerely,

Miss Eugenia Haggis

     (*Pause.*)

PK. Well...

MBJK. Oh well. It's fine. It's fine. It doesn't matter. I'm almost gone anyway, you see. Or halfway done at least...

PK. And now she's gone...

MBJK. No. No. Better always. Better always to know the truth and to accept it. I know the truth and I accept it. God has punished me with life but redemption will come before long. I accept the truth...In fact. In fact. I will. I will surrender myself to the dream world now...Goodnight Miss Pauline Khenghis...

PK. It won't come for me. Redemption.

MBJK. Oh now. It'll come for you. It'll come after many many years of suffering. (*he he*) Goodnight Miss Khenghis.

     (MBJK *begins to get up. The snow toboggans rev up somewhere in the distance.*)

PK. Please. Stay up late and finish your book...

MBJK. Oh no. No. No point really...I've uh...Read it before.

     (*The noise comes closer.*)

PK. Stay with me...Please! Please!

MBJK. What?

PK. Tell me something! Talk to me! That book you're reading. What is it about?!

MBJK. Oh. Always the same. Always the same ending…

PK. (*PK walks over and opens the door. She contemplates the outside world.*) Does anyone die for love in your book?

MBJK. HA! Good Lord. No. No. It's nothing like your novel. This book is not nearly so…melodramatic.

PK. Why don't the characters die for love and do away with themselves…

MBJK. It's just. The way they are. They're actually fine when they don't expect too much. (*He begins to laugh. He laughs and laughs. It stops abruptly.*) I'll bet. I'll bet Miss Haggis is thanking her lucky stars she got away from me. I can't even stand the sound of my own voice… Say. There's a real chill in the air. Do you have the door open…?

> (*There is a silence. The motors rev up again in the distance. PK looks out into the night.*)

MBJK. No. No. The *real* story is just…It's just a dull story about. Decent lakeside folks. Who shouldn't expect so much…

> (*She shuts the door and lies back against a chair with her eyes closed.*)

Miss Khenghis….(*No response.*) Well then. Goodnight Miss Khenghis…Just the two of us now…All winter…Who knows…Who knows…(*In a singsong voice as he makes his way out of the room:*) Who knows who knows who know who knows…

> (*PK shivers visibly as she sits alone on stage. She blows fog onto the window and writes in the final words.*)

PK. The-secrets-fate-might-hold.

> (*The sound of the motor toboggans somewhere off in the distance.*)

End of Play

FREAKSHOW

by Carson Kreitzer

For more information about rights and permissions, see p. 10.

BIOGRAPHY

Carson Kreitzer's *The Love Song of J. Robert Oppenheimer* won the Rosenthal New Play Prize, the American Theatre Critics' Steinberg Citation, the Stavis Award, and is published in Smith and Kraus' "New Playwrights: Best Plays of 2004." *SELF DEFENSE or death of some salesmen* has been produced in Providence, Minneapolis, New York, Chicago, and Los Angeles, and is published by Playscripts and in *Smith and Kraus' Women Playwrights: Best Plays of 2002.* Other work includes *1:23, The Slow Drag* (New York and London), *Valerie Shoots Andy, Slither,* and *Take My Breath Away,* featured in BAM's 1997 Next Wave Festival. Ms. Kreitzer has received grants from NYFA, NYSCA, the NEA, TCG, and the Jerome and McKnight Foundations, as well as a BA from Yale University and an MFA from the Michener Center for Writers, UT Austin. She is a member of the Workhaus Collective, The Playwrights' Center, the Dramatists Guild, and New Dramatists, and proud to be a Clubbed Thumb affiliated artist since the very first Summerworks.

Other Clubbed Thumb credits: *Hervin/e (Keep Us Quiet)* (Summerworks '96); *Dead Wait* (Summerworks '97); *The Love Song of J. Robert Oppenheimer* (reading, Summerworks '01); *Flesh and the Desert* (Commission '02, Boot Camp at Summerworks '04); Clubbed Thumb Affiliated Artist.

ACKNOWLEDGMENTS

Freakshow was originally produced by Clubbed Thumb at the HERE Arts Center, New York, in July 1999. It was directed by Pam MacKinnon, with the following cast and staff:

AMALIA	Meg MacCary
AQUABOY THE HUMAN SALAMANDER	Shawn Fagan
THE PINHEAD	Frank Dowd
MR. FLIP	Steven Rattazzi
JUDITH	Lisa Rothe
MATTHEW	David Wilcox
THE GIRL	Carla Harting

Sets	Hallie Zieselman
Lights	D.M.Wood
Costumes	Jeanette MacDougall
Sound	Reed Robbins
Music	Grant Stewart
Dramaturg	Kathleen Tobin
Stage Manager	Thomas Rybert

CAST OF CHARACTERS

AMALIA, The Woman With No Arms Or Legs

JUDITH, The Dog-Faced Girl
> Rather, ex-the dog faced girl.
> Older now, she no longer performs, but takes care of Amalia, the new star of the show.

MR. FLIP, ringmaster/owner

MATTHEW, Whole
> He cleans the animals' cages.

THE PINHEAD

AQUABOY, The Human Salamander
> In a tank of water.

THE GIRL

David Wilcox, Meg MacCary, Lisa Rothe
in *Freakshow.*

Produced by Clubbed Thumb at the HERE Arts Center, 1999.
Photograph by Scott Adkins

FREAKSHOW

Scene 1

Vaudeville placard: THE WOMAN WITH NO ARMS OR LEGS. *Lights up slowly to reveal, atop a pedestal,* A WOMAN WITH NO ARMS OR LEGS. *She is dressed simply but well. After a while, she speaks.*

AMALIA. You are wondering if I have ever had sexual intercourse.

(*Pause.*)

Of course.

If it has occurred to you already, having only just met me, don't you think it would have occurred to someone before you? Some man some time, who would have found it quite easy to find me alone some night? Of course. Although I have no arms or legs the rest of me is quite normal. My face is even beautiful. I know this. People are not afraid of flattering me or giving me a swelled head, because I have no arms or legs. They don't even say it *to* me, really. I just hear them as they walk by. "MY GOD SHE'S BEAUTIFUL," they say to each other in varied tones of incredulity. How could a freak, they ask themselves, have been blessed with such beauty? That is why people are afraid of me.

I have a lover. As a matter of fact. A very sweet man. He is the man who cleans out the animals' cages. His name is Matthew. Good, solid, Biblical name. Ran away to join the circus. Or, more precisely, Mr. Flip's Freakshow and Travelling Jungle. Matthew said he fell in love with me the minute he saw me, but I think he just made that up later. I think he just wanted to get out of that little town. But he is in love with me now. Every night after he is finished shovelling out the elephant shit, he comes to see me. He washes himself thoroughly first. I am the only person who gets to see him clean. He spends all day in the mud. If you were to pass him by when you leave this tent, you would never guess he is my lover. He looks just like any other muddy boy during the day, but ah, you must see him at night.

He parts the curtain and tiptoes into the Hall of Freaks. I watch him walking toward me, hair still wet, clean pressed suit, love in his eyes. We are silent so as not to wake the others. Often the Pinhead is awake anyway, singing little songs to himself. Matthew lifts me up and carries me out, back to his bed. Pallet of sweet straw in the wagon. Listening to the animals settling into their sorrow for the night. Sweet good straw and to be off this...DISPLAY for precious moments, held. It's a bit of heaven. A small, manageable bit. Sometimes he takes me for a walk in the woods at night. If the weather is good, sometimes he lays me down and we make love in a field.

(*Smiles conspiratorially.*)

This is exciting because of the danger. How would he ever explain it if we got caught? It would look pretty bad for him. I would never be blamed—I have no arms or legs. I think the old farmer who discovered us would have a heart attack and die on the spot. Thinking he'd have to chase off a pair of young lovers and instead finding a man and a torso.

(*Laughs to herself. After a moment, turns her attention back to the audience.*)
You can tell that I am well taken care of. My appearance is neat. I am properly fed. That is all, by the way, because I am beautiful. I've no doubt that if I were born ugly I'd have been thrown in a pit before I was five. But, as I say, I am well taken care of. My hair is brushed. My teeth are brushed. I am washed. I am well taken care of. But there are some days, sitting here silent hour after hour being stared at, when I would gladly commit murder to be able to scratch my nose.

Only once have I been taken against my will. The night that Matthew sold me. It's actually not a very interesting story. I'd rather not go into it. Just what you'd think. You can fill in the details. Rich man in some town we passed through got that idea about me, the one we discussed earlier. Asked around, the boys shrugged, said Ask Matthew. Coincidentally, Matthew and I had fought bitterly the night before, about the Pinhead. I had hurt him very badly, so Matthew decided to hurt me back. He came in and warned me first, though. He was crying already. When the Rich Man came and took me, I didn't say a word. Didn't make a sound. I could have been the Mute with No Arms and No Legs for all he knew.

(*She finds this amusing.*)
In the end, it was much worse for Matthew. He cried at the foot of my pedestal all that night, and for many nights to come. It took me a while to forgive him. That was really a rotten thing to do, after all.

I was, uh, very frightened.

But I was morally in the right, and Matthew was not. That's why it was worse for him. He learned something about himself, something he didn't want to know. I certainly would never have guessed it was in him. After it happened I knew I shouldn't have been surprised, but I really believed that Matthew was one human being without that astounding capacity for cruelty.

I am in love with the Pinhead. That is the tragedy of my life. And perhaps it is also the tragedy of the man who cleans out the animals' cages, but I don't think so. He is still young. As am I, but I seem much older because I have never moved from this spot.

Matthew will leave the freakshow, whereas the Pinhead and I will not.

He is young and filled with belief. And love for me.

Jesus, he practically bursts with it.

One day he will notice the cruelty of an absent God and he will leave.

I know the Pinhead has the capacity for sexual intercourse because they have to put something in his food to keep him from playing with his thing while the audience is here.

(*Lights fade up on the* PINHEAD, *rocking and singing to himself. Frail and blonde, his head lolls a bit to one side.*)

PINHEAD. (*The song is simple but beautiful.*) La la la la. La la la.

AMALIA. I love to hear him sing.

I have never told him of my love because that would break his heart. He is neither tall enough to reach me here nor strong enough to carry me. If he were aware of the possibilities, he would go mad in his cage.

I am the only one strong enough to suffer in this love of ours.

Sometimes we speak. I ask him to sing songs for me. He likes that.

He is proud when he remembers things.

You've no idea what it takes not to go mad.

Many are. But I cannot go mad.

I have responsibilities.

(*Starts:*)

Oh—how rude of me.

Allow me to introduce my fellow abominations.

I believe you've already met—

THE PINHEAD

AQUABOY, THE HUMAN SALAMANDER.

(*Lights rise on a young man in a tank.*)

Kept in water from twelve to fourteen, who wouldn't turn some luminous pale shade of green, eyes growing bigger, breathing slowed. More often than not, the water was quite cold. Bringing up the blue blush under his translucent skin. Like a salamander, shifting blue to green. Biggest eyes you'd ever seen. After a year in the water, they begun to fleck with gold. Bulging beautiful like the eyes of a toad. The angle of his neck, head floating on water. Everything changed. Once you got used to it, it was even colder out than in. He'd piss in the water, trying to make it warmer. If only for a minute. Then drink so he could do it again.

Eyes green gold above the water, mouth open slightly, taking the water in. Warming it for a time on his insides.

THE HUMAN SALAMANDER. Drain this tank and you pour my soul out on the floor.

AMALIA. Isn't he beautiful? You'd never guess he showed up here just an undernourished boy with a bit of extra skin between fingers and toes.

Takes an artist to make a transformation like that.

It takes—

MR. FLIP

> (*Lights up suddenly on* MR. FLIP, *in ringmaster regalia, caught sneaking between two cages.*)

MR FLIP. I am not a bad man.

> (MR. FLIP *continues on his way, crossing paths with* MATTHEW, *filthy but whole, carrying a bucket of slop for the animals.*)

AMALIA. He always says that.

Oh, and here is Matthew, on his way to feed the dumber of the beasts in this place.

> (MATTHEW *looks embarrassed to be caught onstage, but smiles gamely to* AMALIA.)

He feeds them. Waters them. Brushes their coats. Drags away their shit in buckets. And when they die (*She coughs*) he buries their exotic bodies (*Cough*) by the side of the road.

> (*She has a coughing fit.* MATTHEW *looks terrified, but remains frozen on the spot.* JUDITH *enters with a glass of water, brings it to her to drink. Holds it up to her lips. Brushes the hair out of her eyes. Lights fade on them.*)

Scene 2

MR. FLIP. I am not a bad man.

I know you think I am. You've got your minds all set. This is a bad man. He profits from the sale of Freaks. Runs a glorified peepshow for the sick. Exploits these poor freaks who have been deformed by SIN OR GOD.

Well, who paid to take a peep, you sick bastards?

I know you. You love me and you hate me. You blame me for their deformities because I am the only one standing up here unscathed. It's as though I somehow caused the pain and suffering and maimed lives just so I could run my fantastic little show.

But you also love me because I'm the only one you can look at without looking away.

You do not fear me as you fear them, as you fear BEING one of them, as you fear waking up one of them, drool running out of your mouth eyes glazed BUT STILL ALIVE INSIDE. That really makes you shit, doesn't it. That's what you come here for. It's for the fear.

And I am only here to serve YOU.

> (*Lights up on* MATTHEW, *finishing slopping the animals [the animals are painted behind bars].*)

MATTHEW. Oh, you don't really want to hear from me. I'm not smart or beautiful as Amalia is. I'm just the man who cleans out the animals' cages. I'm just some guy who happens to be the luckiest man in the world I can't believe she lets me remain in her presence, even, but that she lets me love her.... If you were to kidnap me and take me away from this place and tell me all this never happened, I couldn't argue with you.

I am in love with the most beautiful woman in the world. She won't let me feed her or brush her hair, but she lets me take her out for walks. She loves the countryside.

And I can hold her in my arms that way for hours. She hardly weighs a thing—like a baby lamb.

(THE HUMAN SALAMANDER *spits a stream of water straight up.*)

JUDITH. I feed her. I wash her. I brush her hair. I put it up in the morning, take it down at night. I change the little cloths beneath her that time of the month. I tend to all aspects of her life.

I make sure she is the beautiful creature you see.

She confesses to me. After she has heard all the others.

I hear her private sins.

Such as? you want to know.

Oh, grave ones. Quiet and heavy in her beat-clutching heart.

She loves the pinhead, who is weak. Too weak to hold her.

MR. FLIP. Tell them about the old days. Tell them you were not always so invisible. Used to be the star of the show.

JUDITH. I never speak unless he gives me permission. It's an old habit.

MR. FLIP. Used to be the star of the show.

JUDITH. In my nightdress.

MR. FLIP. (*Smiling:*) Ah—that's when nightdresses were nightdresses. When a nightdress meant a certain state of undress. Nowadays a nightdress is apt to be the most decent thing in a woman's wardrobe, such is the state of bitter turpitude to which we've fallen.

JUDITH. You always talked like that.

I can't remember a time when you didn't talk like that.

MR. FLIP. Tell them about the old days. When you were the star of my show.

JUDITH. Not now.

AMALIA. (*Surprisingly peevish.*) Oh come now, don't make us *all* wait.

JUDITH. It's not the time.

You are beautiful now. When you're older you'll learn patience.

AMALIA. Do you speak to *me* of patience?

JUDITH. (*Soft, looking down.*) You're right. I've no right.

AMALIA. (*Same.*) All right.

(THE PINHEAD *stirs in his cage.*)

PINHEAD. I *like* Amalia. (*She turns her head away.*) She is the Woman With No Arms Or Legs for your sins.

AMALIA. Daniel. Would you…sing something for me?

PINHEAD. What?

AMALIA. Oh…Lavender?

PINHEAD. (*Sings:*) Lavenders blue, dilly dilly
Lavenders green
When I am King dilly dilly
You'll be my queen.

> (*The* PINHEAD *sings this verse several more times, getting softer each time, then goes to sleep. BLACKOUT.*)

Scene 3: THE NEWS OF THE WORLD

MR. FLIP *reads to* AMALIA *from a newspaper.*

MR. FLIP. The politicians are arguing again.
Money's bad.
Continued Threat from Bandits and Brigands.

AMALIA. Why don't you read me a nice story?

MR. FLIP. BLAST IT!

AMALIA. What's the matter?

MR. FLIP. Barnum's got a mermaid.

AMALIA. Well? We've got The Human Salamander. (*He lurks, listening.*)

MR. FLIP. He hasn't got tits, does he? (*Agitation in the tank.*)

JUDITH. (*Entering:*) Neither does Barnum's.
It's a monkey sewn to a fish.

MR. FLIP. And how do you know so much?

JUDITH. Hear things.
It was all the talk among our clientele today.

AMALIA. You see, we're a much better show.

> (*Sadly:*)

Because everything here is true. All true.

Scene 4

MATTHEW. How about I make you up a story?

AMALIA. No. I don't want a made-up one. I want a real one. Words off the page. Pages turned. I want the truth.
Judith.

> (JUDITH *enters, brushes the hair back from her eyes. Exits.*)

MATTHEW. I could do that.

AMALIA. I don't want you to.

Scene 5

Spot on MR. FLIP.

MR. FLIP. I only pay for babies so their families don't THINK they're throwing them away. Oh it was hard times too many mouths to feed we had to sell the freak baby. Sounds better on the conscience than WE DROWNED THAT THING.

Originally, I had a man to scour the countryside, looking for freaks, the outlandish, the physical phenomena lurking away in those backwoods backwater towns. But I had to let the man go, because the freaks were coming to me.

Or rather the parents were. We heard about you, Mr. Flip sir, and we thought perhaps you'd have a place for our boy. He's a lovely child, except for his head's so small.

There are those I have to turn away.

Not strange enough to pay what it costs me to keep them.

Scene 6: THE BALLAD OF THE HUMAN SALAMANDER

AMALIA. You're quiet tonight, Salamander

THE HUMAN SALAMANDER. I'm dead.

AMALIA. Don't be silly. I can hear you sloshing around.

THE HUMAN SALAMANDER. Today a…girl came to the show.
She saw me.

AMALIA. That's what we're here for.

THE HUMAN SALAMANDER. NO. Saw me.

AMALIA. Oh.

THE HUMAN SALAMANDER. She did not see a marvel of nature. An amphibian man. She saw me. Run away from home and sitting in a tank of water.
I'd almost forgotten.
You really start to believe your own press. You have to. Without pride…well, they wouldn't pay, is all.

AMALIA. I'm sorry. I forget—

THE HUMAN SALAMANDER. Yes, no-one doubts your credentials.

I am a mutation. That means change. Changed. And I have mutated. Into this half-human creature. Because just a bit of skin between the fingers and toes is fine for back home but it doesn't keep the crowd leaning in for a glimpse. So I became the Human Salamander.
Until she saw me.

Staring eyes. Burning.

The Human Salamander does not blush. The intricate network of veins and capillaries works differently than in ordinary humans. But there it was. I felt my skin growing hot. Under her gaze.

How could she see me? Inside my guise?

If it's happened once, it could happen again. That show could come when suddenly, an entire audience sees me. Some skinny kid, bloated with water. Sad. An entire audience suddenly overcome with revulsion and...pity.

Now I know fear.

She has ruined my life. A wandering pair of eyes, set the lie to the whole thing. She's cracked my tank. I won't notice the waterlevel sinking slow, just one day will come and I'll be naked.

She doesn't even know what she's done. A day trip, idle staring. One moment of recognition—oh, that poor kid. He's about my age. Sitting there in a tank of water all day while people stare. Then moving on to see the other marvels. Then home.

Cracked my tank and went about her life. Left me here to leak.

AMALIA. Salamander—

THE HUMAN SALAMANDER. She was pretty.

I was...staring at her first. That's how come I noticed. That she...saw me.

Usually I can stare at whoever I please. One advantage of the tank. No-one notices. They think I'm waiting to catch a fly. Hardest part of the job, learning how to do that. I had to practice for six months after the people had gone before I could do it in front of them.

AMALIA. You'd never guess you weren't born to it.

THE HUMAN SALAMANDER. But this time...burned. Her eyes burned. Because she caught me. She saw me.

AMALIA. It'll never happen again.

She'll never come back.

THE HUMAN SALAMANDER. (*Soft:*) I know.

    (*BLACKOUT.*)

    (*Water music.*)

    (*Lights up on* MR. FLIP *and* AMALIA.)

      Scene 7: WERE HER ARMS VERY BEAUTIFUL?

MR. FLIP. Why do you want to hear it again?

AMALIA. I don't know. It makes me feel strange.

MR. FLIP. She fell in the river.

AMALIA. And she could not kick or swim or grab her way to safety?

MR. FLIP. Hit her head on a rock.

AMALIA. How long had you been married?

MR. FLIP. Four years.

AMALIA. No children?

MR. FLIP. God didn't see fit to bless us.

AMALIA. She did something, didn't she? To make sure?

MR. FLIP. Do you know, I don't honestly know. I can't say I knew that woman's heart and soul, much as I loved her.

AMALIA. Were her arms very beautiful?

MR. FLIP. Yes.

(*BLACKOUT.*)

Scene 8: THEY STICK TO THE TREES

JUDITH *feeds* AMALIA *a pomegranate, pip by pip.* AMALIA *nibbles, then spits the pit into* JUDITH's *hand.*

MATTHEW. And I heard of another place so cold they live in snow. Blocks of snow piled up to give shelter from the wind. Everything they wear is the skins of animals, so they look like great furry beasts themselves.

JUDITH. Yes. I saw them once. Laplanders, they were called.

MATTHEW. How can you live in snow?

JUDITH. Oh, I don't know if they really live in snow.

MATTHEW. They pack the snow very hard, is what I heard.

JUDITH. Still. How would it stay up?

MATTHEW. I don't know…we used to build snow fortresses—

JUDITH. That's walls, yes? Not a roof.

MATTHEW. No, but—

JUDITH. And then do they light a fire inside?

MATTHEW. ——

JUDITH. And melt their house?

MATTHEW. Maybe there's—

JUDITH. No fire?

MATTHEW. Yes.

JUDITH. On a vast plain of snow and ice? They would die. These Laplanders were human beings, not beasts. Not so different from you and me.

MATTHEW. Perhaps not outwardly, but with a different interior circulatory system, different physical requirements for life and breath—

JUDITH. Matthew. You must stop believing in everything.

MATTHEW. Still. I would like to see it for myself. Great plains of snow and ice. Jungles filled with singing frogs and monkeys. Pygmies I would not have believed had I not seen them with my own eyes. They are true enough.

JUDITH. Yes, certainly. True enough.

MATTHEW. Singing frogs. They say. Not like ours. They stick to the trees. Climb right up the side. Can you imagine the heat and the green and a jungle full of singing frogs—

AMALIA. (*Erupts:*) Just go.

MATTHEW. (*Beat.*) I don't want to go.

AMALIA. Yes. Yes you do.

> (*Chorus of* SINGING FROGS: THE HUMAN SALAMANDER *and the* PINHEAD. MATTHEW *goes out. Light on the* PINHEAD.)

Scene 9

PINHEAD. Amalia.

AMALIA. Yes, darling.

PINHEAD. My mother came to see me today.

AMALIA. She did?

PINHEAD. Yes.
I could hear her crying in back. (*He becomes agitated, rocking.*)
I couldn't see her, but I know she was there.
I could hear her crying. (*He bangs his head against the bars.*)

AMALIA. Daniel? Daniel? Could you sing something for me?

PINHEAD. (*Quieting down.*) Yes.

AMALIA. Lavender?

PINHEAD. (*Thinks very hard.*) I can't remember.
I can't remember. (*Begins hitting his head again.*)

AMALIA. Something else then—

PINHEAD. I can't remember anything.

> (AMALIA *looks at* JUDITH, *who goes to him, putting her hands around the bars in front of his head. Softly, she begins to sing to him. "Perrine Etait Servante". He begins singing. Once she's gotten him started, he knows all the words, in perfect French.*)
>
> (*Note: this is abridged from a longer version available on Kate and Anna McGarrigle's "Dancer With Bruised Knees."*)

JUDITH.

Perrine était servante	Perrine was a servant
Perrine était servante	
Chez Monsieur le curé,	At the curate's house
Digue donda donaine	

(*The* PINHEAD *joins her.*)

BOTH.

Chez Monsieur le curé,	At the curate's house
Digue donda dondé.	

Son amant vient la voir,	Her lover came to see her

(JUDITH *drops out. She leaves* PINHEAD *and returns to* AMALIA.)

PINHEAD.

Son amant vient la voir,	Her lover came to see her
Le soir aprés l'dîner...	At night after dinner
Perrine O ma Perrine,	Perrine, O my Perrine
Perine O ma Perrine	
Voidrais-tu m'embrasser	Would you kiss me?
Digue donda dondain	
Voidrais-tu m'embrasser	
Digue donda dondé.	

AMALIA. Would you—

JUDITH. Of course.

(*Over next verse,* JUDITH *strokes* AMALIA's *hair, then pulls a heavy red velvet curtain around her perch.* AMALIA *is completely hidden.*)

(JUDITH *sits and listens while the* PINHEAD *finishes his song.*)

PINHEAD.

Voilá l'curé qui arrive	Here comes the curate!
Voilá l'curé qui arrive	
Ou vas-to bien t'cacher	Where can we hide you?
Caches-toi donc dans la huche,	Hide yourself here in the pantry!
Caches-toi donc dans la huche	
Elle l'avait oublié	She has forgotten him
Digue donda dondain	
Elle l'avait oublié	
Digue donda dondé	

(JUDITH *joins him for the last verse.*)

Voilá la triste histoire	Here is the sad story
Voilá la triste histoire	
Les rats l'avaient mangé	The rats have eaten him
Digue donda dondain	
Les rats l'avaient mangé	
Digue donda dondain.	

JUDITH. That was beautiful.
Now you should sleep.

PINHEAD. Does Jesus want me to?

JUDITH. Yes. Jesus wants you to sleep.

(He lies quietly. Loud voices offstage. MR. FLIP *comes charging in, followed by* MATTHEW.)

MATTHEW. Do you think you own her?

MR. FLIP. What, as a means of production? Or do you mean her soul?

MATTHEW. Go ahead, throw your words around. I'm not afraid of you, even if you do reek of the devil's pitch.

JUDITH. Voices—she is asleep.

MR. FLIP. Come, come, boy. I was joking. Surely even you can—

MATTHEW. YOU CAN'T OWN ANOTHER HUMAN BEING.

JUDITH. Please—

MR. FLIP. Are you telling me? Or yourself.

 (MATTHEW makes a fist. Shaking with rage.)

Go ahead. Hit me. It'd feel good, wouldn't it? Wouldn't it feel just wonderful to release that fist from its coiled spring.

But you won't.

Because I'd fire you.

And then you couldn't be around HER.

And then. Where would you be?

If you were not in her presence?

 (MATTHEW drops the fist and strides offstage, still coiled with fury. MR. FLIP *watches him go.)*

JUDITH. Why don't you fire him?

MR. FLIP. What do I care who she's fucking?

JUDITH. Max...

MR. FLIP. I *cannot* care. It is not my business to care.

JUDITH. Max.

MR. FLIP. It is not good business for me to care.

JUDITH. Ah. The last word.

MR. FLIP. Not so last as it used to be.

JUDITH. You do not fire him because

MR. FLIP. Because I do not care.

JUDITH. Because if you fire him she will love him forever.

MR. FLIP. *(Smiles:)* You always had

JUDITH. animal instincts

MR. FLIP. Wisdom beyond your years.

JUDITH. The years are catching up.

MR. FLIP. With your wisdom? They never will.

(*They exit A moment of silence. The* HUMAN SALAMANDER *stretches in his tank, idly spits some water. The* PINHEAD *turns in his sleep. Mutters:*)

PINHEAD. He forgave the Magdalene.

(*The* PINHEAD *settles down again. There is a noise from offstage— "psssssst." The* HUMAN SALAMANDER *looks* around. *A* GIRL *sneaks onstage, looking over her shoulder.*)

Scene 10

THE HUMAN SALAMANDER. You...
You can't be here.

THE GIRL. I had to see you.

THE HUMAN SALAMANDER. Well, now you've seen. It's true. I live in this tank. We're not fakes here. You can report back to all the kiddies in town.
Maybe the reception will be better when we pass through next year.

THE GIRL. Kiddies? You're no older than I am. (*Beat.*)
You know what I mean.
I had to see you.

(*He won't look at her.*)

I'll be whipped if I'm caught sneaking out. The least you could do is act glad to see me.
Don't you remember me.

THE HUMAN SALAMANDER. (*Soft:*) Yes.

THE GIRL. It was just this afternoon.
That I...fell in love with you.

(*He looks up.*)

You must have known.
My god, I felt transparent. When I saw you were looking at me. Seeing me. Looking at you. My love stupid all over my face. My face went hot. I was so ashamed I had to walk on.

THE HUMAN SALAMANDER. You—

THE GIRL. But I kept thinking about you. All day. I didn't see anything else here. No matter what I stood in front of. All I could see was you.
I should take a look around, now that I'm back.
Paid good money this afternoon. I was gypped.
Falling in love with you.

(*The* HUMAN SALAMANDER *begins to laugh.*)

Yes, laugh at me. I'm an idiot. Going to be whipped sure for sneaking out to declare my love to a circus freak in the middle of the night.

THE HUMAN SALAMANDER. (*Grandly:*) You love the Human Salamander.

THE GIRL. No, silly. I love you.

THE HUMAN SALAMANDER. Oh. How do you know?

THE GIRL. I suppose this happens to you all the time.
Farm girls sneak away from their homes in every town you pass through, just to pay homage at your tank.

THE HUMAN SALAMANDER. no—

THE GIRL. Run away with me.

THE HUMAN SALAMANDER. What?

THE GIRL. You've done it before. Had to run from somewhere to end up here.
Run again. Only this time, with me.

THE HUMAN SALAMANDER. I...can't leave this tank.

THE GIRL. You don't think I—

THE HUMAN SALAMANDER. I couldn't breathe.

THE GIRL. I'm not a rube, you know.

THE HUMAN SALAMANDER. I...couldn't breathe.

(*Quickly, not looking at her, he recites his Pitch.*)

I sit in a tank of water because otherwise my delicate amphibious skin would parch and crack. The gills—see them?—need to be kept moist or I could not breathe. Being a half-human mutation, I breathe through lungs and gills. But the one system would be insufficient without the other. Just as I cannot fully breathe when completely submerged in water, so I cannot fully breathe when completely out of the water. The one system of breathing supports the other.

THE GIRL. Isn't the water cold?

THE HUMAN SALAMANDER. No. The air...is cold.

THE GIRL. I want to kiss you.

THE HUMAN SALAMANDER. I don't turn into a prince.

(*She kisses him. After a few moment, she puts her hands on his neck, behind his ears. He cannot breathe. Begins to shake until she lets him go. He gasps for breath.*)

THE GIRL. Oh my god

AMALIA. (*Speaks from behind her curtain:*) Young woman.

(*The GIRL jumps.*)

Open up this curtain.

THE HUMAN SALAMANDER. (*Still breathless:*) I'm sorry we woke you—

(*The GIRL pulls back AMALIA's curtain.*)

AMALIA. I never sleep. Just shut it all out for a while. (*Looks at the girl:*) So. You have discovered his gills.

      (*The* GIRL *nods, speechless.*)

He's not gaffed. They're real.

      (*She nods again.*)

We wouldn't have put them on him, anyway. Everybody knows salamanders don't have gills.

THE GIRL. So he was—

AMALIA. No, he wasn't born with them.
He grew them. Here.

      (*Looks at the* HUMAN SALAMANDER:) She *is* pretty.

      (*The* GIRL *looks between them.*)

THE GIRL. You told her about me?

      (*The* HUMAN SALAMANDER *nods.*)

Then you did notice me!

THE HUMAN SALAMANDER. I have…thought of nothing since.

THE GIRL. Come away with me!

AMALIA. Do you want to, Tom?

THE HUMAN SALAMANDER. (*Soft:*) I can't.

AMALIA. Didn't you hear? She says she loves you.

THE HUMAN SALAMANDER. (*Agonized:*) I *can't.*

      (AMALIA *turns her attention to the girl.*)

AMALIA. Young woman. Are you truly prepared to run away?

THE GIRL. Yes.

AMALIA. Leave behind those who love you?

THE GIRL. Begging your pardon, that's not what's involved.

AMALIA. Have you ever run away before?

THE GIRL. No ma'am. I aim to do it once and do it right.

AMALIA. If you've never run away before, you can't know what's involved, the difficulty, the fear—

THE GIRL. If I said I'd done it before youd've said I'd just turn around and go home again.
There's no right answer to that one.
Right?

      (*This almost gets a smile from* AMALIA.)

AMALIA. Can you cook?

THE GIRL. Yes.

AMALIA. Count money?

THE GIRL. I'm good at that.

AMALIA. All right.

You can stay.

(*They both look up at her as though she is an apparition from God.*)

THE GIRL. I— I—

THE HUMAN SALAMANDER. Really?

AMALIA. I'll talk to him. (*She cocks her head.*)

Go to Judith. She'll hide you till then.

(*The* GIRL *starts in that direction, then runs back for a last kiss.*)

THE GIRL. (*Exiting:*) Thank you!

(*Beat.*)

AMALIA. Beware of her, Salamander.

Anyone who tries to steal you from your home. Is evil or an idiot or both.

You know where she comes from.

THE HUMAN SALAMANDER. Yes. (*Beat.*) Why did you do that?

AMALIA. What?

THE HUMAN SALAMANDER. Say she could stay?

AMALIA. (*Beat. looks down:*) I was afraid you'd go after her.

We'd find you asphyxiated half a mile down the road.

THE HUMAN SALAMANDER. I wouldn't have gone.

AMALIA. Mmm. And you'd have wished you had.

(*He acknowledges this possibility.*)

This way you can observe her.

Get to know who she really is.

So that when she leaves, you won't be sorry.

THE HUMAN SALAMANDER. Oh.

AMALIA. But you must learn to breathe again, Salamander.

Autonomy is not a thing to be given up for comfort.

(*He nods.*)

THE HUMAN SALAMANDER. (*Soft:*)

It'll be nice having her around for a while.

I'm not in love with her, though. I don't think.

AMALIA. Just a stomach ache?

THE HUMAN SALAMANDER. (*Surprised:*) Yes.

(AMALIA *laughs. The* HUMAN SALAMANDER *smiles shyly. Slowly, slowly he begins easing himself out of the water. Once a significant amount of his skin is exposed, he begins to shiver and submerges again.*)

(*Lights fade on him, rise on* AMALIA.)

Scene 11

AMALIA. So. Has it crossed your mind yet? Don't tell me it hasn't. Wondering what it would be like. To have me. While I have no arms and legs, the muscles of my interior regions are unbelievably strong. Did it occur to you to wonder what I do up here on this perch all day long?
I do my strengthening exercises. Tighten and release my interior muscles. Thousands of times a day.
Matthew could tell you things… Oh but he never would. Not under pain of torture. He would never speak ill of me. He loves me.
And now you know why.
I can clench a cock so tight you couldn't pull it out.
Sometimes I can even make myself come. If I get my weight positioned just right. It takes hours. But then, I have hours. I have all day. Every day. Eyes staring rips through my skin. It makes me laugh. That they don't know what I'm doing with my precious anatomy.
This strange perhaps funny gift of god.
Does he laugh? Does he think, Finally. I have created the perfect woman.
I never take it in my mouth. I think that's disgusting. I know there are those that do, but I myself think that is disgusting. A mouth is for kissing. And were you to kiss me, on my mouth, on my warm pink open mouth, you would become intoxicated. Kissing me, you would become intoxicated and after that, after one kiss or two you could not fail to be so intoxicated by my kisses that you would have to lift my skirt.
No fear of what lies under could match the passion of my soft warm breath. My tongue, inside my teeth. Inside my mouth. You would need, at least, to put your hand beneath my skirt. And once your fingers find what they seek you would find, Yes, she is like other women. She is like all other women. and you would not be afraid.
I never take it in my mouth because that is disgusting. And because rules are important. Some. Modicum of control. Is important.

Scene 12

MR. FLIP *crosses the stage, eating an apple.* AMALIA *watches him.*

AMALIA. There's a new girl.

MR. FLIP. We don't need anyone.

AMALIA. I want her here.

MR. FLIP. Good lord, woman, we can't just go around picking up strays. I'm running a business, here.

AMALIA. I'll quit.

(*He looks at her.*)

Walk away from my whole career.

MR. FLIP. (*Cracks a smile:*) Does she cook?

AMALIA. Yes.

MR. FLIP. Can she sell tickets?

AMALIA. A head for figures and a figure that turns heads.

MR. FLIP. (*Laughs:*) All right. You've got your pet.
As if I could deny you anything you want.
I'm sick of Matthew's Anything Chowder, anyway.

> (*He smiles at her, takes another bite.*)

MR. FLIP. Don't know why you think you can order me around.
There's a human torso in England who paints miniatures, you know.

AMALIA. (*Lofty:*) So hire her, if you can afford her fees.

MR. FLIP. Hm. She is, I've heard, rather unusually plain.

> (*Takes another bite.*)

AMALIA. That looks good.

MR. FLIP. It is. Shall I send Judith to get one for you?

AMALIA. Yes.

> (*BLACKOUT.*)

Scene 13

> JUDITH *is there, with an apple and a knife. Cuts slices for her.*

AMALIA. What was she like, his wife? Was she nice?

JUDITH. Nice not the word I'd use. She was always good to me.

AMALIA. What was she called?

JUDITH. Bet.
She was a good, sensible woman. Liked animals better'n people. Guess that's why we got on so good.

AMALIA. You were friends?

JUDITH. We got on.
Used to stay up later than anyone. Watch the fire burn down to coals. Sometimes talk. Sometimes not.

AMALIA. Did she do something? So as not to have a baby?

JUDITH. Yeh. I showed her. Which plants to use. After my Grandmother showed me. My mother said What ya tellin her that for? She's not gonna need it.
Ha.
I've had more men than she has, that's for sure.

AMALIA. And did she... Did she mean to do it, do you think? Disappear beneath the water and never come up?

JUDITH. (*Thinks about this:*) I don't know.

I didn't know all her secrets.

(*BLACKOUT.*)

(*Music over next.*)

Scene 14: TRAVELLING SCENE

JUDITH *points the* GIRL *in the direction of the cook shack. She starts across the stage. The* HUMAN SALAMANDER *sticks his head up.*

THE HUMAN SALAMANDER. Where you—?

THE GIRL. Kitchen. Wanna—?

THE HUMAN SALAMANDER. (*Slightly miserable:*) Can't.

THE GIRL. Right.

(*She pauses by his tank.* JUDITH, *still pointing, gives a little growl.* The GIRL *jumps, continues on her way.*)

I'll see you later, then.

(*She disappears into the cook-shack.*)

THE HUMAN SALAMANDER. (*Alone:*) Yeah.

Scene 15: THE CHANGING OF THE GUARD

Music out. MATTHEW *and the* GIRL, *in a tiny makeshift cooking area. He shows her around.*

THE GIRL. What do you make? What do they like?

MATTHEW. Chowder, generally.

THE GIRL. Chowder? Of what?

MATTHEW. Beef. Corn. Crawdads. Depends where we are.

THE GIRL. And that's the Circus Favorite?

MATTHEW. Well, we haven't got much money to spare for fancy ingreedymints. Depends what's cheap at the market.

THE GIRL. Well, there's always biscuits and gravy. Can make that from next to nothing. Or is everybody sick of biscuits?

MATTHEW. Uh, no. I don't make biscuits.

THE GIRL. (*Teasing:*) Your mama never taught you to make biscuits?

MATTHEW. (*Defensive:*) She never taught me how to make chowder, neither. (*Beat.*)

I...don't even know if it is chowder, really. I just...made it up. It's not exactly soup, right? More hearty.

THE GIRL. I bet it's wonderful.

MATTHEW. Well, I was gettin' better. (*Beat.*)

They're never gonna need you like you want them to, you know. There's a thousand thousand like you. You'll always be replaceable.

THE GIRL. Naw. Not like me.

MATTHEW. That's what I thought, too. Till I saw the spittin' image of me walk in here every third town we pass through. Jaw droppin' to the floor, eyes all over everything, tryin' to memorize.

THE GIRL. Well, I don't want them all to need me.
Just him.

MATTHEW. He'll never leave.

THE GIRL. Yeh he will.

MATTHEW. This is where he lives.

THE GIRL. He'll leave it for me.

MATTHEW. You really wanna do that?
Dry him out?
Keep him all to yourself?

    (*Beat.*)

THE GIRL. I think I can take it from here.
Less there's anything else you need to show me.

MATTHEW. Naw. I guess you gotta learn it for yourself, anyway. (*At the door:*) Maybe you're just…better suited to the job than I ever was.
Maybe you'll do just fine.

    (*Lights fade as* MATTHEW *walks into next scene.*)

Scene 16: SUNDAY

    All are gathered round.

MATTHEW. Since when can't we show on a Sunday?

MR. FLIP. One of the fascinating things about rules, Matthew: their ever-changing, ever-twisting, shimmering permutations.

MATTHEW. What's that supposed to mean?

MR. FLIP. Almost nineteen hundred years after his death and incontrovertible resurrection, Jesus himself has whispered in some local deacon's ear that our little show is a sin. A sin and a shame.

PINHEAD. (*Suddenly bursts out in song:*)
Glo-ooooo-ooooo-ooooo-ria
In Ex Celsis Deo

MR. FLIP. It's not their souls, but their coins the clergy are concerned for.
That sweet hard clank on the collection plate.
Sunday was our biggest day.
Back in the day.
Remember, my dear?
When a Sunday meant crowds packed in sweat tight?
As many shows as we could fit into a day?

JUDITH. We put the fear a God into um.
Better'n any church.

MATTHEW. With the Dog Girl routine?

MR. FLIP. Routine, he says.
She *was* the Dog-Faced Girl.
Tell him, Jude.

AMALIA. Yes, now is it time for the terrible tale?

JUDITH. I don't know—

AMALIA. Please...

JUDITH. All right, then.

(*She begins the story to* MATTHEW, *but is soon lost in the rhythm of telling.*)
I was I was the uglymug with the Harelip. But Mr. Flip saw I was blooming.
About to burst. Out. Uglymug attached to sweet. Ness. Sweet ripe flesh.
Down on all fours in the dirt.

I was one of the last ones he bought. After they was comin after him from all
the villages, sayin Mr. Flip take the deformity. Make you good money. Here,
take. Take the freak baby. In the magic glamour caravan so we never have to
look at the sin we've spawned. What sin spawned. The sick. Please. Look
what a freak. Make you good money. Make you good money, Mr. Flip.

An he saw me. Sweeping up in the corner.

Me, he had to pay for. They didn't want to let me go. Had all my limbs fine.
Just the split lip just the face like an animal. Nevergetermarriedoff, but she
works just fine. Uglymug but she's a strong 'un.

Mr. Flip said I'll Pay. Saw he'd soon get a return. Soon be getting a return on
his investment.

MR. FLIP. You were the most beautiful creature I had ever seen.

JUDITH. No you aint getting away with that

MR. FLIP. I am not saying I am a good man.

JUDITH. He always comes on romanic about things past. It was ugly being
there. It was black and ugly.

MR. FLIP. I am merely saying that you were the most beautiful creature I
had ever seen.

JUDITH. I knew
I thought I knew
He thought I was pretty. That he was the only one saw me pretty.

MR. FLIP. Pretty is cheap and useless. You were the stuff of saints.

JUDITH. I knew when men put up money like that, they thought you was
pretty.
Don't ask how I knew, half-animal, sweeping up in the corner. I'd seen, I'd
heard. I'd seen the way he looked at me.

He thought I was pretty. So he bought and paid for me. And the world was changing.

Then he threw me in the cellar.

MR. FLIP. (*Shrugs:*) Perfection does not grow wild.

JUDITH. Threw me in the cellar with my friend. Her name was

(*She barks.*)

HAURT. my friend. My only companion. No human contact, no speech, fed from the same dish on the floor. Six months, nine? A year? Meat scraps and dirt. Slept curled together for warmth.

No-one had ever loved me like that. She would have killed anyone who tried to harm me.

She told me so.

Aourt howt houuuuu.

When I was sick and almost dying she chewed the meat for me and put it in my mouth. My own mother would not have—did not know how to love a child like that.

And when he had me tempered in the forge, when he'd made me her child, when it was time to put me in the cage he kicked her out onto the streets.

She came howling, following my cage from town to town.

MR. FLIP. How else would they have believed that I'd rescued you from a pack of wild dogs?

JUDITH. Rescued me.

In my filthy outgrown nightdress.

MR. FLIP. Ah, yes. The nightdress.

JUDITH. More rips than dress.

Caged up, men starin' down at me.

I'd see the sick thing swelling in their drawers. And me, and me down on all fours. I'd sniff over to him givin' the evil eye an' I'd set up a howlin

AAAAOOOOOUUUUUU

Then you'd see 'um shrink and quiver, yes

Then you'd see a True Believer. Scared on back to wife and kinder. Never see her in her night-dress with the light on.

Never see her down. In the dirt.

Gotta pay to see a woman debased. With 'r ass in yer face. Licensed, like. It's all right. Gotta pay to see a woman down. In the dirt.

Course you could just knock down the one you got. Many do. There's lots do that. Knock the one you got in the dirt.

In front of God and Kinder.

All in all, this's Easier. A woman so ugly you can't look her in the face. You can't help but look her in the face. Can't help but stare.

GOD SHE'S UGLY and all that Beauty down Below.

Swollen pink and white and muddy. What's that? Glimpsed a bit through her nightie. Sure, that's a nip.

Godawmighty what an ugly. What a beauty.

It starts stiffing in their pants and I come a howling. Dog girl can sniff out sin in ye pockets.

MR. FLIP. It was a good act.

JUDITH. Act, he says.

MR. FLIP. We could stay two weeks in one spot. Word spread like greasefire. Men walking miles, pockets heavy with coin. Two weeks in one spot!

> (MATTHEW *rouses from his shocked silence to stutter a few stunned accusations at* MR. FLIP.)

MATTHEW. How can you—

How can you look another human being in the face

you—

you—

MR. FLIP. (*Calm:*) I made her. Created her.

MATTHEW. How can you—

JUDITH. He did.

> (MATTHEW *storms off.* AMALIA *sighs.*)

AMALIA. Can't you leave him alone?

> (*BLACKOUT.*)

> (*Light up on the* PINHEAD, *rocking. He sings:*)

PINHEAD. Hush little baby don't say a word

Papa's gonna buy you a mocking bird.

If that mocking bird don't sing

Papa's gonna buy you a diamond ring.

If that diamond ring is glass

Papa's gonna buy you a looking glass

If that looking glass gets broke

Papa's gonna buy you a billy goat.

If that billy goat falls down

You'll still be the sweetest little baby in town.

If you're the sweetest little baby in town

> (*He stops, confused.*)

Scene 17: EPISTLARY MISSIVE

JUDITH. MR. FLIP *enters with a letter.*

MR. FLIP. How were profits today?

JUDITH. Not bad for a Monday.

MR. FLIP. Sweet Jesus.

JUDITH. It's the same every time we come through here. Farmers don't have money to be throwing away on foolishness—

MR. FLIP. Bite your tongue!

JUDITH. Or even living wonders of the world. If there's no money, there's no money.

MR. FLIP. They drink, don't they?

JUDITH. Home brew.

MR. FLIP. Hmm. And commit sins upon their own livestock for amusement, I suppose.

JUDITH. Got a letter, hey? That's a rare thing.

MR. FLIP. Indeed, indeed.

> (*Beat.*)

It's not for me.
It's for you.

JUDITH. For me?

MR. FLIP. From your sister.

JUDITH. My sister.

> (*Beat.* JUDITH *soaks in this information.*)

MR. FLIP. Shall I read it to you?

> (*He tears the envelope.* JUDITH *jumps.*)

JUDITH. Let me see the hand.

> (*He hands her the letter. She looks at it, smells it, runs her fingers over the paper.*)

Oh look. Look! She's done it herself.
I thought she would have had someone in town write it out.

MR. FLIP. (*Looking over her shoulder.*)
Mmm. Unless she's gotten a chicken to do the scribing.

> (JUDITH *stares at the words on the page. Finally, she hands the letter back.*)

JUDITH. Read it to me.

> (MR. FLIP *makes a production out of arranging the paper, clearing his throat, etc. Begins to read theatrically.*)

MR. FLIP. Hello my only sister in this world. I hope this letter finds you well.

> (*Breaks.*)

Well, it certainly did find you well, in and of it found you at all. Probably been chasing us through the last six towns.

> (JUDITH *looks at him. He returns to the letter.*)

I have troubles. I married Bill Parker you remember him last year. I had a baby that was not right. Bill took off and left me now they're saying I was touched by the devil and they want to take my poor darling who is so precious to me tears are dropping onto this paper now. I fear their evil minds. Please come home to your family Mama is dead it's just me now and the baby.

Your loving sister,
Ruth Anne.

　　　　　(*Beat.*)

So tantalizing. No mention what the deformity could be.

JUDITH. Hermaphrodite.

MR. FLIP. (*Staring at the paper.*) How do you—

JUDITH. No he. No she.
Also, though, no "it." She'll be a good little mother.
Hardly more'n a baby herself when I left.

MR. FLIP. You're not going to leave us—

JUDITH. Of course not. Not while Amalia needs me.

MR. FLIP. Though your sister will need help. All alone in the world. Why, as soon as the babe is old enough to travel—

JUDITH. You'll not have the child.

MR. FLIP. But Judith, think! Where else could he—

JUDITH. Put it out of your mind. You'll not have the child.

　　　　　(*She exits.*)

Scene 18: THREATS

　　　　　MR. FLIP. *The* GIRL *crosses with a sack of potatoes.*

MR. FLIP. Put that down a moment, girl. I like to get to know my new employees.

　　　　　(*She stands, polite, as he appraises her.*)

Name?

THE GIRL. Louisa.

MR. FLIP. Why are you running away? Dad got his hands in your knickers?

THE GIRL. My parents are dead, sir.

MR. FLIP. Ah. Then everybody's had their hands in your knickers, eh?

　　　　　(*She clenches her fists and looks away, shaking.*)

Well, that's a good enough reason. Won't happen to you here. Cos nobody here would want to upset the Salamander.

I know you're here for him. Saw you starin' in his tank. Obvious as a rash, you are.

If you've got any crazy ideas about stealing him from me, drop 'em right now.

He's the only adolescent in the history of the world to sprout gills. A scientist was gonna pay me good money for him, much as we make in a whole season, and I refused.

So you see I'm not gonna let him go for free. Not to you, nor any other piece of flesh takes a liking to him.

Try and take him, I'll send a man after you with a razor. Make another exhibit of you.

Well. That's all. You'd better get started on them potatoes.

> (*She picks up the sack, heads for the kitchen. Begins to peel the potatoes.* The HUMAN SALAMANDER *raises his head slightly above the waterline and follows* MR. FLIP *out with his eyes.*)

> (*The* PINHEAD *stirs in his cage.*)

PINHEAD. Jesus was a magician. He passed a camel through a needle. Passed a camel, threw a needle. Pulled loaves and fishes out of his hat.

> (*Makes fish-faces.*)

The fishes must have been beautiful.

> (*More fish-faces. Continues, sing-song.*)

Out of his hat. Out of his hat. Jesus fishes out of his hat. Oh, Jesus. Oh, Jesus what have I done? Dear lord I know I'm a sinner but why'd ya have to take it out on an innocent babe. Never done no wrong. Why couldn't you just a struck me dead, leave my babe alone. Look at the sweet thing. Sweet thing.

> (*He settles back down.*)

THE HUMAN SALAMANDER. He shouldn't have spoken to you like that.

THE GIRL. Ah, well.

THE HUMAN SALAMANDER. I'll kill him.

THE GIRL. (*Comes toward him:*) I'd have said the same.
If you were mine. And someone tried to take you away.

THE HUMAN SALAMANDER. I am. I am yours.

> (*He reaches out of the tank—takes her hands.*)

THE GIRL. Oh—don't. I'm all dirty.

> (*He brings her hands to his face, kissing them. Getting muddy potato dirt on his face.*)

Oh.
Oh.

> (*She brings his face to hers. They kiss, both now dirty-faced as she brushes back her hair, leaving streaks of dirt on her cheek.*)

You can't take that back, now.
Don't ever take that back.
You're mine.
THE HUMAN SALAMANDER. Yes.
> (*He lurches up to kiss her, splashing water out of the tank.*)
> (*Lights dim on them, come on* AMALIA. JUDITH *is doing her hair.*)

Scene 19

JUDITH. She did love him. I know that.
He'd of liked it if she made more of a fuss over him, but that wasn't her style.
And he'd of done anything for her.
Made me for her.
Not cos that's what she wanted. But to put food on the table. To take care of her. Came up with the whole crazy works.
We all ate good outta me in the cage.
Don't know how much was guessing and how much he knew, but he turned out right. Made money.
Four years I had enough saved up to buy me a little house somewhere, live quiet. Had enough.
Then came the accident and I saw him drown like she had, but inside himself. You could hardly tell it was the same man. He looked just the same, only he wasn't there.
I'd seen him look at her and there was boy in him, in his eyes and his face, and now that was all gone there was old man taken over.
So I couldn't leave him just then. Wait till he could take care of himself again. And the rest. By then there was more to worry about than just me. Everyone depending on me to bring em in.
Then one day and he came home with you. The minute I saw you, I loved you. Little thing that you were.
I knew. Now I was free. I could get out of the cage.
> (*Touching her hair.*)
I thought I'll just stay and help her adjust. Three weeks or so. Then I'll be gone.
You lookin' brave as hell and scareder'n that.
> (AMALIA *smiles.*)
Three weeks, I said.
Been the longest three weeks I ever heard of.
AMALIA. Oh, it hasn't been three weeks…

JUDITH. (*Smiles:*) No, I suppose not yet.
(BLACKOUT.)

Scene 20

Spot on MATTHEW.

MATTHEW. She doesn't have to do this, you know.
She's one of the smartest people I've ever met. Could do anything she set her mind to, I believe. I'm sure she'd know how to read, except for the turning the pages.
I could turn them for her.
But she doesn't like you to do things for her.

Scene 21

Lights up on MR. FLIP *and* AMALIA. *He is eating a plum.*

AMALIA. (*Coy:*) You must do something about the weather, sir.
At the next spot I'd like a bit more rain.
This dust is irritating.

MR. FLIP. I'll speak to the authorities.
(*Takes a bite.*)

AMALIA. That looks good.

MR. FLIP. It is. Shall I send—

AMALIA. Can I have a bite?
(MR. FLIP *is shocked, but tries hard not to betray this.*)

MR. FLIP. Of course.
(*He approaches her. Holds the plum up to her mouth. She takes a bite. Chews. He cannot help watching her, captivated. She swallows.*)

AMALIA. Thank you.

MR. FLIP. Another?

AMALIA. Yes.
(*He returns the plum to her mouth. She takes a bite.* JUDITH *becomes visible in the shadows, watching. She doesn't make a sound.*)
(*BLACKOUT.*)
(*Dim light on the Human Salamander. He practices breathing.*)
(*Lights come up behind the canvas. We see* MR. FLIP *in silhouette, being threatened by local toughs.*)

Scene 22: PAYOFF

MR. FLIP. This is nonsense. We've already paid twice what we paid last year, for half as many days.

TOUGH. That was rent on the spot. You didn't pay to make sure you don't have any kind of problems.

MR. FLIP. We've never had problems here.

TOUGH. You do now.

> (*They beat* MR. FLIP, *leaving him gasping on the ground.*)

Scene 23

> JUDITH *tends to* MR. FLIP's *wounds, bathing his face, putting a poultice on his eye.*

JUDITH. How long ya gonna keep this up?

MR. FLIP. For Ever.

JUDITH. We barely pull in enough to feed them anymore.

MR. FLIP. And *what* would you have me *do?*

JUDITH. Cut 'em loose.

MR. FLIP. (*Shocked:*) Judith! You know what it's like out there.

JUDITH. They would learn.

MR. FLIP. Judith...

JUDITH. She's a draw. The rest aren't pulling their weight and you know it.

MR. FLIP. What do you propose I do with the Pinhead? Leave him on the church steps in a basket?

JUDITH. He knows all the hymns.

MR. FLIP. If by some miracle these *were* good Christian people who didn't stone him or beat him out of fear or chase him into the woods to live like an animal, if they decided to let him live in a small room at the back of the church and sing hymns in a voice that makes the angels cry, HE WOULD BE TREATED WITH REVULSION AND PITY THE REST OF HIS LIFE.

> (*Beat.*)

JUDITH. The salamander can make his own way.

MR. FLIP. (*Pleading:*) Judith, the boy grew gills. He grew gills...for me. Out of fright. Because he thought he might be let go.

> (*Beat.*)

JUDITH. I used to think you were a good businessman. Now I know it was just a good time for the exhibition of Freaks.
And any fool could have made a go of it.

Scene 24

AMALIA. Sometimes I wish I had a cage.

When I can feel what they're thinking. Looking at me. Breathing through their mouths. Crowding close, dangerous many of them. I can feel their thoughts. Sometimes I hear something straight from a man's mind and I blush and look down. That is the worst humiliation. My long swan-neck bent. Because if they can see that…if they can see that I am not impervious. I can be affected. They will realize. Someday. One will realize that he could reach out. With his hand. And touch me.

Then my heart beats hammers in my chest and my eyes dart. Only by superhuman effort do I retain my cold look, just over their heads. And another day goes by that it does not occur to anyone. To reach. To grab.

For weeks after, I long for iron bars. To keep them out.

Scene 25

MR. FLIP *approaches* AMALIA.

MR. FLIP. How's my angel?

AMALIA. What happened to your eye?

MR. FLIP. Oh, nothing. Just a bit of a territorial dispute—they sought to displace us, I was forced to call upon my more pugilistic nature to prevent them.

AMALIA. So it's all right?

MR. FLIP. (*Smiles:*) Of course it's all right.

(*He looks around to make sure they're alone.*)

We got some oranges. Shall I peel you one?

AMALIA. I'm not hungry.

MR. FLIP. A pear? It won't be good by tomorrow. The flesh gives just slightly to the touch. It's perfect, lightly freckled skin like—

AMALIA. All right.

(*Beat.*)

Like what?

MR. FLIP. What?

AMALIA. Skin like—

What were you going to say?

MR. FLIP. Like your own.

AMALIA. Mm. I thought so.

(*He goes to get the pear. She smiles a little smile to herself.* MR. FLIP *returns with the pear and a small knife. First holds it under her nose to smell. She approves, nods him to proceed. A long slit is cut in the pear, then another.* MR. FLIP *holds up a perfect wet shining slice. Slips it into her mouth. Waits, watches as she chews and swallows. Dabs at the corners of her mouth with his pocket-handkerchief. Cuts again. He has just placed another slice in her mouth when* MATTHEW *enters with a bouquet of wildflowers.*)

MATTHEW. How could you?
From his hand.

(AMALIA *chews, caught.*)
FEEDING FROM HIS HAND!

AMALIA. (*Swallows:*) Careful, Matthew, he's got a knife.

MATTHEW. A fruit knife.

AMALIA. Mr. Flip.

MR. FLIP. Yes?

AMALIA. Will you please leave us? We have things to discuss.

MR. FLIP. Of course.

(*He exits,* MATTHEW *staring daggers in his back.*)

MATTHEW. (*Sadly:*) Never. You would never take food from my hand.

AMALIA. Matthew—

MATTHEW. WHY? WHY WOULD YOU NEVER TAKE FOOD FROM MY HAND?

AMALIA. (*Tired:*) You know why.

MATTHEW. Judith only. You always said Judith only. And the hair, and the... Not even a drink of water. Would you take from my hand.

AMALIA. Matthew—

MATTHEW. Come away with me. Come away from this wicked place. Let me take you away. You don't have to do this—

AMALIA. Matthew—

MATTHEW. I can support us easy. Able bodied. Lots of things I could do. Let me take you away from this evil and shame. You don't need to be on exhibit like this. It's disgusting. We could get married...

AMALIA. (*With gentle humour:*) Where would I put the ring?

MATTHEW. Around your neck. On a golden chain. I'd take care of you. My love. Feed you. Wash your sweet face with cool water. Give you to drink.

AMALIA. Could you show me?
Matthew?
Could you talk them in? To see a living marvel, a monstrous atrocity of God?

MATTHEW. I told you, you don't need to do that anymore. I can do all kinds of stuff, get a job with good pay.

AMALIA. And leave me alone, twelve hours a day?

I need a man who can show me, who depends on me for his feed. His livelihood. Who will stick close by me every day. Yes and love me. Concern himself with my needs and my happiness. Take pride in my strength, my ability to work long hours, my skill at captivating an audience, charming the extra coins from their pockets in a music of metal rain.

I am the center of the universe. I am the means of production. I am the goods.

You think you can take me away from all this?

Save me? From the shame of exhibition?

Save me? By leaving me alone, day after day, staring at a spot on the wallpaper or god knows what, diapered helpless lying on my back?

MATTHEW. (*Faltering:*) Judith could come with us, then.

AMALIA. DON'T YOU KNOW ANYTHING?

She longs to be free of me. I can hear it in her blood, pulsing just under her skin.

I could not leave and steal her with me.

It's she who will leave. Not I.

I…will not leave.

I'll never leave him

    (*She looks at him:*)

You must have known.

    (MATTHEW *turns away.*)

You act as though I am telling you something, but you must have known this.

Matthew.

Would you like to brush my hair?

MATTHEW. (*Choked:*) Are you sending me away?

AMALIA. Yes.

    (MATTHEW *exits.*)

    (*Over next scene, he returns with a hairbrush and, with heartrending gentleness, brushes her hair. The* PINHEAD *sings a little song to himself, then goes to sleep.*)

Scene 26: ABANDONMENT

    JUDITH *enters in travelling clothes, carrying a bag. There is a scarf draped over her mouth.* MR. FLIP *sees her, stands, horrified.*

JUDITH. She has picked you.

MR. FLIP. Damn you, don't leave me. I mean, us. I mean, what will I do?

JUDITH. You'll do just fine.

MR. FLIP. YOU CAN'T LEAVE. I know, I know the news from your sister a shock…

JUDITH. I've been leaving for a long time, Max.

MR. FLIP. TRAITOROUS BITCH. Bring me the child!

JUDITH. Bitch, yes. You saw to that.

If her blood stops, send for me.

Other than that, you're ready.

MR. FLIP. (*Frightened:*) No. What if she won't feed?

It's only been a fruit or two from my hands.

JUDITH. She has chosen you.

Now it will be you. She'll feed from no-one else's hand.

(*They stand and stare at each other a long moment.*)

,R. FLIP. Where's your pride, girl?

(*He crosses to her. Gently, he pulls the scarf down, away from her mouth. Re-drapes it over her shoulder.*)

JUDITH. Goodbye.

Scene 27: MATTHEW WHISPERS
TO THE PINHEAD AS HE SLEEPS.

MATTHEW *strokes* AMALIA's *hair one last time. Walks away. Her face is wet with tears.* MATTHEW *stops, stands by the* PINHEAD's *cage, almost hidden in shadows. He whispers to the* PINHEAD *as he sleeps.* JUDITH *enters. Dries* AMALIA's *tears. Puts her hair up exactly as it had been.*

AMALIA. Did I keep you too long?

I couldn't bear—

JUDITH. I know.

AMALIA. I can't. I changed my mind. Bring everything back. Don't go. I can't

JUDITH. Don't you trust me?

(AMALIA *nods.*)

JUDITH. Well, then. It's time.

(*Turns to go.*)

AMALIA. Judith—

JUDITH. Yes?

AMALIA. My hair. Teach him to do my hair before you go.

JUDITH. Didn't he devise the style himself?

AMALIA. Yes, but can he do it?

JUDITH. He used to do mine. That's how I learned.

(JUDITH *kisses her forehead.*)

I love you more than any creature has the right to ask. If anyone hurts you I'll track them and kill them. Rip their neck out with my teeth.

(*She exits.*)

Scene 28: THE FUTURE

The GIRL *enters from the cook shack, with a scarf around her head and mason-jar rings dangling from freshly pierced ears. The* HUMAN SALAMANDER *stands a bit when he sees her.*

THE HUMAN SALAMANDER. Pssst. Louisa.

(*She looks at him.*)

Tonight. We can go tonight.

THE GIRL. What?

THE HUMAN SALAMANDER. I can do it. I can breathe.
We can leave this place. I can get work on a farm. Or in a factory. We can leave tonight.

THE GIRL. Why?

THE HUMAN SALAMANDER. You wanted to leave—

THE GIRL. No!

THE HUMAN SALAMANDER. Your ear…it's bleeding.

THE GIRL. (*Reaching up:*) Damn! (*Loud voice:*) Mr. Flip.

(*He turns to look at her, taking in her new garb.*)

I have decided you can be trusted with the secret of my parentage. My mother knew the dark arts. For we come of a dark people. She was full-blood gypsy. Through her blood was passed to me the ability to see into the future, which all our tribe possess deep within but only a few know how to bring up to the surface. My mother taught me, before she died. How to read the future in the lines of a hand. Also in tea-leaves. Every time my father caught her teaching me the ancient secrets of her tribe, he would beat her severely, and me as well, but she took most of the blows, shielding me with her body. Until one night he shot her, then himself. As I lay shaking in my bed.

MR. FLIP. So that is how you come to us.

THE GIRL. Yes.

(*He shows her his palm.*)

MR. FLIP. And what does my hand say?

(*She studies it for a moment.*)

THE GIRL. Good. This is very good. This line here shows success. You see it is broken here… Business is good. And bad. And good again.
But you see this line? All the way, curving off the side. Love. Till you draw your last breath.
The hand does not lie.

MR. FLIP. Hm.

Well, I'm glad you have deemed us trustworthy with this…secret. And I see no reason to keep your gift hidden from the public.

THE GIRL. (*A little panic-ed:*) Once we're away from here—

MR. FLIP. Yes, of course, once we're away from here.

THE GIRL. I would not wish to—

MR. FLIP. Of course—

THE GIRL. Shame my mother's memory.

MR. FLIP. I understand. We'll pick up what you need on the next jump.

THE GIRL. (*Relieved:*) Yes.

MR. FLIP. Well. If you'll excuse me…

> (*He exits to the cook-shack.*)

THE HUMAN SALAMANDER. (*Wondering:*) Why didn't you tell me that before?

AMALIA. Because she just made it up.

THE GIRL. Well, not all of it. Just the gypsy part.
Damn! Don't tell him—

AMALIA. My dear, he knows.

THE GIRL. Then what's he waiting for? Why doesn't he tear into me? Rip me to shreds?

AMALIA. Don't be silly.
You're family now.

THE HUMAN SALAMANDER. (*To The* GIRL:) I thought you wanted to run away.

THE GIRL. No…
(*Understanding:*) No! I wanted you to be with me.

> (*The* HUMAN SALAMANDER *sinks back into his tank in relief.*)

So you can get out of that tank now?

> (*Shy, he nods.*)

Well. Why don't you show me around?

> (*With great trepidation,* The HUMAN SALAMANDER *stands, breathes, steps gingerly out of the tank. Stands there dripping water. He's okay. A bright smile cracks across his face. The* GIRL *takes his hand. They walk into the shadows.* MR. FLIP *enters from the cook shack, shaking his head.*)

MR. FLIP. That girl's got guts. Pierced her own ears with a nail and a potato. Looks like she slaughtered a chicken in there. (*Beat.*)
Reminds me a me when I was that age.

Wasn't much older when I found Judith. We always say I invented her, but she just about equal invented me. I never was a talker before her. But she was something people had to see. A wonder of the universe.

(*They look at each other.*)

AMALIA. So now it's just us.

MR. FLIP. Yes.

　　　(*Beat.*)

Are you hungry? Can I get you something?

AMALIA. No.

MR. FLIP. Thirsty?

AMALIA. (*Irritated:*) No. (*Relenting:*) Maybe later.

You're making me nervous. Hovering around like an invalid's nurse.
I'm fine.
Go run the business.

MR. FLIP. All right.

　　　(*With a lingering smile, he exits. The* PINHEAD *stirs in his cage, wakes.*)

PINHEAD. Jesus came to me in my sleep.
He said I'm locked up. Am I locked up?
Caged. He said. Treated like an animal.

AMALIA. Daniel, we love the animals

PINHEAD. (*Happy:*) Oh, yes.
(*Troubled again:*) Jesus said this place was full of sin. A hell. And like hell, it
should burn.

AMALIA. Daniel.

PINHEAD. A great cleansing fire—

AMALIA. You just had a bad dream.

PINHEAD. (*Feeling around in the straw:*) No. He left matches.
(*Holds, triumphant, a box of matches:*) See—

AMALIA. (*Frightened now:*) Daniel. No. Put them down.

　　　(*He lights one.*)

PINHEAD. Ah!

　　　(*He stares at the flame, mesmerized.*)

Scene 29: THE END IN FLAMES

A fanfare. MR. FLIP *bursts out, every inch the ringmaster.*

MR. FLIP. You know, that new kid's got a great act.
Because while people may or may not delight in an aquatic human, a saucy
torso, or a boy with a very small head, everybody wants to know
THE FUTURE.

　　　(*Just before he's burned, the* PINHEAD *tosses the match out through his
bars.*)

What's to become of us? What lies in store?

A thousand thousand tent shows more
or one tremendous blaze of glory
FLASH against the night-sky all they saw
because the jilted lover in our tawdry little story
left a box of matches in the Pinhead's straw?

> (PINHEAD *strikes another match, stares at the flame. The* HUMAN
> SALAMANDER *and The* GIRL *return, summoned by the light.*)

Or are we just run out of town by crowd and clergy
because the sight of some monstrosity
caused a pregnant woman to miscarry?

So. What do you think?
What will it be?
Am I burned in effigy?
Or in cage number three?
And does my lady love stand fast beside me?

AMALIA. Of course, darling.
I've got no legs.

MR. FLIP. (*Looks at her.*)
How could you not love a woman like that?
But returning to the question at hand:
on reflection that's too much demand
placed on our Pinhead's thin shoulders—
the destruction of the universe. No

Ladies and Gentlemen, it's up to you.
Won't one of you STEP FORWARD and dip the first match to the tinder.
No?

Sign a petition, brand me a sinner?

> (*Steps forward, sotto voce.*)

I'll let you in on a little secret.
We did not end in flames.

> (PINHEAD *blows out the match.*)

Economics did us in
I think it was the Calvinists really and their bloody Speechifying
scared the good people away
to cultivate the perversions of their souls at home, in private.

And all these beautiful creatures you see behind me
hand-plucked from the most exotic corners of the earth
are now
Unemployed.

> (*They look down, embarrassed.*)

Not much, is it?

Sad, small and tedious.
Barely worth the price of admission.

We can't let it end like this
Not after all we've been through
Ladies and Gentlemen, that's not a fitting end for us
And certainly not for you.

So come, children.
Let's show them what should have been.

> (MATTHEW *and* JUDITH *return, carrying a model of the sideshow. They set it down in front of the others.*)

THE END IN FLAMES.

> (*Creatures all strike matches and burn model of the sideshow. Lights fade slowly to black over next, as flames dance on their faces.* MR. FLIP *crosses to put an arm around* AMALIA.)

MR. FLIP And will you die with me, good lady?

AMALIA. I never considered anyone else.

> (*They kiss. As lights fade, a cacophony of animal squeals, etc. The* PINHEAD *sings his song.*)

THE HUMAN SALAMANDER. It's hot. It's hot.

> (*All noise cuts at the same moment.*)

MR. FLIP. And so, goodnight.

> (*BLACKOUT.*)

End of Play